MORGAN'S MISSION

A Novel

By

Edward G. Schultz

ISBN: 1-4107-6114-2 (e-book)
ISBN: 1-4107-6113-4 (Paperback)
ISBN: 1-4107-6115-0 (Rocket Book)

Library of Congress Control Number: 2003093723

This book is printed on acid free paper.

Printed in the United States of America
Bloomington, IN

1stBooks – rev. 08/01/03

Dedicated to
My loving and patient wife Frances,
my children Barbara, Ed, Jim
and Bill
for his significant assistance

PREFACE

Religion...the zeal to propagate it, or the need to flee from it...has been a major cause of human migration since the beginning of recorded history. Each of the great religions or cultures has, at one time or another, forced itself on others, by outright intrusion, and more often, by migration.

So it was with the formation of "America". In the "colonies" the English and Dutch had come to the new land to escape European "state religions". They then promptly established their own Protestant religions, trying to convert the natives or newer immigrants, often insisting that their religion be revered as a condition of the founding of any new town in their colony.

The French entered North America through eastern Canada, and with Catholic Jesuit Missionaries in their parties, they explored the Mississippi River valley, trying to convert the Native Americans to the Catholic religion. To the south, the Spanish, with Dominican and Franciscan Friars in their groups, were settling Florida and had explored as far north as Tennessee. Since gaining control of the territory was their prime objective, educating the natives in Spanish culture and religion would be the means to accomplish this end.

Meanwhile, at the very time that the "American" eastern colonist were trying to shed the yoke of King George, the Spanish were beginning to colonize Alta California, from their base in Nuevo Espanola, Mexico. For several centuries before, they had controlled Central America and large parts of South America, having subjugated several Native American cultures in order to do so.

Expecting that the Russians would soon colonize Alta California from the north, the Spanish felt compelled to move into this potentially rich region, which their explorers had claimed several centuries before.

The political leaders implemented the same plan that had been proven to be a successful technique in Central and South America. The Mission Padres would become the "teachers" of the natives, converting them to Catholicism, while at the same time the government would gain political control over them. This clash of cultures occurred not only between the Spanish and the California natives however, for even in this early period, New England "yankees" were already on the western seacoast of California, and their "American" culture would also have an influence on the development of what would become, 79 years later, the 31st of the United States.

"Morgan's Mission" relates the involvement of one of these "yankees", personified in the character called Charles Morgan, who was born in Massachusetts in 1784 and arrived in California in the early 19th century. While this narration is generally based on many true events, some of the incidents, dates and characters are fictitious.

"Morgan's Mission" is an historic-novel, but it is only a novel. While it tries to depict the historical events with accuracy, the main intent is to present a dramatization of life in very early California. Some readers may feel that an attempt is made to "romanticize" the Mission Era of California, but the actual intent of the novel is to present both sides of the philosophical debate regarding the Padre's culture and the culture of the aborigine Native Americans. Which side the reader favors depends on many factors, but the main point of this novel is that these events did happen, and are now part of our history. While the events described may be subject to opinion as to why they happened, we record here only that they did happen.

CHAPTER ONE
The Priest In Hell

'My God! that sun is hot. This has to be as hot as hell will ever be. Or am I already in hell?' Morgan's mind was wandering. The intense heat of the sun and lack of water was making him weaker by the hour. How long has it been now? 'Let's see, I was staked here all day yesterday in this hot sun, and it must be mid-afternoon now, 'cause the sun's right in my face'. In between periods of near blackout, Morgan could still recall the events of the past two days. Sometimes he would lapse into thoughts of his boyhood years in Massachusetts. But now he was under the terribly hot sun of central California in August of 1802.

Morgan dimly remembered two nights back when he had slid over the side of Bouchard's pirate ship, very quietly so that the sailor on watch wouldn't see or hear him. He was a good swimmer, so that by first paddling quietly for about fifty yards, then swimming strongly, he had gotten to shore in ten or twelve minutes. It must have been sometime past midnight. He waded up onto the sand, rested just a few minutes, then darted to concealment in the bulrushes, inward from the beach. He was generally familiar with the terrain, as he had studied it through the ship's glass many times. In fact, once that he had decided that he was going to jump ship, he had spent a lot of time studying most of this part of the California coastline. He knew that it would be risky to get caught deserting Bouchard, and he knew too, that it would be equally dangerous if he came ashore where rebellious natives were camping. All in all, he had decided that this place, with the quiet Mission just a thousand meters or so inland, would be the best place to come ashore. He knew that the Mission south of here, called *Santa Barbara*, had a *Presidio* with a garrison of fifty or more soldiers, who could easily capture him. But this Mission, they called it *"La Purisima"*, was far enough away from *Santa Barbara* that he could very likely approach it at night, steal some food, and maybe even a horse, and head north to Monterey. From there, with any luck at all, he might catch a Yankee ship going back to Boston, and he would sign onto her.

Well, the first part of the plan had worked. He did get to shore without anyone on Bouchard's ship noticing him and he knew that they wouldn't come after him now. After all, he was just one lowly sailor in a large crew of ruffians. Even when they discover him gone, they'll decide not to risk their own capture just to retake this timid Yankee kid. No, Bouchard wouldn't waste time with a shore party to find him, but would more likely continue his to plan to attack *Santa Barbara* again. So after another few minutes of rest in the thickets he proceeded cautiously up the hillside toward *La Purisima.* After pushing through the brush and tripping a few times on fallen branches, he realized that his feet were bleeding because he was barefooted. In all of his planning to desert the pirate ship he hadn't figured out how to take his boots with him. On board ship for the past two years or so, he had worked barefoot on the decks, only wearing his boots when he occasionally went ashore. Of course as a boy in Massachusetts, like all the children, no shoes were worn during the summer months. With all that, he didn't think that walking barefooted was going to hurt so much, but he hadn't reckoned on this tangled brush. As he moved uphill and the Mission buildings came into sight, he forgot all of his discomforts.

'It must now be between three and four in the morning', he thought. If he was going to steal food tonight he'd better get to it pretty quick because the daylight would be coming soon. He crept quickly and stealthily to the edge of a large vegetable garden. He remembered thinking that it was much larger than the vegetable patch on his father's farm back in Sturbridge. He was creeping as quietly as he could but a dog barked and a Native American hollered. Then he saw the sentry. Only one, but he was shouting wildly in Spanish and soon two others, shirtless and hobbling as they tried to run while pulling up their trousers and putting on their boots, came running from the barrack. Morgan turned to run but as he glanced back he saw that the emerging sentries had retrieved their muskets and were looking in his direction. He jumped up to run just as the first soldier got off a shot. It missed him by quite a bit. Morgan kept running but now he was crouching low in case of another shot. During the half-year that Morgan had sailed with Bouchard he learned a little Spanish. He heard one soldier declare, "Don't bother to shoot anymore, you can't see him well enough. We'll let the dogs track him and after daybreak we'll catch him".

Well that told Morgan what he must do; backtrack to the surf, wade a good distance to get his scent lost from the dogs, then find a safe place for hiding during the daylight hours. His plan was good

3

but the dogs came faster than he had expected, and wading in the surf had tired him to the point of exhaustion. He waded ashore again and fell to the sand. He thought about his feet again. Now they were really painful, with the salt and the sand in the cuts. No time to think about that now, he had to decide his next move. Looking up and down the beach to determine his best chance for cover, he decided to head north. He remembered that there was an outcropping of rocks and trees, and it can't be too far from here. He started to run along the beach staying in the waters edge, hoping that both his scent and his footsteps would be erased by the lapping waves. Soon the outcropping was in view. He waded into the water a little deeper while still moving as fast as he could against the water's force. He had now reached the rocks and scrambled up them (oh, how his feet hurt) and at the top he moved inland where the trees and brush were thicker. He found what he believed to be a good thicket and slid in as low as he could. He was gasping for air and was now aching all over, not just his feet. As he lay gasping, he was trying to quiet his breathing so that he could listen. He didn't hear the dogs or any voices, only the soft splashing of the waves well below him. He realized that the sky to the east was just beginning to show the first signs of light. He thought, 'I made it!' and in a few seconds, in spite of wanting to stay awake, he was asleep.

He awoke abruptly to find two Spanish soldiers standing over him and a few Native Americans surrounding him. The two dogs that had tracked him were yelping while the natives restrained them. One of the soldiers was a Corporal and was giving terse orders, not to the soldiers but to the Native Americans. "Take him to your campsite! Don't let Padre Payeras know anything about this! I'll tell him we were chasing a wild animal that was ravaging his garden. He'll believe it". The Native Americans responded in excited statements that Morgan could not understand. They appeared to be asking the Corporal what to do with him. "I don't care! Just take him to your camp. Can't you see, he's a troublesome *yanqui*. I don't want Padre Payeras to know about him or he'll just make more work for me to escort him to the *Presidio*, or worse yet, keep him here as a prisoner for me to watch day and night! I don't want that kind of bother. He's only a *yanqui,* and probably a pirate. He should be killed". Although Morgan did not understand all that the Corporal had said, he did understand the last statement with no doubt, and it was what the natives wanted to hear. Now they knew that they were directed by the Spanish authority to take his life.

As he now slumped against the post that he was tied to, Morgan knew that he was not going to live. Why don't they just kill him. Why keep him tied here to die of the heat, thirst and starvation. Apparently they just wanted him to die by this slow torture. After marching up the foothills in what seemed like several miles well beyond *La Purisima*, the natives had tied him hand and foot to this post in the middle of their meager campsite. They're were only five of them, all males. This was not a tribe, just a renegade gang that were apparently followers of the Spanish Corporal and not the Padre at the Mission.

Morgan had fallen into unconsciousness again. When he awoke he estimated that it was about five in the afternoon. If it was, he had now been tied here for more than thirty-six hours and it was more than two full days since he had eaten or drunk anything. A breeze from the ocean made it a little cooler but the afternoon sun was now full in his face. He was facing west but as he looked downhill he couldn't see the ocean because of the large trees surrounding the natives' camp. There was a large field of grass in front of him. The heat vapors that rose reminded him of what he thought hell would look like. When he was a boy in Sturbridge his Papa and Step-mama Anna would occasionally take him to the Congregationalist Church where it seemed that Reverend Dawson often preached about the fire and heat of hell. Morgan did not now see flames but he expected that they would suddenly flare up right in front of him. It was so damned hot! He longed for a drop of water. He had had a few drops on his lips from the dew last night but that was all that he had had for two days. He first thought, 'if I live 'til tonight I'll get a few more drops', but then he thought of the cold he had felt during the night. In August the contrast between the day's heat and the night's cold was severe and especially when your out under the open sky and wearing only a tattered shirt and trousers. Uugghh! Now he was shuddering just thinking about the oncoming cold night again. He didn't think that he could last through another night like that. His thoughts about the cold soon disappeared as he became aware again of his present heat and thirst.

Dwelling on the thought of water brought him more reminiscences of his boyhood. He particularly remembered that he and his brother Albert would often take a quick dip in the pond between the schoolhouse and his Papa's barn. Even though Papa was expecting them home immediately after school to do their chores, he and Albert would take a real quick dip, then dress and run all the way home. By the time they reached home they were all heated up again, but the dip felt good anyway. He thought more about Albert. Gosh he loved his brother. How he wished that Albert had not died. Then none of this would have happened. He remembered the last dip that he and Albert had taken. It was Indian Summer, must have been mid-October. Was it really three years ago?. Yes, it was October, nearly three years ago. As usual they had left the one-room schoolhouse and headed home. He asked Albert if they could go in for a quick dip because it was just as warm as a summer day. Albert was a year older so Morgan always did what Albert said. At first Albert said, "No, we better just get to home". But as they came to the pond Albert said, "Charlie, do you really want to?" Morgan replied excitedly, "You bet, Al". So they quickly stripped and jumped in. Even though the day was hot, the water had cooled considerably in the last few weeks. They jumped in and out much quicker than usual. That evening Albert began to sneeze and cough and during the night had a fever. The next morning Step-mama Anna said that he should stay home from school, but Albert wanted to go, and said he'd be alright. Papa left it to Step-mama to decide, like he always did. She knew that Albert was smart and very serious about his schooling. She had said more than once that Albert would probably become a lawyer someday. Albert kept going to school, but his cold got much worse until one day Step-mama Anna sent

Morgan to ask Doctor Markham to come by. He said it was pneumonia. In early December Albert died.

Morgan thought some more about his family. His father, a hard working tenant farmer, always kept so busy with the many, many farm chores, that he never had time for Albert or himself. Papa did talk a lot to Morgan's older brother George, but mostly about farm activities. George had left school after seven grades and had now been helping Papa full time for four years. Mary, his sister was the oldest child. She had been working in town now for two years for widow Pennington who ran a boarding house. Mary had also only gone through seven grades, so Morgan felt that was as far as Papa and Step-mama Anna would let him go. That would be only one more year. Harold, his young half-brother was just starting school, so it would be many years before he could help Papa on the farm. Morgan himself didn't know if he wanted to go any further than the seventh grade, but he knew that Albert would finish all eight grades and then likely go to the Free Academy in Brimfield, the next town west of Sturbridge. Then, somehow he would probably also go to that college up at Amherst, or maybe even Harvard. Albert knew that Papa couldn't afford to send him to any college, but at least he wouldn't hold him here on the farm, and somehow Albert would work for the tuition money. Morgan sure looked up to Albert and knew that someday he'd be proud of his lawyer brother. But Albert died…even here in his own misery Morgan felt the pain in his heart again as he thought about Albert…but Albert died…that's why Morgan decided to run away to New Bedford to become a sailor. That was March of 1798. Morgan had turned 15 years old the previous December eleventh, just five days after Albert died.

Morgan's reverie was abruptly disturbed by sudden activity of the natives. One of them had a stoneware jug and a stick, and was vividly describing to the others what he intended to do. The others all jumped to their feet in great excitement and urgings to the first man. That one approached Morgan with the jar and stick. As he came close enough Morgan recognized the smell of the contents. It was honey! He didn't have to guess the next move of the native. Daubing the stick into the honey, he applied it first to Morgan's feet, then to his arms, chest, neck and face. Morgan knew that by evening he would have been bitten and stung by enough insects that he would certainly not live 'till dawn. Damn, why don't they just stab him to death! Why this terrible heinous method!

As the Native American continued to daub the honey, Morgan looked all about to imagine how he might escape. As he looked across the heat-hazed field he saw a figure, a person, he thought, but he couldn't be sure. Or was it the devil coming to get him? Maybe this really was hell, as he had imagined before, and this was the devil coming. But no, this figure was not in red as he had envisioned the devil from Reverend Dawson's sermons. This approaching figure was wearing a long gray robe. He had stepped from the forest surrounding the campsite and had a few other natives following him. As he approached he shouted from the fifty or so yards remaining between him and the renegade Native Americans.

"What are you heathens up to? What did that *demonio Cabo* Rivera put you up to?" The renegade natives stood silent. While they obviously did not regard this Padre as their leader, as many of their fellow tribesmen did, they did have trepidations because of his authoritative manner. "Release this poor man…now, I say! Release him!" Because the Padre had spoken in the native's dialect, Morgan hadn't understood what was said, and he was so weakened and stunned by the heat, he thought he must be hallucinating. This can't be a Monk coming into hell to retrieve him. This must be all part of death's agony. He remembered no more it seemed, for a long time.

When he gained consciousness several Native Americans were wrapping cool wet leaves all over his body. My God! It felt so good! They were also giving him water from a jar to sip. He thought, 'I think I am alive! I don't know how, but I am alive! Oh yes, now I remember, the Monk came to hell to free me!'. The priest spoke in Spanish, "Do you feel better, my son? I hope you feel well enough to walk a few kilometers, as we have to leave now for the Mission compound. We have only a few hours or so until darkness and it will be best if we are inside the Mission by then". Morgan understood some of the words, enough to get the intent. 'So, it must be well after seven in the evening. I must have passed out again', Morgan thought, 'because the sun was still up when I first saw the monk.' *"Si, esta bien"*, Morgan was trying to speak Spanish. Although during the last two years or so he had learned to understand some Spanish, he had seldom tried to speak it. He did not know if the priest would understand him. *"Ah, bien, bien! Me ilamo is Padre Mariano Payeras.* But I believe that you are a *yanqui,* and I can speak a little *Englis.* So, what ees your naame?". 'Oh, this will make it much easier', Morgan thought. As he lifted himself from the ground to indicate his readiness to travel, he responded, "My name is Charles Morgan and I'm originally from Massachusetts." "Mach asoo setts?", the priest replied in obvious amazement, "How in the name of *Dios Todopoderoso* did you arrive here?" the priest asked, but continued, "ah well, we do not need to discuss that now, there will be time enough to speak during your recuperation at the *Mision*. But what I am wondering even more right now is, why did Almighty God send you to me?"

As Morgan had only begun to take his first few steps, this statement stunned him, and he hesitated. 'Why did God send me to this priest? What in the hell is he talking about? God didn't send me to him, I got here because of my own stubbornness and stupidity.'

Two of the natives that had arrived with the Padre had started to walk back toward the trail with Padre Payeras following. He turned to Morgan, "Come, my son. Are you alright? Why do you hesitate. I hope that you can make this short walk to *Mision La Purisima.* It is not far."

"Yea, I'll be alright", Morgan responded. He followed the priest with the other two natives following him. They walked a narrow path through the woods, then came to clear land again. In the distance Morgan could now see the ocean in the twilight. They descended the sloping hill and kept walking on a well-worn path. After a half hour or so, they joined another even more worn pathway. "We have reached *El Camino Real*" the priest said. Morgan understood the words but not the meaning. "What did you call this?", he asked. The priest replied, *"El Camino Real,* The Royal Road. This footpath was established several decades ago by our *Presidente,* Padre Junipero Serra. It extends from our first Mission, *San Diego de Alcala,* in the south, all the way north to *San Francisco de Asis.* We travel it often, mostly to go to *Mision Santa Barbara".* It certainly looked well traveled, as the path was worn below the level of the surrounding topsoil. It reminded Morgan of the cow paths to his Papa's barn back home.

Soon they reached a split in the trail. The lead Native American left *El Camino Real* and followed a different pathway, not as well traveled. The priest spoke, "In another half hour or so we will be at *Mision La Purisima* and we will find you a place to spend the night. Then in the morning we can further examine God's design for you". 'There he goes with that "God's design" stuff', Morgan thought. Doesn't he know that things just happen, some for the good and some for the bad? At this point Morgan had obviously decided that his being rescued from certain death by renegades was a good thing, but he was beginning to wonder if the fate he was getting into might turn out to be another bad thing, even if not as bad as these last two days. 'What would be good', he thought, was 'if I can complete my original plan to get to Monterey and find a ship heading out to Boston'.

They were approaching the Mission compound. Many natives came out to greet their Padre and to learn why he had left in such a hurry a few hours earlier. When they saw the tall young light-skinned youth with the Padre, they stood in some awe. Morgan stood a half-head taller than most of the Native American men

12

and nearly a full head taller than Payeras. His body had the look of the strength of a vibrant youth, and his physique was well developed because of doing farm chores from his boyhood. He was a great contrast to Payeras who, though not rotund, was certainly a bit flabby with middle-age girth. In fact, now as Morgan looked about, he remembered being amused while following Payeras on the trail, as the priest looked a bit comical with his rope-cincture tight around his waist. It tended to hold his robe tight to his buttocks, exaggerating their flabbiness.

As he thought about Payeras' raiment he realized that most of the older women were bare-breasted, with only the lower part of their torso covered with skirts made of tule or animal hides, tied about their waist with a thong of animal hide. It wasn't too much different from the mode of dress of that he had seen while visiting some of the South Pacific islands, both as a cabin-boy on the whaling ship he sailed out of New Bedford, and later as a crewman on Hippolyte Bouchard's pirate ship. He did notice that the younger maidens wore a cloth band that covered their breasts and some had cloth skirts or deerskin dresses instead of the tule skirts. The men were all generally dressed in an animal skin skirt that covered only their groin and buttocks areas. What a contrast to the priest who was covered from head to toe with that heavy and uncomfortable-looking robe.

Payeras now spoke to the natives in their language, explaining that he had recovered the *yanqui* from the renegades, and that he would be staying at the Mission to work for God. Morgan did not understand what he had said or he would most certainly have been upset again. He did, however, feel a bit of awe towards this priest's ability to speak to the natives in their own language, as well as to speak to Morgan in his language. 'Obviously,' he thought, 'this is a smart man'. He did not know then that the future would prove the priest to be an expert in languages, architecture, farming, vineyards, and not the least, a wonderful sensitivity towards his flock. Morgan would remain intimidated by this man's capabilities for quite some time to come.

Payeras was now rubbing his chest and Morgan noticed that the priest was suddenly looking pale and uncomfortable. A stout middle-aged native woman stepped quickly forward, looking to the Padre for instructions. "Ah, Cimkonah, please bring me some of your *espina blanco (Hawthorn)* tea…*pronto! pronto!*". Cimkonah turned and with the acknowledging statement *"Si, Si, Padre"*, hurried away. Everyone stood motionless in apprehension as they watched Payeras continue to rub his chest. In just a few minutes Cimkonah returned with the small jug of tea and anxiously passed it to the priest. After drinking and resting for a few more minutes, Payeras looked more comfortable and his color returned. With a little strain in his voice he said, "Now Cimkonah, will you please find Carlos something to eat, then let him sleep in the wheat storeroom." Then, turning to Morgan he said, "I'll see you in the morning Carlos. We can discuss your welfare in more detail after you have rested. Good night, my son".

Cimkonah motioned and Morgan followed her. They went to her cooking area where she quickly found food for him. She offered it while exclaiming,

"Pan!, queso!" He thought that bread and cheese had never tasted so good. Offering a jug, Cimkonah exclaimed, *"Vino!".* Morgan drank so fast that he dribbled the delicious drink down both sides of his mouth.

After Cimkonah thought that he had his fill, she motioned again for him to follow her. They walked under the portico for some distance, then she motioned for Morgan to wait. She went quickly into a room, returning with two beautifully woven blankets. *"Manta",* she explained, displaying them to Morgan. She continued to lead under the portico until they reached the far corner of the compound. She opened the gate to a room which was apparently the wheat storage room that Payeras had mentioned. Cimkonah gave the two blankets to Morgan, backed from the room saying, *"Buenas noches, Carlos",* and was quickly gone.

Morgan remembered waking only once during the night, being aroused by the scurrying of mice as they feasted on the wheat kernels. He rolled over, repositioned the blankets, ('thank God for Cimkonah's thoughtfulness') and quickly fell back to sleep.

When he awoke the sun was high in the sky and was shining through the fenced doorway and the one window of the storeroom. He sat up quickly. He had been so tired that he slept very hard, but now he felt great stiffness and realized how hard the floor of the storeroom was. Just as he lifted himself to stretch, an arm extended itself through the fenced door and dropped a pair of moccasins. *"Por Carlos, de Cimkonah"* a soft female voice said. Morgan heard the soft steps leaving his doorway. He quickly stepped through the gate and saw a young Native American girl hurrying along the portico. He involuntarily exclaimed out loud, "My God, she is so beautiful!"

CHAPTER TWO
Meeting An Angel

Morgan returned to the storeroom, sat on the floor and put the moccasins on his bruised and cut feet. Oh, they felt good. They were deerskin, lined with the fur. As he looked at the place on the floor where he had slept he thought, 'this ain't even as good as the hammock I had on Bouchard's ship', and he couldn't help imagining how comfortable Padre Payeras' bed must be. As he was wondering what kind of quarters the natives must have, he suddenly realized that there was a lot of commotion going on outside. It wasn't the kind caused by a disturbing incident, it was just the activity of many people moving about and chatting. He moved to the doorway, looking all about. He was surprised at the number of people. There were several dozen natives moving about in apparently normal chores, while others worked in the gardens. Many women were clustered around a large pool, washing garments or filling jugs with water from the nearby fountain.

He wondered what he should do now, but didn't have to wait long to find out. Cimkonah was walking toward him under the portico. *"Buenos dias, Carlos"*, she said as she reached Morgan. He smiled and replied *"Buenos dias"*, trying to show appreciation in his voice, since he did not know enough Spanish to tell her fully how he appreciated her great concern for his welfare. He rolled up the two *mantas* and now proffered them to her. She took them back with a smile and motioned for him to follow her. She led him again

17

to her cooking area where she served him ample amounts of food and coffee, all the while flitting about in a solicitous manner. It appeared that she just couldn't do enough for this handsome young *yanqui*.

When he had finished eating she again motioned to him to follow her. They crossed a short open-air distance to the portico and she entered the first doorway that they came to. At the inner door she knocked gently. Padre Payeras' voice from within said, *"Ascentar"*. She entered with a slight bow of her head to the Padre. He was just rising from a kneeling bench in the corner of the room. As he rose, he kissed the figure that was attached to the wooden cross hanging on the wall. Morgan recognized the figure as Jesus Christ. He had seen pictures of this figure in Sunday School books that he had sometimes used at the church in Sturbridge.

"Ah, good morning to you Carlos my son", Payeras greeted, *"Buenos dias* again to you Cimkonah." 'Of course', thought Morgan, 'she has already served him his breakfast'. For the first time he wondered what time of morning it was. The sun was well up in the sky, so he knew that he had slept later than he usually did, and he was apparently the last person in the Mission to rise.

With words of dismissal, *"Muchos gratias,* Cimkonah", the Padre excused her and turned to Morgan. "Sit down my son, how did you sleep. Well I hope." Morgan just nodded and with half-sincerity said, *"Bueno"*. The Padre sensed Morgan's true feelings and said, "I hope that you realize that because we arrived so late last evening, there was no time to prepare better quarters for you. Also, I must be concerned that I do not over-extend our facility on your behalf or I will bring the ire of some neophytes and the sentries upon both you and myself." 'Oh yes, jealousy is everywhere', Morgan thought. "That's alright priest", Morgan replied, "I know that you didn't feel well yourself last night. I hope you feel better this morning". Payeras just nodded slightly and smiled. Morgan continued, "But I didn't understand a word you used, what are the neophytes?" "Oh you have not heard this expression?", Payeras asked. "'Neophyte' is the term we use to describe a native who is receiving my instructions in the tenets of the Catholic faith. Here at *La Purisima* we have several hundred neophytes, with more arriving from their villages almost daily. I take it that you are not yourself of the Catholic faith then." "No", replied Morgan, "I am not".

Payeras commented, "Well, I am not surprised because I have not yet heard of a *Yanqui* who is of our faith. But I'm sure that you did attend a church in your village".

Morgan did not reply, but instead asked, "How in the world do you feed all these people?" "Oh we have many cattle, sheep, and a few swine for food, as well as a few horses for plowing and tending the wheat fields", Payeras replied. The word 'horses' registered well in Morgan's mind. Perhaps his plan to get to Monterey can still be accomplished. "We also prepare the hides of the cattle to sell to the *yanqui* traders. When we have sufficient quantity we transport them to Monterey, fetching a good price for them" 'My, this is sounding better than I had imagined' thought Morgan, 'I oughta be able to find a way to get to Monterey. But

I must bide my time. I may not even have to steal a horse, then I won't have to elude the authorities'.

While they were speaking Morgan was glancing about the room. Noting Morgan's inquisitive gaze, Payeras explained, "This is my quarters, my study and my bedroom combined. Here I pray, direct the Mission efforts, and sleep." The simplicity of the room surprised Morgan. He had thought that a man with such an important position would have a much more *grandios* sleeping quarter and a managerial office. He was especially surprised at the bed which was nothing more than a wooden frame with rope cross-netting. Not even a straw mattress was in sight. He wasn't so sure that this bed was any more comfortable than the floor that he slept on last night. "You are no doubt wondering, Carlos my son, how I came to find you at the camp of the renegades. Well, fortunately for you, the neophyte who had first seen you near our garden in the early morning, decided to come and tell me of the incident. He had spent much of two days in great distress, but finally in the late afternoon yesterday, came to seek my counsel. He wants you to know that his outcry which alerted the sentries, was a startled reaction to your presence. He did not intend that you become hunted like an animal. He is very distressed and seeks your forgiveness. I have already given him mine. When we meet him, I trust that you will find your heart open to his plea. His name is Juan Bautista." Morgan nodded his understanding and concurrence, but he wondered why a native lad would have a Spanish name.

"Now come, Carlos, my son, I will show you the *Mision* complex, *Mision La Purisima Concepcion de Maria Santisima,* in *inglis,* 'The Immaculate Conception Of The Most Pure Holy Mary'". You will see how self-sufficient we are and how efficient the neophytes are in their duties". Padre Payeras led him out of the room and under the portico again. Looking along the portico, it seemed to extend a few hundred yards. Beyond the end of the portico Morgan could see a building that appeared to be a church. Looking away from the portico, across a large open plaza, he saw the fountain that he seen earlier, and the pool still surrounded by many native women. Several tiled pathways criss-crossed through flowered gardens and in the distance he could see a large wooden cross and several more buildings. The land on which the Mission was built was flat but just beyond the buildings the terrain in the east changed to gentle hills. Even though the central Mission grounds were surrounded by a wall, over the top of this he could see the wheat fields and the large garden patch that he had tried to approach two nights ago.

Payeras led Morgan across the plaza, pointing out certain items as they walked. Many species of flowering bushes and cactuses were flourishing. The Padre identified many and indicated why they were selected to be part of the garden. Most had edibility or medicinal purposes, as well as adding beauty to what the somewhat bland color of the mud-brick buildings.

"How long ago were these buildings erected?", Morgan asked. As they strolled toward the large wooden cross Payeras narrated the history of *La Purisima.* "This is the eleventh Mission in the chain that was first conceived by our former *Presidente,* Padre Junipero Serra. Unfortunately he passed away, oh my, it is eighteen years this month, since his death. He died before seeing the completion of the full chain. He had been assigned the task of extending our country's domain northward into Alta California by the Governor of *Nuevo Espana*, Jose' DeGalves. DeGalves feared that Alta California would be populated from the north by Russian soldiers and pioneers, so he ordered Padre Serra and a small group of *soldados* to proceed to Monterey, establishing Mission settlements along the way. This Mission was established as soon as we were sure that *Mision Santa Barbara*, which is two days journey to the south, was self-sufficient. It took only one year for *Santa Barbara* to flourish. *Mision La Purisima Concepcion* was established at the end of 1787 by our present *Presidente*, Padre Fermin Francisco de Lasuen." Morgan thought about that year, 'I was only five years old then'. Thinking more of his childhood, he remembered that when he was about six years old George had told him that 1787 was the same year that Papa returned from Springfield, after Daniel Shay's rebellion was crushed when they tried to capture the arsenal there. Papa left Shay's 'army' just before that, when he heard that Shay was about to attack the Arsenal, and Papa knew that that was a hanging offense if they got caught'.

"He is a remarkable man." Morgan was listening to Payeras again, finding the commentary quite interesting. "You will enjoy him when you meet him", Payeras continued. "He has distinguished himself in service to God and our Country by correcting problems at Missions in both *Baja* California and *Alta* California, especially quelling problems with the natives at *Misions San Gabriel y*

San Diego". Without comment Morgan thought,' quelling native problems?, What caused that I wonder'. Payeras continued, "After using temporary buildings here for a number of years we were able to obtain enough craftsman from *Santa Barbara* and enough neophyte laborers, to begin these permanent buildings".

Again Morgan's thoughts were contrary to what Payeras believed were laudatory remarks. 'Neophyte laborers?, or slaves?. Permanent buildings? They don't look all that permanent to me.' Extending his arm in a sweep of the Mission, Payeras continued, "These buildings took about four years to construct and were only completed a few years ago. Our next need is to stucco the outer walls to prevent erosion by the wind and rain in the spring. Just two days journey to the north is the beautiful *Mision San Luis Obispo De Tolosa*. It has been in existence now for about twenty five years. You see, it was *Presidente* Padre Serra's plan to maintain a Mission at the distance of one day's journey apart so that travelers would always find a haven for the night. The distance also gave each Mission sufficient land area to maintain itself and support the neophytes within that area. We now have eighteen Missions established and need to establish a few more in order to accomplish Padre Serra's plan. Padre Fermin Francisco Lasuen, the successor to Padre Serra, has founded our last eight Missions. He is a most holy and devoted man and it is he who established the methods under which we prosper today." They had reached the far end of the plaza.

"Now look, my son," Payeras continued, "from here you can see the fields of wheat, and beyond in the hills are the ranges where the cattle graze." It was true, Morgan could see the enormity of the operation. 'And this is only one of eighteen', he thought. He had never seen such a farm in Massachusetts; in fact he thought, mistakenly, that all of the farms in Massachusetts put together would not equal the acreage and herds of this one Mission. 'This must be what the farms in Indiana Territory and in the Northwest Territory are like. No wonder so many farmers from Massachusetts are leaving for the western territories'.

Most of the view that the two had was east and southward, but turning to the north Morgan saw long rows of buildings that were constructed of timber and covered with tule, tree branches and boughs. These buildings were mostly hidden when one stood at the Mission plaza. Almost as if by intent, Morgan thought. "That is the native village", Payeras explained. "It is quite large as compared to the individual campsites that these people lived in before." Morgan wondered to himself if "these people" were now better off than in their former family groups. Inwardly he doubted it.

They continued walking, coming to buildings that Payeras described as "our *carpinteria*", "our *texturia*", "our *calenderia*", "our *alfararia*", "our *herbario*", and so forth. Although he did not know the meaning of all the names that Payeras had spoken, Morgan recognized the activity of each area, as they were similar to the same activities necessary to his household and farm back home. But these were on a massive scale, understandably he realized, with many hundreds of people needing these necessities. The two came to another building with a portico. At the first door Payeras said, "This is the *soldados* quarters. Next to it is the room of the *Cabo* who is in command of the three sentries assigned here. At that very moment a soldier with corporal's insignia on his tunic came out the door. Payeras spoke to him in Spanish. By the soldier's reaction it was not hard for Morgan to understand. "Ah, *Cabo* Rivera. I want you to become acquainted with *Senor* Carlos Moorgaan, who is my guest and will be remaining at *La Purisima* for some time. I expect him to be treated with courtesy. I trust that you understand." Morgan recognized the soldier as the leader of the group that had captured him three days earlier. The Corporal gave Padre Payeras a nod of his head, accepting, though obviously reluctantly, the "orders" from the Padre.

As they continued walking Payeras explained, "I have a rather tenuous control over the sentries. It is more the respect of my priesthood to which they accede, since I have no civil or military authority over them. They are stationed here as an outpost of the Company of *Capitan* Marco Hernandez at *Santa Barbara*. Each Mission has at least a few *soldados* assigned to act as *policia* in the event of any unruly neophytes. Of course, in the unlikely event of a more major problem, *soldados* from the *Presidio en Santa Barbara* would be dispatched here immediately. But with regard to Rivera, he is a trouble-maker and not worthy of holding the advanced rank of Corporal. I have requested *Capitan* Hernadez to transfer him back to the *Presidio* on several occasions. Apparently Hernandez doesn't want the attendant difficulties either, so that he will not transfer him. My serious fear is that Rivera wants to attain a position of important leadership so badly that he is willing to cultivate a following of renegade natives. So far, he has only been successful in finding a very few followers. But you already know that don't you, Carlos." Indeed, Morgan did know this and wondered if the Padre's instructions to Rivera were really going to end Morgan's troubles.

They passed several more doorways which Payeras described as various storerooms. Morgan recognized the one in which he had spent the night. At the last doorway of the building the Padre stopped. "This is the *monjerio,* ah *dormitorio*, that is, the private room of the neophyte maidens. It is forbidden for any males to enter this room. If they do, they must suffer not only my wrath, but also that of Cimkonah, who is their *duena*. As you can imagine, she has strength enough to assail any male who dares to intrude. Unfortunately, she has had to eject some of our own sentries who dared to enter on 'official business'".

'So, this is not the serene "village" that it appears to be', thought Morgan. Still, as they had been walking, he heard the native women singing Spanish hymns while they washed their clothing or worked in the gardens. They certainly seemed happy enough. As he finished speaking, Payeras looked straight in the eyes of Morgan. The look clearly said "you understand me well, do you not." Morgan felt a little embarrassed by the Padre's hard stare. Yes, he understood, but his mind went immediately to the young native maiden that he had seen at rising this morning.

Of course, the Padre had no way of knowing that this shy young yankee had not yet ever held a girl in his arms nor been kissed by any other than his step-mother and sister. In fact, while sailing with Bouchard, each time that they entered a port he was the butt of many jokes and remarks by the lascivious crew. It wasn't that Morgan did not have the urges and desires, it was more that he could not find comfort with the kind of women that the other sailors "enjoyed". It was this discomfort with the life of a pirate band that led him to decide to desert the ship, even at the risk of his life.

They had now reached the building that was obviously a church or chapel. The entrance door was at the center of one side wall, not at the rear as in most churches. Just inside the door the Padre dipped his finger tips into a water bowl attached to the wall and made the sign of a cross, touching those finger tips to his forehead, his waist and then each shoulder. This was the second religious action that Morgan had observed of the Padre today. He had heard that Catholics had many strange beliefs and customs, but these did not seem so terribly harmful. At least, Padre Payeras did not seem to expect Morgan to follow his actions.

They walked down the center aisle to about the center of the church. The Padre stopped, looked all about, then said to Morgan, "Do you like the decorations? They have been done by the neophytes, using berry and fruit juices, as well as ground pigments of earthly materials. They have only recently completed these decorations, in time for our *adviento* liturgies, which will start in a few months in preparation for *pascua de navidad.*" Morgan was surprised at the beauty of the decorations, painted on every wall. These had obviously been accomplished using crude stencils, but the designs were attractive and adorned the areas above each window and around each roof beam. Other, more geometric designs were stenciled along the entire length of the church just above the wainscoting. But by far the most beautiful were those adorning the *reredos,* the areas behind the altar, consisting of a large central niche and two smaller niches to either side. The frames of these niches, as well as the adjacent panels and roof beams just above the altar, were even more profusely decorated.

There were no pews or benches; the floor was covered with large but uneven tiles. Other devices were attached to the walls. They seemed to be a series of pictures, each one including a figure that looked like Jesus Christ. The whole effect was confusing and a bit overwhelming to Morgan who had only seen the inside of one other church in his life, his own Congregationalist church in Sturbridge. That one was starkly simple except for a few gold ornaments on the chandeliers. And his church had pews so that everyone could sit comfortably while Reverend Dawson droned on with his lengthy sermon.

"What do you think, Carlos?, Are you not impressed by the artistic ability of these neophytes?" They were now standing immediately in front of the altar, so that the decorations and the obvious intricacies of the art work were more apparent. "I'm amazed", Morgan replied, as he turned himself in a circle to review the whole effect again. "I never conceived of a church looking like this, and certainly not to be so beautifully decorated by pagan Indians." Padre Payeras corrected him somewhat sternly, "These are not pagans, Carlos, they are neophytes, and they will soon be baptized into our *Catolico* faith. Further, I sense a tone in your voice when you say 'Indian', that is patronizing. Remember, my son, that we are all children of God, made to His own image, and are all equal in His eyes. It is our actions and failures on earth that will cause Almighty God to treat us unequally in our final judgment. Further, while you are my guest, I do not wish to hear you speak again of pagan natives unless they are not of our Mission family." 'My word', Morgan thought, 'I sure touched his peevish spot.' "Alright", he replied, "alright, I understand the distinction." Payeras moved very quickly to the side doorway again, seeming to want to end this conversation by leaving the church.

Outside, Payeras pointed out the cemetery beside the church, then pointed to another cemetery just outside the Mission wall and explained, "This cemetery is for the Padres and others who may die here, while across the way is the native's burial ground." Morgan believed that he knew that by "others", the Padre meant Spaniards. The cemetery within the Mission wall had white crosses marking each grave while the cemetery outside the wall had a few crosses but most were marked with a stick that had feathers or animal bones attached. Other animal bones or shells lay on the mounds. Morgan wondered to himself, 'What is this then? If all are equal in God's eyes, as Payeras had just said, why not one cemetery? He decided not to ask about this discrepancy just then.

Instead he followed after Payeras who was now walking toward the building where Payeras' quarters were located. It was a long building and as they walked the Padre explained the rooms. "This is *cuarto de instruccion*, a school-room, where our children are taught to read and write Spanish, as well as to learn their prayers and their new religion. We are attempting to interpret their Chumash tongue and to transcribe it, but it is most difficult. Do you realize that even though their language is thousands of years old, it has never been put into written form because they have no alphabetic characters. Only a few native cultures have developed an alphabet for themselves. While I was stationed in *Nuevo Espana* however, many of the native tribes that I encountered there had written characters for their language."

Morgan peered into the room through the open doorway. There were nearly two dozen youngsters seated on the floor, being taught by a Spanish-looking lady. The most noticeable thing about the room, other than not having chairs or desks, was its darkness. There was only one window, so for lighting many tapers were being burned, giving the room a smell of smoke and burning tallow. Through the smoky darkness though, Morgan did get a glimpse of the native maiden that he had seen that morning. From her position she also saw Morgan, and looked at him rather long he thought. Because she was departing from him that morning, he had not seen a full view of her face until now. He thought, 'her face is as beautiful as her body'.

"How old are the children in this class?", Morgan asked, trying to sound casual. He was hoping that she was not too young; she certainly had not looked immature this morning in her deerskin dress which clung to her body. "They are as young as six years, and our oldest student, Angelica, is sixteen years." It pleased Morgan to hear that she was that old;

30

he himself would be twenty in just a few months, and he thought how well her Christian name suited her lithe, full beauty.

They moved further along the portico. At each doorway Payeras explained the room's function. There was an additional *cuarto de instruccion*, several guest's bedrooms and the wine storage room. This was the only room that Morgan noticed having an iron gate with a lock. "To forestall any trouble, this wine storage is next to my quarters and I am the only one holding a key for the room. In this way we eliminate any temptations that the neophytes, or the *soldados* for that matter, may have."

"So, Carlos my son, now that you have seen *Mision La Purisima Concepcion*, we must next determine what is God's plan for your presence here." Morgan felt that uneasiness again, even aggravation, at Payeras' persistence on this point. It was as if Payeras was some kind of spirit that had the power to determine how the rest of his life was to be lived. Payeras continued, "Join me for *almuerzo,* luncheon that is, and we shall discuss the matter. But first we must get your clothing washed. Since you have no others, come with me to the guest room next to my quarters and I shall provide something for you to wear while Cimkonah tends to your clothing".

As soon as they reached Payeras' room he left for a few minutes, returning with a large white garment. "Take off all your clothing including you under garments. I am sure they are just as salt-laden and odorous as your outer garments. Then wear this *blanco prenda de vestir* for a few hours. Ah...your English speaking priests call it an Alb...By mid-afternoon the sun will have dried your clothing. You can wear the Alb while we take *almuerzo* and while you *siesta* for a few hours, here in this guest room." "What is an Alb?", Morgan asked, while examining the voluminous garment. Payeras explained, "It is one of several liturgical garments that a priest wears during the celebration of Holy Mass. I am sorry that I have nothing else to provide you right now. I did not think that you would want to wear one of my heavy, course robes. The alb will be cooler for you and it is only for a few hours."

Morgan thought the garment to be very frivolous and bulky but he did not argue with Payeras' reasoning. His clothing was indeed dirty, stinking and uncomfortable. The priest left, Morgan stripped, and feeling very foolish, put on the alb. It was only a few minutes before Cimkonah knocked on the door. "Enter", Morgan called. Cimkonah entered and quickly picked up Morgan's clothing from the floor. She tried not to look at Morgan but from the corner of her eye she could not help but see him. As she departed, Morgan was sure she was giggling to herself.

While waiting for lunch-hour Morgan inspected the bookcase that was well stocked with books of many kinds. All were in Spanish, but glancing through the pages and the illustrations, he recognized that there were books on engineering, architecture, agriculture, art, Shakespeare, as well as other famous writers. Not that Morgan was a "scholar", but he had heard the names of some of the authors, and was a generally inquisitive person. He made a mental note to ask Payeras if he could borrow some of the books to take to his storeroom "quarters".

From the room next to him, Morgan heard Payeras call him to lunch. As he entered, Cimkonah and Angelica were carrying in the meal. Comkonah tittered again but Angelica broke into an embarrassed laugh. Morgan blushed and was very uncomfortable. Payeras explained to the two women why Morgan was wearing the liturgical garment, but the explanation did little to end their amusement. As they left the room together they joined hands in an expression to each other of the merriment of the situation.

As the two men sat at the table Payeras said, "Carlos, my son, we must say grace before partaking of this meal. Perhaps the only prayer that we both know is the *Pater Noster*. Oh, sorry, you would know it as 'The Lord's Prayer'". Yes, Morgan knew it, but it had been a long time since he had said it. Payeras prompted, "I will have trouble saying this prayer in English, so why don't you lead and I'll follow as best I can." Now Morgan felt even more uncomfortable. He had never been put in the position of having to lead a prayer, and especially with a clergyman as his associate.

"Our Father, which art in heaven", he began. Payeras spoke the words simultaneously, if a little falteringly. Morgan continued all the way through the prayer, closing with "for Thine is the kingdom, the power and the glory for ever. Amen." Payeras had not expected the last sentence, but then remembered that Protestants concluded the prayer with that sentence, although Catholics did not. He had faltered a little although Morgan had not realized it. They had both stated the "Amen" simultaneously and strongly. Morgan felt quite good about himself.

While they ate Payeras asked Morgan many questions about his background and was especially interested to know how Morgan had gotten involved with the brigand Hyppolyte Bouchard. Morgan told the priest how, after the death of his brother and a misunderstanding with his stepmother, he had left home, regrettably without saying goodbye to anyone except his brother George. He told how he was so upset with his stepmother because she always seemed to favor Harold, her natural son, over either Albert or himself. He was also upset with his father for having married this woman who seemed to have no love except for Harold. He felt that she did not even have love for Papa, only marrying him to get a roof over her head. He did admit, though, that since leaving home, he realized that she may not have been so bad as he thought, that it was natural that she would favor Harold as he was really very young. Still, while in a confused state, he had traveled to New Bedford and signed on a whaling ship. At first the new life was exciting and sailing in tropical waters was certainly pleasant. They had been at sea for about ten months, then put into the island of Maui in the Hawaiian Islands group, to replenish their fresh water and food stocks. On the third or fourth day there a sailor from another ship spoke to him in glowing terms about his ship and the wonderful places that they had sailed. Their next port-o-call was to be the Sandwich Islands, where there would be abundant opportunity to secure treasure and gold, enough to live the rest of his life in comfort. He was barely eighteen. He had no idea that he was joining a band of pirates, but once aboard he had no opportunity to leave for almost a year, until his escape two nights ago.

Payeras listened in rapt amazement that such a young man had already seen so much of life. "And what is your hope now, Carlos?", the priest asked. Morgan decided to divulge his plan to steal a horse and to flee to Monterey as a means of returning to New Bedford or Boston. "Oh, my! That could have gotten you killed! Do you realize that?", Payeras asked. Yes, Morgan acknowledged that the plan was not without risk. He was now secretly hoping that Payeras would offer to provide a horse to him.

"Well, Carlos, my son, neither of us knows what the Good Lord has in mind for you, but I think for now that it is best that you stay here at *La Purisima* for a while. You see, after observing you for only this short time, and listening to your experiences, I believe that God wants you to help me for a few months." At this statement Morgan suddenly felt very desperate and could not help wondering if it was "the Good Lord" or Payeras himself that was deciding this 'help' matter. "What do you mean, 'help you", he asked. "If you have any concern at all for my welfare, you will want to help me return home to Massachusetts", Morgan stated.

But Payeras explained, "You see, my son, each Mission is supposed to have at least two Padres, one who attends to the religious instruction of the neophytes, while the other concentrates on running the temporal aspects of it's large rancho. Unfortunately, due to the reduction in the number of missionaries from *Espana,* and because our seminary in *Nuevo Espana* is still preparing seminarians for ordination, I am laboring here alone. I pray that I will soon receive the assistance of another Padre, but in the meantime I believe that you can be of great service to God, and incidentally to me. Further, I promise that after you have completed these tasks, if you still wish to leave, I will aid you".

'Well', Morgan thought, 'I guess I can't go wrong by agreeing to this arrangement'. "Alright, I'll do what I can for a few months, but no later than springtime. I want to be on my way by then". The priest was jubilant. "Very well, my son, I am sure that God will bestow blessings on your efforts in His behalf. And now I must say my mid-day prayers in thankfulness to The Lord, and you need to *siesta* for a few hours. We shall discuss this in more detail later. In the meantime I will have Cimkonah prepare the guest room for you to occupy." Morgan started to leave the room, but near the door he hesitated. "How is it that you speak such good English?", he asked. "Ah, I thought you would be curious about that", Payeras replied. "You see, my son, when I was about to be ordained a priest, Spain had regained control of *Florida* from the English. I was to be assigned there by my Order, I was therefore tutored extensively in the English language, since there were both Spanish and English speaking inhabitants."

"Oh, I see", Morgan replied. Then with further thought, and looking straight into Payeras' eyes he said, "I've been thinking. Since I'm not of your faith, and I'm not your son, I don't like you to call me 'my son'. And I don't see how I can call you 'Padre' since you ain't my father. I think I can only call you like I would a professional man back home, like 'Reverend' or 'Doctor', so I'll call you by your profession, 'Priest'. And,...like I told you yesterday, my name is Charles, not Carlos."

Morgan waited for the priest's reaction. He had decided that if Payeras wanted him to stay so badly, he might as well get these things off his chest. The Padre looked a little surprised, but not stunned. Morgan turned to leave and Payeras said, *"Adios Sharlezz,* my so..., ah, good afternoon *Sharlezz."* Morgan replied pleasantly, "Good afternoon, priest." As they turned away from each other both men were smiling. Neither saw the other do so. Morgan was very pleased with himself for taking a stand against what he felt was the priest's attempt to dominate him, while Payeras smiled because he couldn't help but like this brash young yanqui.

CHAPTER THREE
From Farm Boy To Seaman
To Pirate To...

It was now nearing the end of September. Morgan found it hard to realize that he had been at the Mission for over a month. Still, with the pleasantness of his new surroundings and activities, he was not as displeased as he thought he would be. Padre Payeras had allowed him to live in the guest room where he had plenty of reading material on subjects that he enjoyed. He was making more sense of Spanish each day, as well as beginning to understand some of the Chumash words. Payeras had now assigned him to supervise the natives in the blacksmith shop and saddler. For the first few days Payeras had put him to work in the gardens, then a week or so tending the cattle herds, and even made him work in the tallow shop. That was the most distasteful, with its pungent odor and dense smoke. But his present job was enjoyable because he felt that it demonstrated the need for skill, more than the other activities; the skills that he had practiced on the farm since he was only seven or eight years old.

And he was thoroughly enjoying teaching the natives. Especially the one they called Juan Bautista, who was about the same age as Morgan, and was very eager to learn anything that Morgan could teach him. Morgan had expressed his "forgiveness" to Juan for that first night alarm, as soon as Padre Payeras had introduced them. Juan Bautista was an apt student, a fine fellow in his manners and had a very pleasing personality. He appeared to Morgan to be just like the drawing of an Algonquin warrior that he had seen in a book at home. Juan had a fine physique, wore deerskin breeches, usually was shirtless and had long black hair arranged in a long braid. Morgan "conversed" with Juan by a mixture of Spanish words, some English, occasional Chumash, and if all else failed, by hand motions.

Adding to the pleasantness of the situation, Morgan often saw Angelica. Of course it was only as she passed by while performing her general duties as Cimkonah's helper, but he thought that each time she passed, Angelica's smile became more friendly. Even when she wasn't present, Morgan thought of her often. He could not remember knowing a girl that had affected him the way Angelica does. (Well, maybe Becky Reynolds in the fifth grade.) But this was the first time that he felt inner arousals, the kind that his pirate shipmates had so vulgarly and so often expressed. There had been a couple of times when Bouchard's ship had put into Caribbean ports that a woman tried to seduce Morgan, and he had felt the urges to respond, but something in his puritanical upbringing inhibited him. He remembered that one or two of these women were quite attractive and the manner of their dress was certainly revealing of their female attributes. Morgan realized however, that his instinctive reactions to these women were not his true feelings.

Angelica, on the other hand, was causing both physical and emotional responses. Could it be that he was truly in love? Yes, he felt so. But what should he do about it? Should he approach Angelica, hoping that she may respond with the same emotions? Should he arrange a secret rendezvous? No, he instinctively knew that Angelica would only feel revulsion to this suggestion, not only because of her belief in her new religion with its rigid moral code, but because she was, he felt, a virtuous person in herself.

Several days later, however, Morgan came to a disheartening realization. He knew that each time that Angelica had smiled at him she was sincere, but he now had to accept the fact that Angelica was only displaying her innate friendliness, not any amorous signals toward him. This realization became apparent when he recognized that Angelica was coming by the blacksmith shop more often when Juan Bautista was there. And now he realized that those longing smiles she displayed were directed at Juan, with a different, only courteous smile for Morgan. Then yesterday, shortly after Angelica passed by, Juan had left the blacksmith shop to join her.

Morgan watched after them as they walked along a pathway toward the edge of a wooded area. They disappeared behind a large tree. Morgan saw them embrace just before completely disappearing from view. They remained out of sight for only a moment then walked hand-in-hand back to the blacksmith shop. With their hands still engaged, Angelica departed slowly, allowing her finger tips, rather than her lips, to express her love for Juan. Juan came into the shop smiling like Morgan had never seen him smile before. Morgan was very envious, but he smiled to his friend, placed his strong hands on Juan's shoulders and said, "You love her very much, don't you?". Juan replied with a nod of his head and an even broader smile. Morgan felt heartsick when he added, "and she loves you very much, too." If only she had felt that way toward him, he would be as elated as Juan was, rather than feeling so dejected. But of course, Angelica would prefer one of her own culture, and Juan was certainly a handsome and physically attractive young man. Why should she not fall in love with him.

So now the days seemed to drag on and became very monotonous. Teaching Juan was no longer exhilarating. Thoughts that Morgan had forgotten for awhile, to get to Monterey to find a passage to Boston, came more often again. Each day Angelica and Juan had their very brief tryst. Morgan thought that surely their time together would become longer and longer, but it did not. Only the brief moment to embrace, then back they came. As Morgan thought about it, he realized that Angelica was certainly a chaste girl, and would nodoubt remain so until her wedding day. Perhaps it was this realization of her strong character that had attracted him to her to begin with. Well, yes, she really was extremely physically attractive too. He could not deny his yearnings for her. Suddenly he realized that for all those nights that he had thought about her, Juan too, no doubt, was having the same torment. How long can Juan control himself?, Morgan wondered.

Both Morgan and Juan were keeping plenty busy in the blacksmithshop. Payeras was always asking for more door and shutter hinges, latches and candle holders. Then too, there was the constant repair of the farming implements and horses harnesses.

41

Although the buildings had been constructed some years earlier, more extensions were being added and most of the original buildings never had doors or window shutters installed because Payeras had not been able to obtain the services of a carpenter or a blacksmith. Recently though, a carpenter had arrived from *Santa Barbara*, so now many unfinished projects were getting tended to.

Payeras was smiling more these days it seemed to Morgan, nor was he rubbing his chest as much. Morgan asked Payeras about what must be his heart pains and the priest had explained that he had a condition that a doctor in *Nuevo Espanola* had called "coronary thrombosis". Although the doctor knew of English and French physicians who were able to treat and alleviate this condition, Payeras could not avail himself of their cures. He relied on the therapeutic effect of Cimkonah's *espina blanco* tea, which greatly eased his pain.

The other disconcerting element remaining at the Mission was Corporal Rivera. Morgan realized that Rivera's eyes were forever gazing at Angelica, also. He had first noticed this during the time that he worked in the garden. Each time that Angelica had come to pick vegetables for Cimkonah, and while Morgan himself was starring at Angelica, he came to realize that Rivera was leering at her from the portico in front of his barracks room. At first Morgan believed that Rivera was smitten by her beauty, just as he himself, but he grew uncomfortable about Rivera. Then Morgan discovered that Rivera was aware of Angelica's and Juan's rendezvous location and was often positioned where he could observe them. Morgan had warned

Juan to be very careful, but Juan was too anxious to meet Angelica each day, so he paid no heed to Morgan's warning.

It was the end of another work day. Morgan returned to his room to wash for *cena,* the evening meal. For the whole month that he had been here, he had taken both lunch and dinner with Payeras. Breakfast however, was taken separately because Morgan ate immediately after rising, whereas Payeras celebrated his first Mass at dawn and could not yet partake of food. This Mass was attended by many of the neophytes before they began their daily tasks. A second Mass, celebrated one-and-one-half hours later was attended by the soldiers, the Spanish craftsmen and their families, as well as by a few neophytes whose duties allowed them this time. By Catholic regulations, Payeras had to abstain from breakfast until he had finished this second Mass.

Morgan and Payeras enjoyed each other's company most of the time. Payeras was especially happy to have a meal companion that he felt offered intellectual stimulation and was able to discuss a wide variety of subjects. Morgan had not realized himself how conversant he was on many of the subjects raised by Payeras. They often discussed the history and political conditions of Morgan's young country, the United States, and Payeras was especially curious about Morgan's own life and home.

Morgan described how his grandfather, Seth, had come from England in 1760, bringing his wife Elizabeth and infant son Paul. Grandfather had a brother who had come from England a few years earlier and was farming in Charlton, the town just northeast of Sturbridge. But Seth and his family had moved into Sturbridge where Seth became a tenant farmer on land owned by a wealthy man named Aldrich. When the trouble started in Boston in 1775, Seth and many of the village men had marched to Concord to protect the arsenal that the farmers had secreted there. He remained in the Colonial Army all the way to Valley Forge, where he died in that terrible winter. His widow Elizabeth died soon after, and Paul was on his own at age 17. He worked as a farm hand, and the next year he married Catherine, an immigrant girl. They had four children, but Catherine died of influenza just a few days after Charles' birth. All four children were left in the care of Mr. And Mrs. Pennington, who had a nice house in the middle of the village. The children remained with the Penningtons for almost three years.

The Penningtons had wanted to legally adopt them but Papa said no, he was going to marry again and could bring them home to the new farmhouse that he was renting. Papa and the boys all worked hard to develop the rented land, while Mary and Stepmama Anna tended to the home, the cooking, making clothes, preserving food for the winter, and dozens of other necessities. Morgan described how, as a five year old, he helped Papa, George and Albert to move boulders from the field so they would have more farming area. The boulders were placed around a field that Papa hoped would someday be the grazing area for a cow or two, when he could afford them. Morgan remembered how Papa told George that when he got the cows he would then be able to vote in the town elections, but until then the law was that he could not. A year later

Harold was born and Morgan felt that Stepmama Anna never had time for him after that.

Morgan asked Payeras about his boyhood in Spain but Payeras only replied, "Oh we can discuss that at another time." He then asked Morgan to leave him so that he could say his evening prayers. One evening during their discussions Payeras said, "I have some clothing for you. I knew that you must be uncomfortable wearing the same clothing every day, so I sent a trusted neophyte to *Santa Barbara* to obtain additional clothing for you. I knew that RobertoMendez, a craftsman there, was almost as tall as you, so I sent a note to his wife Margarito, asking if she might send me some of Roberto's old clothing. I'm afraid that because the request came from me, Margarito has sent some of Roberto's best clothing. But take them, and someday you may have an opportunity to repay Roberto and Margarito. In the meantime please remember these two finepeople in your prayers, as I do in mine."

The matter of prayer had arisen at each meal because Payeras would not partake of a meal without giving thanks to the Almighty. They had maintained the practice of saying "The Lord's Prayer" as their common offering. Recently however, Payeras had been insisting on saying the prayer in Latin and was urging Morgan to express the words in this very foreign tongue. *"Pater Noster, qui es in caelis: Sanctificetur nomen tuum..."*. Payeras waited as Morgan tried to twist his tongue into these unusual words. Payeras would go on, one sentence at a time, until Morgan caught up with him. Over several weeks, Morgan had memorized the strange words, but never knew the exact translation of each word into English.

Still, he enjoyed the company of Payeras, even if the priest always seemed to be pressing him in some way. Each noon for instance, Payeras would ask Morgan if he had attended Mass that morning, even though Payeras knew that he had not. Morgan would always reply that he had not, nor did he intend to do so.

Following the evening meal Morgan would return to his room spending several hours browsing through the library of books before retiring. Except for his yearnings for Angelica, life here at the Mission wasn't too bad. By early November the weather was cooling, the occasional rains were starting and the winds from the eastern mountains were very strong at times. Payeras had cautioned everyone about outdoor fires because a spark carried by the wind could easily start the dried tule roofs afire. He commented to Morgan several times that in the spring they must start making tiles for the roofs of the major buildings, both for better weather protection as well as safety from possible fire. The tiles would also protect the tops of the adobe walls from erosion caused by the rain. The Padre had already started many neophytes on the project of applying stucco to the walls to prevent crumbling, also caused by the rains.

The clay for the stucco had to be carried from the foothills some distance away, kneaded into a pliable consistency, then have pieces of cactus needles or other chafing mixed in. While this laborious task was going on, other natives were scoring the adobe walls so that the new outer layer would adhere better.

It was obvious to Morgan that even though half a hundred neophytes were engaged in this project, it would take years to stucco all of the buildings. This formidable task, plus the future manufacture and application of the roof tiles, struck Morgan as being slave labor of the natives. He and Payeras now discussed the matter more often, sometimes heatedly. Payeras insisted that the neophytes were not slaves by any definition of the word, that they were doing the work voluntarily for the love of the *Jesuchristo*, and that they could return to their original villages at any time that they wished.

While Morgan reluctantly agreed that the latter was true, still, the neophytes had now become very dependent on the Mission for their food, clothing and even the direction in their lives. Only the older ones would be able to now return to the life-sustaining methods of their forebears. None of the younger North American natives had ever foraged for themselves. Even Juan Bautista, who had been left at the Mission when he was only six years old by his widower father, had never gathered acorns or trapped small animals for food. These, and occasionally caught fish, had been the staple commodities for the inland Chumash for thousands of years before the Padres arrived. But now, in just one or two generations, the Chumash were being changed forever.

During their dinner conversations Morgan became more and more tenacious in his views that the Missionaries and the Spanish government were taking advantage of the availability of the large native populous to perform servile tasks for the enrichment of the Spanish treasury. The more agitated and vocal that

Morgan became, the more calm and deliberate Payeras became in explaining that the primary objective of the Missionaries was the welfare ofthe Native Americans, and admittedly, their conversion to the Catholic faith. For after all, Payeras explained, our toils on earth are but the prelude to our eternity with our Maker, *Todopodoroso Dios*, Almighty God.

Payeras also related how, more than two hundreds year earlier, Spain had tried to occupy the area now known as the Carolinas of the new United States, as well as the now Tennessee Territory, by military conquest. In spite of the Spanish armies the natives had repulsed the invaders. Payeras explained that, in his opinion, had missionaries been included in those parties, converting the natives, peace would have been established and that by now the natives would be well educated and share an equal status with the white settlers.

Then he asked, when the English or Dutch came to the New World, did they provide for the welfare of the Native Americans? For that matter, did the New England settlers provide for the natives in any way. Indeed not, they had only taken the Native American's land from them, forcing them further and further westward, into unknown territories where even others of their own culture often did not accept them. Is it not better that we teach these neophytes to provide for themselves in the new ways of the world. And indeed, if we had not, the Russians would have been here by now and who knows what might then have been the fate of the Native Americans and their culture? Well, Morgan did have to concede that the New Englanders really had not done much for the

Native Americans except in a few places where Ministers had tried to teach them, but without much support from the local population.

Once Morgan had tried to complain about the practice of changing the native's names to Christian names, but as soon as he brought up the matter, he remembered reading in his history book about Metacomet, who first befriended the Pilgrims at Plimouth and christianized his name to Phillip. Later this same chief, then known as King Phillip, had changed his mind and massacred hundreds of whites after they took more and more of the Wampanoag's land. Then Payeras reminded Morgan that even the Apostles had changed their names when they became followers of Christ, so what was so strange about the neophytes taking a Christian name?

After these discussions, Morgan would usually come away feeling that he failed to convince Payeras of any of his points. But then, what did it matter, he wasn't going to change the intentions of the Spanish government or the Catholic Church anyway. The only thing that he felt he could do is to be kind to the natives and teach them as best he could to cope with their new conditions.

In late November Padre Payeras informed Morgan that he had to relocate Morgan to the blacksmith's quarters, that is, the room adjoining the blacksmith shop itself. Of course, Morgan had seen this room, which not having been previously occupied, was not in a very livable condition. Morgan was inwardly convinced that Payeras was retaliating against him because of the argumentative mood that he had now been showing. But Payeras explained with some excitement however, that a new Padre was due to arrive before *Navidad*, and he would naturally require the 'guest' room for his quarters.

So Morgan, with Juan Bautista's help, had finished the blacksmith's room and manufactured a few pieces of furniture for it. Morgan did not like the new quarters, but what bothered him more was not having access to the library of books in the guest room. Payeras had also explained that it would be necessary that Morgan take his meals with the Spanish craftsmen. Many of these did not readily accept Morgan because they felt the he had been given preferential treatment by their Padre.

One morning in mid-November, Morgan was summoned by Juan Bautista to report immediately to the Padre's quarters. When he entered the room he saw Corporal Rivera, Cimkonah, Angelica and a Spanish officer all standing, somewhat nervously, in front of Payeras' desk. Payeras spoke, "Ah, do come in *Carlos*." Morgan felt that he had stressed the *"Carlos"*. Payeras continued, "I wish to introduce *Capitan* Marco Hernandez, who has ridden all the way from *Santa Barbara Presidio* to meet you and speak about you." For his part, the Captain seemed to ignore Morgan's presence, addressing only Payeras. "PadrePayeras, I find it hard to accept your explanation for the presence of this *yanqui* here at *La Purisima* for these past several months. You have not reported his presence to me, and from what Corporal Rivera has reported to me, he is a *pirata* that should have been sent to my *Presidio* for trial and punishment. Had I not inquired why *Senora* Mendez had dispatched some of Roberto's clothing here, I would not even have know of this *yanqui's* existence. But now that I do know, and now that I know his background, I find it hard to believe your statement that you are tutoring him to become a padre"

Morgan was astounded! Payeras had told this Officer that he was preparing to become a priest? What ungodly statement had Payeras made anyway? Me!, a priest! Before Morgan could blurt out a protest, Payeras spoke. Seeming to give an emphasis to certain words so that Morgan would understand the situation, Payeras calmly asked, *"Carlos*, have we not said prayers together?, Have I not been teaching you Latin?, Have you not worn a liturgical robe at an appropriate time?, Have we not discussed the Catholic church's teachings at length?"

Turning to Hernandez, he continued, *"Capitan* Hernandez, in my opinion this young man has abundant qualities and abilities to become a fine padre, and after I have continued instructing him, and after baptizing him into the Church, soon I hope, he may be enrolled in our seminary in *Nuevo Espana*. So you see, he has repented for any misconduct in life, and it is *my* judgment that it is not necessary to subject him to any civil trial. Now,…Carlos, Cimkonah, Angelica, can you attest to the truth of my statements so that *Capitan* Hernadez can report to his superior that this young man has participated in all of the activities that I described?" As Hernandez looked around, each nodded assent.

Hernandez made a quick judgment. He did not feel that he wanted to create a jurisdictional dispute between the civil and religious authorities, especially with him in the middle. A bad outcome could thwart his chances for promotion or even ruin his military career entirely. With a quick nod to the *Padre* and a hand signal to his underling, the Captain and the Corporal turned and hastily left the room. Watching through the doorway, Payeras and the others saw Hernandez speak a few words to Rivera, nod his head towards Payeras' quarters, then mount his horse. While Rivera stood in an attentive salute, Hernandez rode out of the Mission.

Morgan was the first to speak, "What in the world did you mean by telling him that I was going to become a priest? What ever gave you such an idea?" His tone was one of great annoyance. Calmly Payeras replied, "Now Carlos, my son, did we not do all those things that I described?" Cimkonah and Angelica, looking at each other amusedly, nodded their heads again in agreement with the Padre's words. "Furthermore, did you prefer that I let Hernandez take you to the *Santa Barbara Presidio* for trial as a pirate?"

"But you know that you are lying", protested Morgan. "Yes we did those things that you told Hernandez, but we never talked about me becoming a priest!". "No, it was not expressed by either of us, but my prayers have daily included this supplication. And there is still time for the Lord to inspire you and to grant my request". At this, Morgan went to the doorway, and with obvious anger showing in his departure, said, "Priest, I told you before, I am not your son and my name is not *Carlos*!. And I certainly do not intend to become a *Padre!*"

In late November Payeras did indeed obtain the services of a new Padre. The new priest and his native guide looked tired from the long walk from *Santa Barbara.* They were greeted at the Mission entrance by a large and somewhat joyous group of neophytes who quickly led them to the Padre's quarters. Payeras heard the commotion and came out in an excited mood. He embraced the new Padre with gusto. He first directed Cimkonah and Angelica to prepare food and drink for the Padre and his guide, then quickly summoned Morgan to come meet Padre Manuel.

Morgan ambled slowly from the blacksmith building which was located some distance from the Padre's quarters. He did not want to appear anxious to meet the man who had caused him to lose his "position" with Padre Payeras. In fact, he really wasn't anxious to meet the new priest at all. But on the other hand he thought, perhaps now Payeras will not have time to pursue his intent to convert him.

When Morgan arrived in view, Payeras shouted to him, *"Sharlezz*, my s…, *Sharlezz*, come! I want you to meet Padre Manuel Castellanos who has come to help us minister to the neophytes". The new Padre smiled and extended his hand to Morgan. He looked so young that Morgan found it hard to believe that he really was a priest. "Ah, I am pleased to meet you *Sharlezz,* Padre Mariano has told me of your great assistance to him. I hope that we will also be good friends". Morgan was surprised that the young priest also spoke English. Morgan took his hand, gave it a modest shake, nodded, but said nothing. Payeras led the trio into his quarters, whereupon Cimkonah arrived with refreshments. While the three ate and drank, Payeras excitedly outlined the duties of the new Padre, which were to be mostly of a religious nature, then added, "*Sharlezz*, I will continue to depend upon you to assist me in the operation of the rancho and shops". Morgan nodded with a half smile. He suddenly felt the best that he had felt in several weeks. Payeras seemed to genuinely want his help, and it was to be in the non-religious part of the Mission's operation. That would suit him fine.

For the next week, each day Payeras would escort Castellanos through a section of the Mission. Sometimes Morgan would be invited to join them. At these times it became apparent to Morgan that Padre Castellanos was well qualified in religious matters, and did not have a "technical" mind. He showed total amazement at some of the techniques that had been employed to make the Mission a town, with all of the needed features to provide its residents with water, food, living accommodations and the means to survive.

Castellanos had, for instance, assumed that the water in the central fountain emerged from a sunken spring under it. But Payeras described how the water from a great number of springs, some from distant locations, was conducted through underground clay pipes which led to a central filtering system, and was then conducted to the central fountain. In addition to providing the necessary water for drinking and washing, the water was also conveyed in this way to the garden area where it irrigated the land for vegetable and herb growth. The pipes, Payeras explained, had been made by the neophytes, from clay obtained at the base of the nearby hills.

The clay was also used to make the many utensils required for cooking, drinking and eating. A large number of neophytes, under the direction of a

Spanish craftsman, were constantly manufacturing these items, not just for the increasing population, but to replace the items that were broken every day.

They walked by the area where Morgan labored each day, the blacksmith shop, then the tannery, then the vats where the unused parts of the slaughtered cattle were melted over huge fire pits, to render the tallow used for the manufacture of the hundreds and hundreds of candles that were regularly needed.

Surely, Morgan thought, this young Padre must have had similar activities in his town in Spain. But he seemed so overwhelmed by it all. Morgan would discover why in a few weeks. Morgan now realized why Payeras had stated that Castellanos would be assigned to the religious education of the neophytes. Payeras must have known that this young man would not be of much help in running the day-to-day life-sustaining activities of the Mission.

But now it was time for Morgan himself to begin to realize that he could be educated in new events and culture as well. The next several days were surprising and enlightening to him, for *posadas* had started. Of course, he had never heard of the custom of *posadas* before. This tradition of pre-Christmas celebration was filled with excitement for both the Spanish and neophytes, especially the children. The excitement was contagious and Juan Bautista, who had experienced the *posadas* for several years previously explained the custom to Morgan. He even convinced Morgan to join in the procession of search for shelter, in simulation of Mary and Joseph's journey to Bethlehem.

For nine evenings the group enacted the journey of Mary and Joseph, but were told by the inhabitants of each quarter, "This is no Inn, continue on your way." Those outside continued their journey, holding candles and singing hymns, until Payeras motioned the children to return to their quarters. On the ninth evening, after several planned refusals, one door was opened to them. It was the home of the Mission's carpenter, Ignacio Remirez and his wife Rosa. As the pilgrims gently knocked and continued their plea for shelter, Rosa's voice joyously called from inside the door, *"venir, viajeros, bienvenido!"*

As the processioners crowded into the small quarters, expressing their great pleasure by both their voices and their eyes, Juan explained Rosa's greeting to Morgan. The young mother-to-be and carpenter husband, who were to be the parents of Jesus, were welcomed into her home. As Morgan entered he could not hide his absolute amazement at the holiday decorations, the arrangement of religious articles and the food that Rosa had managed to display in such small quarters. Everyone entered joyously, singing hymns, embracing each other, then eating the many delicious special foods that Rosa had prepared, the recipes for which had been passed down to her from her mother and grandmother. Morgan had never experienced anything like this. Even the traditional New England autumn thanksgiving meal was never so sumptuous and was certainly not as joyous.

He was absorbing the smell of flowers and fruits, mixed with the delicious aromas of Rosa's cooking, when Padre Payeras arrived with several bottles of wine from his guarded supply. He filled a small glass for each adult, hesitating briefly before three of the Mission's *soldatos*, then with a shrug of his shoulders and a happy laugh, filled their glasses too. The three laughed with surprised joy, as Payeras offered his toast, *"Felice Navidad!"*. With this, all drank, while the children ran onto the portico to knock more of the *pinata* to the floor, breaking them open and grasping the candies and fruits held within.

After just a little more than an hour, and after only two glasses of wine by all, Payeras reminded the revelers that the hour was getting late and that the next day was a very sacred and revered Holy Day, suggesting that they all get a good night's sleep and greet him at the sunrise Mass. Reluctantly all nodded assent, and with happy smiles embraced each other with many repeated *"felice Navidad*'s ", trickled out onto the portico and toward their individual quarters.

Morgan was greatly disappointed. He was enjoying himself so much that he had hoped the party would go on much longer. As he and Juan Bautista walked toward the blacksmith building, Morgan complained that Payeras was dictatorial, that he should not have sent everyone to their beds. Juan tried to explain to Morgan that the main importance of the Christmas season was the next day, *Jesuchristo's* birthday. Never having celebrated Christmas before, Morgan really did not understand any of this, he just knew that he was enjoying himself at Rosa and Ignacio's quarters. When Juan asked how Morgan had celebrated Christmas at his home, Morgan reluctantly admitted that in New England, Christmas was just another work and school day. They reached the blacksmith building. Juan asked if Morgan would like to attend the sunrise Mass with him. Morgan went through the doorway of his room without answering. Juan moved along with a *"buenas noches"*, disappointed that Morgan did not even reply.

At first Morgan slept quite well, but he awakened and realized that it was still dark outside. He rolled over expecting to get back to sleep, but somehow he could not. He thought about the fun of the previous evening and the days before. He began to realize why so many of the neophytes, especially the younger ones, enjoyed the Spanish traditions. Then it came to him that these traditions were not only Spanish, but Catholic as well. So what were the neophytes accepting?; the Catholic church, or the white man's culture. He tossed and turned. He thought, 'I'm not a philosopher, so why should I be concerned? I'll just do as I decided some months ago, I'll treat the natives well and teach them whatever I can'. He finally fell back to sleep.

When Morgan awoke again the sun was up a little. He sat up with a start. He had the feeling that he was supposed to be up earlier and was supposed to be doing something right now. He looked out the window, but saw none of the neophytes in their usual activity. In fact, there were none in sight at all. Suddenly he remembered that Payeras had practically "dictated" that everyone attend the sunrise Mass. Without even thinking about it, Morgan quickly washed, dressed in clean clothing, and walked to the church. He stood outside for a while listening to the hymns that were being sung very boisterously inside, by the larger than usual congregation. His mood softened as he remembered the enjoyment of the previous evening and he then decided that he wanted to be part of that joy again. He pulled open the door which was located at the side of the church instead of the back. Entering as unobtrusively as he could, he weaved his way through the crowd of standing neophytes, hoping that he could find Juan Bautista. Glancing about, every face that he encountered was smiling at him, especially Cimkonah and Rosa. Then he also noticed that Angelica was smiling beautifully and he blushed and lowered his head. He felt a hand grasp his elbow and turned to find Juan, also smiling very broadly.

At the altar of the church Payeras and Castellanos were intoning the Mass prayers in Latin. As was the custom of the time, the Padre's backs were toward the congregation as they prayed to the crucifix above the altar. Morgan was happy that Payeras could not see him. At that very moment Payeras turned toward his congregation and extending both arms toward them and with a booming baritone voice sang out *"Dominus vobiscum"*("The Lord be with you"). Morgan quickly hid behind Juan as the entire congregation sang their reply back to Payeras, *"Et cum spiritu tuo"*("And also with you"). After a few more prayers, Payeras strode to the beautifully carved and decorated pulpit, read from a very large and highly decorated volume, then spoke in the Chumash language for what seemed to Morgan to be several hours, though in reality it was only slightly more than an hour. All this while Morgan was slinking behind Juan so that Payeras would not see him from the vantage point of the high pulpit.

Finally Payeras left the pulpit and again facing the altar, droned on in Latin prayers, both spoken and sung. Morgan wondered whether he should stay or leave. He was both uncomfortable in the surroundings but comfortable with the crowd of friends. After many more prayers, Payeras raised a round wafer high over his head, while bells rang out reverently. Now everyone was kneeling, so Morgan followed their lead lest he be standing alone, for then Payeras would surely see him. Now the priest raised up a bejeweled gold chalice, and although the bells again rang loudly, no one moved or seemed even to be breathing. The church was now extremely quiet and the atmosphere was now entirely different than when Payeras was giving his long sermon during which everyone had to keep shuffling to ease their feet and legs. Morgan was finding it very hard to remain any longer. The congregation now stood simultaneously. Morgan decided that this would be his exit opportunity.

Now Payeras and Castellanos spoke another prayer in Latin, came forward to the railing which separated the altar from the rest of the church, and the entire congregation began to inch forward in several shuffling lines. Morgan decided to get out. He nodded to Juan and started to move through the crowd to the door. He had difficulty moving through the dense crowd so it took him several minutes to come to the vicinity of the side door. He neared the door, protected he thought, by the large standing crowd. But suddenly the entire congregation knelt again, leaving him standing awkwardly alone. Before he could either kneel or get out the door, Payeras turned toward the congregation once more with another loud *"Dominus vobiscum"*. Morgan darted through the door, hoping that Payeras did not see him. He quickly walked back to the blacksmith shop, changed into his old clothes and donned his apron. He hoped that onlookers who would soon be coming by after Mass, would believe that Morgan felt that this was just another ordinary day. He did not know how he was going to handle his first encounter withPayeras today, for he knew the first question Payeras would ask.

Shortly before noon Juan came to find Morgan. "Padre Payeras asks that you join Padre Castellanos and him at *almuerzo*. He says that you should not be working today." Juan waited for Morgan's reply. By way of an affirmative answer, Morgan started removing his apron. After washing again, Morgan went to the Padre's quarters. Shortly after the usual greetings and while waiting for Cimkonah to bring in the food, Payeras asked the question that he had been asking almost every day since the first day that Morgan arrived, "Did you attend Holy Mass this morning *Sharlezz*?" Morgan knew that that question would be coming, in fact the main reason he had accepted the invitation to lunch was to get the matter out of the way.

"You certainly could not have missed seeing me there, priest, standingso awkwardly when you told everyone to kneel." "Oh, no, no, *Sharlezz*. I do not order anyone to perform in any way at Holy Mass", Payeras replied, "they are instructed how to display proper reverence and decorum, then they do as they please. And yes, I was most joyfully pleased to see you at Mass on this, the most holy day of the Church." "Oh come now, priest", Morgan commented, "I knowthat you ordered everyone to go up front and get one of those wafers that you were giving." Payeras smiled and said, "No, *Sharlezz,* I did not order anyone to come to the altar rail. Our Lord *Jesucristo* invited all to receive Him in Holy Communion and thankfully everyone did accept." Everyone except Morgan, that is. "Well, then I guess we both chose to be honest", Morgan replied, seeming now to be more relaxed. Sitting alone, Castellanos appeared to be baffled by the conversation, not knowing that both Morgan and Payeras knew that this discussion would most certainly have to take place.

CHAPTER FOUR
Disaster!...Opportunity!

With the flurry of activity of Christmas now over, a number of other commemorative Masses were celebrated on each Sunday. Morgan wondered how the neophytes could possibly absorb all of these new traditions and their relationship to their intended new faith. Nevertheless, the weeks were passing by and the days were again getting a little longer. Everyone, especially Morgan, was looking forward to the springtime, with its longer days and new growth of plants and trees...and his departure to Massachusetts.

Morgan lay in bed. It was still very dark outside, but he had been aroused by what sounded like a few people moving near his blacksmith shop. Suddenly the door to his meager room was pushed open. Two *soldados* rushed in, followed immediately by Corporal Rivera.

"Seize him!", Rivera ordered. The two soldiers grabbed Morgan by his arm pits and pulled him from the bed. "What are you doing?", Morgan shouted, but the men just kept pulling until Morgan was forced to be in a standing position. Rivera spoke angrily, but somewhat softly. "You have raped the young neophyte Angelica and you will be brought before the tribunal at the *Santa Barbara Presidio* to acknowledge your guilt and to receive your punishment. Hopefully they will have you shot".

"Are you *loco!?* Where did you get such a crazy idea. Why would I harm Angelica! She is a friend of mine". Morgan was protesting loudly. But all the while that Morgan was speaking he was being dragged by the two soldiers. He was absolutely bewildered. Then, terrible apprehension overtook him. Had Angelica really been raped!? Oh that poor girl! Thoughts of great anxiety about her swirled through Morgan's head as he wondered if what Rivera had said about poor Angelica were true. As intense as he was, Morgan knew that it was obviously not going to do any good to try to reason with Rivera, or to protest either. As he was being forced down the length of the lane behind the Mission buildings, Morgan knew that his only hope was that Payeras would arrive quickly and put an end to Rivera's false accusations and madness. Yes, Payeras would certainly know that Morgan was innocent!, wouldn't he? Suddenly it came to him who was most likely the real rapist, Rivera! Yes, Rivera was the one who always leered at Angelica, studied her every action, watched her as she moved through the Mission. He probably had been awaiting an opportunity to attack her, and he likely had a few glasses of the forbidden wine, gaining the bravado that he did not show otherwise. Oh!, where is Payeras?, Morgan wondered anxiously. Didn't someone tell him what Rivera is up to?

Then Morgan realized that at this time of morning Payeras would be in the church celebrating Mass. He would be inside there an hour or more. 'So Rivera hoped to whisk me out of the Mission compound before Payeras even knew what had happened. And poor Angelica! How is she? Who is with her?, Oh, I hope Cimkonah is tending to that poor girl!' Now he wanted to hold Angelica, to try to calm the terrible anguish that she must be feeling, and to assure her that he would never, never abuse her.

And where is Juan Bautista?. 'Oh my God!'. For a fraction of a second Morgan asked himself if it was possible that Juan had perpetrated the terrible abuse. This thought upset Morgan greatly, so much that he almost forgot his own serious situation. 'No, not Juan', he thought, 'it must have been Rivera, he must be the one!' He was now being pushed through the door of Rivera's room and the door was closed quickly behind him. With his hands tied as theywere he could do nothing. 'Oh where is Payeras? Why doesn't he come?' Morgan felt desperation.

Someone must soon discover the situation before he is marched out of La Purisima, or it may be several hours before anyone realizes that Morgan is gone. It might even be mid-day and by that time Morgan and the escorting soldiers will be many kilometers south. In just a few minutes the two soldiers returned with their knapsacks and canteens, obviously prepared for their trek to *Santa Barbara*.

"Alright, take him out of here! *Pronto*!, before someone who thinks he has authority over the military tries to interfere in my area of jurisdiction." It was obvious that Rivera did not want a confrontation with Payeras. He wanted Morgan gone before the priest concluded the morning Mass. Just as Morgan and the two soldiers were passing through the gate of the Mission wall, Morgan heard Juan Bautista shouting loudly. Juan had just come out the church and upon catching sight of the trio, he quickly ascertained that something was wrong. Soldiers should not be escorting Morgan anywhere! Morgan is certainly no criminal.

Without even knowing why the soldiers were acting so, Juan started shouting as loud as he could, hoping to arouse everyone, but especially Padre Payeras.

As soon as he saw Payeras come through the doorway from the church Juan called, *"Padre, Padre! Pronto!. Soldados* are taking *senor Sharlezz* away." Payeras came running toward the gate, shouting as he ran, *Alto! Alto! Soldados, alto!"* Rivera also came running to the gate from a hiding place he had taken behind a large tree. At first he was inclined to tell his men to hurry out the gate, but now, in Payeras' presence, he lost his bravado. Displaying brash authority before Morgan was one thing...but facing Payeras was another. Just like Hernandez, Rivera did not want to create a problem between the religious and the military. If he did, Payeras would likely win, because Rivera knew that his own service record was neither distinguished nor without blemish. Besides, it was rumored that Payeras would be elected the next *Padre Presidente* of the Missions, a position of great importance, even in the eyes of the Vice Governor Ortega.

Payeras arrived at the gate very breathless from his dart across the Mission plaza. Holding his chest as he often did when exerting physical stress, he gasped, "Rivera, where do you think you are taking this man? Have I not made it clear that he is my charge. Unhand him!", Payeras demanded. The two soldiers obeyed immediately. "Now untie his hands!", Payeras ordered. Again, the two soldiers obeyed immediately. After all, Payeras was their Padre and right now his authority seemed more important than Rivera's. "Now Corporal Rivera, just what is the reason that you have apprehended *Senor* Morgan, treating him like a criminal". Payeras was intentionally speaking to Rivera as if he were the lowest recruit of the Spanish Army.

Somewhat meekly Rivera replied, "Padre, neophyte Angelica has been raped and I believe that Morgan is the despicable culprit who did this dastardly thing." "*Oh! mio Dios!, mio Dios!*", gasped Payeras, clutching his chest again. Turning toward Juan he blurted, "Did you hear that Juan?, Oh! that poor child. Where is she? Angelica raped! *Oh, mio Dios*!". He could not seem to comprehend the reality of it.

Now Juan was also devastated. He was white with dismay. He obviously had known nothing of this. Juan immediately turned and ran toward the *manjerio* where he could see and hold Angelica. As he ran he screamed, *"Angelica! Angelica!, mia amore!"* Poor Payeras was now showing deeper anguish and continued to rub his chest. He was looking grayer and grayer. Morgan feared that if Payeras did not get some of Cimkonah's *espina blanco* tea immediatly he might die. Morgan shouted to one of the soldiers, *"Pronto*!, go to Cimkonah's kitchen, find her jar of *espina blanco* tea! Bring it to Padre Payeras' quarters immediately! Hurry! *Pronto!"*

One of the men left on the run. Rivera enraged that Morgan was giving orders to his men. He started to object but Morgan cut him short with an order to the other soldier. "Come, Help me get the Padre to his bed." The other soldier quickly helped Morgan for he was fearful that his beloved Padre might die. They left Rivera standing alone in a state of enraged exasperation. After Morgan gave a few sips of tea to Payeras, he left him in the charge of the soldier. Speaking in the best Spanish that he could muster, Morgan ordered, "He needs a few hours of rest. Let no one except Padre Catellanos enter. Let no one disturb him. Do you understand?, No one!" The soldier nodded that he understood, *"Si Senor Sharlezz."* Morgan ran to the *monjerio* himself. Standing at the door he could see Angelica laying on a bed, her head on Cimkonah'slap. Cimkonah was stroking Angelica's forehead, her cheek, her hair, speaking very softly and motherly. Juan was kneeling beside them, holding Angelica's hand, sobbing and pleading, "Tell me who did this to you Angelica. I will demand retribution!, Justice will be done by my hand." Morgan entered slowly not wanting to disturb Angelica. She did not see him and he was happy for that. He did not feel ready to face her, to try to console her. Upon hearing Juan's plea to be told the name of Angelica's rapist, Morgan knew that Angelica would not respond. She loved Juan too much. She knew that Juan's attempt to seek retribution might well get him immediately killed or later executed. She would rather hold this secret in her heart forever than to risk Juan's life.

The rest of the day was spent somberly with Morgan feeling spells of anxiety, anger, irritation and great anguish. Padre Castellanos tried to fulfill the role of a pastor but it was obvious that he was neither confident enough in himself nor capable of exerting the leadership that Payeras always displayed. But why should he?, for although he was a few years older than Morgan, he was not much more than a boy. And his seminary training did not likely include handling situations including rape, an unknown assailant, an unruly corporal and a pastor-Padre who may be dieing. A few hours later Juan came into the plaza, walking toward the church. Morgan approached him and tried to console him but Juan pushed him away with a strong swing of his arm. 'What?, does Juan think that I assaulted Angelica? Why is he dismissing me in this manner?' Morgan was dismayed. He let Juan enter the church then followed him after a few moments.

Morgan entered the dark church. By the light of the few tapers that were burning he saw Juan kneeling at the altar railing, praying to the hanging crucifix. Morgan came and quietly knelt beside him. For a few minutes they both were silent and motionless. Then abruptly, Juan turned toward Morgan with tears in his eyes and threw his strong arms around Morgan. At first Morgan did not know if Juan was attacking him or hugging him. But it was quickly obvious that Juan wanted his friend's consolation. Morgan then placed his arms around Juan and let him cry on his shoulder. Juan sobbed and cried for quite awhile asking repeatedly, "Why did this happen? Why would anyone want to harm my beautiful Angelica?" Morgan could offer no answer, all he could do was to let Juan cry out his exasperation. After a long while, Juan made the sign of the cross, arose and began to leave. Morgan followed.

As soon as they were outside they met Cimkonah who was still in an intense state. "Juan, *Shalezz!* Please go and stay with Angelica. She has finally fallen asleep and pray that she may stay so for a few hours. Oh! the poor girl. But go, be near her if she awakens. Assure her that she is safe. I must go attend to Padre Payeras. Oh, the poor man has had such terrible tribulations with that *demonio* Rivera. His heart cannot stand many more of these terrible disturbances."

Morgan advised her, "Castellanos is with him, but I'm afraid he has no idea of what to do to help the Padre." "Oh yes, he is only a child. He tries so hard to be a man",Cimkonah replied, "but unfortunately he was raised in such a sheltered manner, he knows little of hardships or how to handle difficulties. Yes, his mother did such a fine job of sheltering him from the world that now he knows not how to face it."

In the early evening Payeras arose and over the protestations of Cimkonah and Casellanos moved toward the door. "Padre, please remain in bed", Cimkonah pleaded. Payeras waved his hand towards her, "I am fine, Cimkonah. What is the time of day?". "It is about seven in the evening Padre," she replied. Payeras moved another step to the door. Castellanos knew that he should either protest or protect, but he knew not how to do either. He just stood awkwardly. Payeras sensed the young priest's futility. "Come, Padre Manuel, help me to counsel Angelica." The young priest hurried to Payeras' side, greatly pleased that Payeras had shown confidence in him, andthat he was asked to help perform a priestly duty. The two walked slowly toward the *monjerio*, with Cimkonah close behind them. When they arrived, Angelica was just beginning to awaken. Payeras motioned for Morgan and Juan to leave. He showed no upset that they were inside this forbidden quarter. Cimkonah hesitated at the door but Payeras motioned for her come inside. She went immediately to Angelica, placing her arm around Angelica's shoulders. The two priests knelt beside the bed and began to pray.

After a long time the two priests came out. Morgan and Juan were still waiting. "Come to my quarters tomorrow morning immediately after Mass, both of you", Payeras ordered. Morgan and Juan looked at each other, then at the serious countenance of Payeras. They nodded assent. With Castellanos supporting Payeras by one elbow, the two priests walked slowly to their quarters.

The next morning, immediately after Mass, which Juan had attended and Morgan had not, they both went to Payeras' quarters. They were surprised that Cimkonah, Rivera, and all but one of the Mission's soldiers were there also, all standing under the portico. They saw the two priests leave the church and walk across the plaza toward them. Payeras was still walking slower than usual and Castellanos was walking close by to be of assistance if needed. Payeras entered his bedroom-office first, followed by Castellanos and the others.

The room was very crowded. Payeras spoke slowly and deliberately. "A terrible offense has been committed against our dear child Angelica and against Almighty God. We all know what that heinous crime was." Rivera shuffled nervously. Payeras continued, *"Soldato Raso* Rodolfo Nunez, I place you in command of the *soldados de Mison La Purisima Concepcion*, and I order you to arrest Corporal Pablo Rivera for the felonious assault and rape of neophyte Angelica."* A stunned silence befell the room until Rivera shouted his protest. "How dare you usurp my authority over these *soldados*, and how dare you accuse me of this terrible crime. You have no cause to make such charges."

Now Payeras replied with anger apparent in his voice, "Considering the circumstances of your malicious conduct, I have no alternative but to take charge of the Mission constabulary. Again, I order them to arrest you!" Payeras was insistent. Immediately, two of the soldiers moved beside Rivera, grasping his arms. Rivera broke from their grasp with a twist of his body while giving his two underlings a sneer. "By what evidence do you dare make this accusation", Rivera shouted at the priest. Strongly and emphatically Payeras stated, "By the words of Angelica herself. She has told us of your assault on her. She has related the incident in great detail, how you followed her to the far edge of the garden, pulling her down and performing your dastardly deed."

"What!, you are violating the confidence of the confessional!", Rivera accused. "You are not worthy to be called Padre! Besides, I deny that any of this is true. And further, since this crime took place in the darkness, how could Angelica know who her assailant was?" Payeras replied, "Well, we shall let the trial authorities at the *Presidio* determine your guilt or innocence. But for now, you are under arrest and will be marched to *Santa Barbara* under guard. Angelica did not make her accusations in the confessional, but rather to Cimkonah, to Padre Castellanos and me, all at the same time. There will be many to testify against you. Further, you seem to be the only one who knew that the assault took place in the dark. And more! Angelica states that she tore a button off of a uniform while the assailant pulled her to the ground." Payeras spoke with emphasis. "Now *Soldado Raso* Nunez, take this *diablo* to his quarters and get yourselves ready for the trek to Santa Barbara *pronto*."

As all looked at the missing button on the front of Rivera's tunic, Payeras dismissed the group but quietly signaled Morgan and Juan to stay. With only the three remaining in the room, Payeras said, "I want you both to know that I did not for one minute suspect either of you as the culprit. I know that you both love Angelica too much to ever harm a hair on her head." 'He is a very observant man', Morgan thought. Realizing Juan's great love for Angelica, Morgan had tried hard not to let his own affection show, but obviously he had not fooled Payeras. The two friends left the Padre's quarters, Juan to the church, Morgan to his blacksmith shop.

Within the hour Morgan saw two soldiers escorting Rivera through the gate of the Mission. He wondered what events would occur before this tragic matter would be settled. He hoped that Rivera would be severely disciplined, maybe even cashiered out of the Army. But he was far more concerned about the effects of the molestation and what the disagreeable future events, would have on Angelica. How would she feel testifying before the Officers of the*Presidio*? And how would she be able to live a normal life after these tragic events.

The next morning Morgan knew that Angelica and Juan were both gone from the Mission. He knew because Juan had told him of their planned departure that morning. Morgan avoided Padre Payeras and Cimkonah because he did not want to divulge to them that he knew that the two were gone and to where they had gone. The days seemed exceedingly long now. Morgan missed Juan very much and especially missed seeing Angelica's smiling face at the Mission. He thought about them often, wondering if they reached their destination safely, and hoped that they were well. At one time he thought of asking some of the older natives if they knew where the village of Juan's father was, but then he remembered Juan's urgent request that he not divulge where he was takingAngelica. Surely, if he asked about Juan's ancestral village, and he then disappeared, word would reach Payeras. He then might follow too. That would cause Juan to know that Morgan had betrayed his confidence.

Morgan thought of speaking openly about it with Payeras, seeking his "permission" to go to Juan's father's village, but decided that that would also show a betrayal of Juan's trust. But why had Juan and Angelica left so suddenly? Apparently Angelica did not even bid *adios* to Cimkonah, her closest friend, or either of the two priest. And from what Juan had told Morgan, he was the only person that Juan was confiding in about their hasty departure to Juan's father's village.

So the days dragged on. Morgan was having his meals with theSpanish craftsmen and they were now more congenial to him, especially Ignacio Ramirez, the carpenter. Ever since Morgan had eaten the *posades* meal which Ignacio's wife Rosa had prepared, and after Morgan's genuinely high praise of the meal, Ramirez had taken a liking to Morgan. Rosa was also so pleased with Morgan's praise of her meals that she now invited him to dine with them more and more often. Morgan was happy that they had become such good friends because it filled the void caused by Juan and Angelica's departure.

Nevertheless, January and February passed in what seemed to Morgan to be a much longer time than it really was. But by March the daylight hourswere lengthening and the temperatures were rising. Morgan had spent the past eight weeks diligently working in the blacksmith shop. It seemed to him that he had made enough hinges, brackets, nails, candle holders and other architectural devices to make an entirely new Mission complex. Now he was bored with the long day of pounding on the anvil. For many of the past weeks he was pounding out his frustrations, and now he was anxious to move on. His promise to Payeras to stay for six months was coming to a close, and he was thinking more and more of getting to Monterey to find a ship going to Boston. Should he steal a horse? Should he ask Payeras for a horse? Should he talk openly to Payeras about his wish to go to Monterey now? Day after day he was struggling with this yearning to get out of *La Purisima.*

Very unexpectedly Payeras came by one morning after Mass andasked Morgan to join him for *desayuno.* It was rather late in the morning for Payeras to be taking breakfast, Morgan thought, but then he remembered that since Padre Castellanos had arrived, Payeras had the luxury of celebrating the later Mass. Morgan hesitated in his acceptance because he thought Payeras was going to want to talk to him about becoming a Catholic, or even that priest thing.

But before Morgan could reject the invitation, Payeras insisted. "Come *Sharlezz,* put down the hammer for a few hours. Let us enjoy one of

Cimkonah's delicious meals." Payeras had just given two good reasons for Morgan to accept. He was boringly tired of hammering, and Cimkonah's cooking was never to be refused. Laying the heavy hammer on the anvil, Morgan smiled, "Yes priest, I will join you for *desayuno*, and I'm extra hungry this morning!" This was true because earlier Morgan had eaten very little because he felt too depressed to do so.

"Maravilloso! Come then", Payeras replied, "I should have asked you many days ago." They walked towards the Padre's room. "You have been exceedingly sad these past several months, *Sharlezz*. I know that you miss your friends very much. I wish that I could have been able to lessen your sadness", Payeras spoke. "I too have missed them greatly. I find solace in praying often for their welfare."

Morgan thought 'I don't see how praying for them can do any good', but then he realized that Payeras must really miss the two neophytes, and if praying eased his sadness, then there can't be anything wrong with that'. "I'm sure that Juan and Angelica know that you are praying for them Padre, and I'm sure that they appreciate it", Morgan replied. 'Did I just call him 'Padre'?, he thought. 'I wonder if he noticed? Why did I do that? Am I now thinking of him like Juan, Angelica and all the others do, as a father?'

Yes, Morgan suddenly realized that he was yearning for a father's love and concern. It had been three years now since he saw his own father and he suddenly missed him greatly. 'Yes', he thought, 'I must tell Payeras that I have to get to Monterey and sail to Boston. I must get home'. He felt relieved that he had come to this decision.

After a few pleasantries about the improving weather, the buds on the bushes, and about the fine treatment given Morgan by the craftsmen and their families, and halfway through the breakfast Payeras said, "*Sharlezz*, let me discuss with you the reason that I wanted to sit with you today. As you know, because of Divine guidance, with your help and the help of our craftsmen, and through the industriousness of our fine neophytes, *Mision La PurisimaConcepcion* has progressed wonderfully. The *ranchos y huerta* are now well established. The cattle herds are healthy and growing, and our wheat fields are producing abundant harvests. The buildings are being stuccoed so that next winter's rains will not erode them, and thanks to the abundant supply of hinges and latches that you produced, we are erecting many doors and window shutters to also protect from the weather. We can now consider this Mission complete, and for that we give great thanks to *Dios Todopoderoso,* ah, that is, Almighty God, and his Son *Jesucristo*. So, after much consideration, and only coming to my final decision last evening after prayer, I have decided to go to Monterey to recommend to *Padre Presidente* Lasuen that a new Mission be established. Because the distance between here and *Mision Santa Barbara* is so great, and because much fertile land lays to the southeast, I will urge *Presidente* Lasuen to approve of my proposal. In a few days I plan to leave for *Mision San Carlos Borromeo de Carmelo* where Padre Lasuen makes his headquarters. What do you think of that, *Sharlezz*?"

Morgan spoke words but his thoughts were way ahead of his words. "Well, I reckon that's a good idea.

I mean, if you think so, it must be right." But what he was thinking was that this was just the break that he had been hoping for. He was about to ask Payeras if he could go with him when the priest said, "*Sharlezz,* the Mission at Monterey has your namesake, *San Carlos,* so I want you to accompany me to Monterey. I want you to see this magnificent Mission compound. It has a beautiful church which was designed by a master mason three decades ago, Senor Manuel Ruiz. He was a very dedicated craftsman and was inspired by God to design a Mission church that will stand for centuries."

Payeras knew that the trip would help Morgan forget his sadly missed friends, but he had other reasons also for asking Morgan to accompany him. But he wasn't ready to divulge these reasons yet. "Well, priest, this is sure a surprise. I never expected to get to Monterey", Morgan replied, as he thought 'at least not this way'. Morgan pressed harder, "But remember our conversation when I first arrived here last August. You agreed that if I stayed and helped you for six months, and after you had an assistant Padre, that you would help me get back to Massachusetts." Payeras looked surprised, then pensive, "Of course, *Sharlezz*, I recall." But this reminder by Morgan set Payeras back a little for it could well upset the plans that he had concocted in his mind. "Well, *Sharlezz*, please do accompany me to Monterey and then we shall see what Almighty God has in mind for the two of us."

'There he goes again with the God will tell us', Morgan thought. Still, he decided that he should take up the Padre's invitation, and when he got to Monterey he could work out a plan for himself. "Alright priest, I'll go with you. When do we leave?" "In a few days, on next Tuesday, March nineteenth, the feast day of San Jose', the protector of *Jesucristo y Santa Madre Maria,"*, Payeras replied happily. "In the next few days we must help Padre Manuel to prepare for our absence of many weeks. Let us meet in my office this evening. And *Sharlezz*, my son, take *cena* with us. I shall ask Cimkonah to prepare an especially fine meal in celebration of this momentous decision."

Payeras was plainly excited about Morgan's agreement to accompany him to Monterey. He placed his arm around Morgan's shoulder, practically pushing him toward the kneeler against the wall, under the crucifix. "Now let us give thanks to Almighty God, beseech His guidance and protection on our journey, and inspire us in our presentation to *Padre Presidente* Lasuen." Payeras knelt on the floor beside the kneeler and by his glances at the vacant kneeler, silently urged Morgan to kneel there. Although with some hesitation, Morgan did kneel.

Quickly Payeras seized the opportunity and began, "*Pater Noster, qui es in caelis...*", he started The Lord's Prayer. Morgan half-heartedly and falteringly tried to follow along with what he could remember. Payeras continued, *"Fiat volunta tua, sicut in caelo..."*, he stopped. Turning to Morgan he said, "That means, 'Thy will be done on earth as it is in heaven.' Truly *Sharlezz*, God will inspire and protect us." He continued to the end of the prayer without further interruptions. They both said "*Amen*" in unison. Morgan rose, not quite understanding why he had so agreeably knelt, but as he turned to say *"hasta luego"*, he did feel that he had done the right thing. 'Payeras is such a dedicated and hard working man. I owe him this support, I guess', Morgan was thinking as he left the room.

Payeras and Morgan had first discussed the plan on Thursday morning. The rest of that day and on Friday and Saturday, Morgan often thought of his own plan. He started gathering the clothing and other items that he would need on the way to Monterey…and beyond. The days were passing faster now, now that he knew that he would be on his way soon.

On Saturday evening, after having a delicious dinner with Ignace and Rosa, Morgan returned to his room in the blacksmith building. He was puttering with a few more items that he might pack when he heard a faint tap at his door. *"Venir!"* he called. With that invitation, Padre Castellanos entered. *"Buenas noches, Sharlezz"*, he said with a nervous smile. "Oh, *buenas noches*, priest. Come in", replied Morgan. "Well, this is kind of a surprise", Morgan continued. "I don't get much company in this little room, and you and I have not spoken very much since you arrived. You are always busy teaching the neophytes and I'm always busy making things here."

"Yes, I know", replied the young priest. "But I came to say that I will miss you *Sharlezz*, when you go to Monterey with Padre Payeras. Although I have not expressed it, I have a great respect for you. You are so talented with your hands and so clever in your thinking. I have never had a brother, but I always wished for one, one like you." Morgan blushed, shifted his stance a few times and stammered, "My goodness, priest, I don't know what to say. I thank you for your compliments and I'm pleased that you would want me for a brother. I had two brothers and I know how reassuring it is to be able to talk to them. In fact, I miss my brothers very much, myself."

"Yes, I can imagine how enjoyable a brother can be", Castellanos continued. "I have only a sister, she is much older and very domineering, almost like a mother. Although we are not very close, I do miss her. You see, the truth of the matter is, I am too young to be a priest, I am barely twenty-two years of age. It was my father's doing. He is a close friend of the Archbishop of Madrid and arranged for me to enter the seminary at a very early age, for reasons that hethought were important. But now I am here, and after next Tuesday I will be in charge of this Mission while Padre Payeras is away with you. I am frightened, *Sharlezz,* for I have no confidence that I can control situations that may arise. I have come here tonight to ask if you would reconsider your agreement to go to Monterey. Tell Padre Payeras that you feel you are needed more here with me. Anyway, he will not travel alone, he will be accompanied by several Chumas natives on his trek to Monterey."

Morgan felt sorry for the boy-priest, but he knew he could not possibly abandon this opportunity to get to Monterey, and Boston. "I'm sorry, priest, but I promised Payeras that I would go with him, I can't back out now." He knew that he was lying, that Payeras was perfectly capable of making the trip without him, just as Catellanos had said.

The young priest looked downfallen, even devastated. Morgan turned away, he could not face him, "I'm really sorry Manuel, but I gotta go. We'll only be gone a few weeks. We should be back by the end of next month." He knew that by "we" he meant Payeras alone.

The young priest said no more, just moved to the door with a feeble wave and said, "*hasta manana*", then left. Morgan felt terrible but told himself, 'If I give in to him, I'll never get to Monterey, and if I give in to Payeras later, I'll never get to Boston.' Still, he felt very sad for this young boy, the one that the neophytes call 'Father'.

CHAPTER FIVE
The Beginning Of A Long Journey Home?

The morning of March 19, 1803 was a bright, sunny morning, with an especially sweet smell in the air. Morgan arose more excited than usual, for today was the beginning of his trip back to Massachusetts. Or so he thought. He went to the Padre's quarters, but neither Payeras nor Castellanos were there. He then realized that they must both still be in the church, celebrating Mass. He sat on the floor of the portico.

Soon the priests arrived, greeting him warmly. Payeras literally beamed, *"Ah! buenos madrugada, Sharlezz.* It is a fine morning to begin our momentous journey, is it not?" Castellanos was not quite so cheerful but he greeted Morgan warmly too. Morgan replied, "Are we to take *desayuner* soon?". He wanted to get going but he was hungry too. *"Si, Sharlezz,* Cimkonah awaits our presence. She is ready to serve *pronto"*. They all went into the dining room where Cimkonah began to serve immediately. As soon as all had their dish of *jamon* and *huevo* in front of them, Morgan grabbed his fork and was about to attack the delicious looking breakfast when Payeras lowered his head, glanced at Morgan, then began to intone a prayer. "Bless us, O Lord," he began in English, for Morgan's recognition, "and for these gifts from thy bounty, we give thanks. And blessed San Jose', we ask your intercession with Our Lord *Jesuchristo* for a safe journey to *Mision San Carlos Borromeo de Carmelo*, which we begin in service to our *Todopoderoso Padre*, Amen". Castellanos spoke a verbal "Amen", but

Morgan just nodded his head and began eating the delicious ham and egg breakfast. He could not help but wonder how the meals on the journey would compare with Cimkonah's.

Within the hour they were all in the plaza, getting their party together. There would be two Chumash men traveling with them. They looked mature enough to Morgan for him to feel confident that they were experienced outdoor travelers and would be of help if nature was unfriendly. With fond *"adios"* and many wishes of *"Vaya con Dios"* the party proceeded to the north side of the Mission where they entered the path called *El Camino Real*, the pathway that had been originated almost forty years earlier by the Spanish soldiers and the Padres who traveled from *Mision San Diego de Acala* in the south, northward all the way to *San Carlos* in the *pueblo* of Carmel, a distance of nearly 500 miles. Morgan was hopeful that there would be horses or donkeys to ride, but at the same time he was not surprised that the long journey would be by foot. After all, Payeras was not one to coddle himself, and the animals were needed daily at the Mission.

After they had been on the pathway for a short time, and barely being out of sight of the Mission, Payeras announced, "To keep our minds off of our feet and to pay tribute to *Jesucristo y Santa Maria*, we will recite the *Rosario*. The first decade we will pray in Spanish, the next in Chumash tongue, the next in English and finally two decades in Latin. In this way we will all feel the *proximo*, how do you say *Sharlezz*, the nearness of the Lord, and of His protection". Payeras began by making the Sign Of The Cross using the Crucifix on the Rosary beads. The Chumash men did the same. Payeras peeked at Morgan, but Morgan did not react. *"Dios te salve, Maria; ilena eres de gracia, el Senor es contigo. Bendita tu eres entre todas las majures y benidito es el fruto de tu vientre, Jesus"*, Payeras prayed. Then the natives joined him in the next portion of the prayer, *"Santa Maria, Madre de Dios, ruega por nosotros pecadores ahora y en la hora de nuestra muerte. Amen."*

Morgan tried to ignore them while he glanced about at the beauty of the countryside. The trail northward had a view of the ocean to the west and he reminisced about his several years at sea. He recalled the day that he left home after a spat with his stepmother about some now forgotten triviality. But once he started walking out of Sturbridge toward New Bedford he did not feel that he could return. And since his father did not come after him, to beseech him to return, he decided that his father didn't care anyway. But it suddenly occurred to him that he left home early on a Satuday morning while his father was in the field. By the time his father came in for supper, he would realize that his son had likely walked ten hours, so it would not be possible to catch up, even if he knew which direction to take. Papa didn't own a horse either, and couldn't afford to hire one, so the fate of his future was entirely up to Morgan himself. He now wondered, though, when I do get back home, will Papa be happy? He didn't care what his step-mother felt, but he was anxious to see the reactions of his brother George and sister Mary.

"Dios te salve, Maria", Payeras continued. Was this the fifth or sixth time that the priest said that

prayer?, Morgan wondered to himself. Although his thoughts were far from California, Morgan was subconsciously aware of the priest's monotonous incantations. Back into his reverie, Morgan was thinking about the day he signed on the whaling ship as a cabin boy. The Captain had promised him much excitement and would teach him to be an able seaman in only a few years. At first it was exciting, everything was new. He had much to learn about seaman's language, the cusses as well as the official names and terminology. The long voyage around Cape Horn was at first frightening, but then became somewhat monotonous after a while. Oh, he had plenty to do, and the Captain was always calling him to demonstrate something new about sails, the hull, navigation and what they would do with the many whales that they expected to harpoon and dress. As he thought about it, he could not believe that he had spent more than a year aboard the "Phoebe Prescott". The Captain had named the ship for his first girl friend, though he had remained a bachelor. He said a seaman should not have a wife, 'though most did. It was indeed a hard life for both the seaman and the wife, being apart often for more than a year at a time.

When they put into port in Hawaii, Morgan was sure that he had made the right choice; a seaman's life was best for him. In the next few months, the "Phoebe Prescott" harpooned many whales, dressed down a full cargo of blubber and loaded all of her vats with whale oil, then headed back to New Bedford. The day they docked was exciting, with many other vessels also docking to unload their cache. New Bedford was indeed a bustling seaport and Morgan expected that after another sailing or two that he might think of finding a nice, maybe even pretty girl, to begin courting, for he would then be prosperous enough.

After the next sailing, he had decided to take one more trip. It was on this trip while taking on supplies at Lahaina on the island of Maui, that he got talked into joining the pirate crew of Hippolyte Bouchard. He had had too many glasses of rum, in fact more than he had ever drunk in his life before, when two burly seamen convinced him that Bouchard would find enough of the buried treasures of "Black Bart" and "Calico Jack" which they supposedly had buried in the islands of Archipelago, that he would be wealthy overnight. After Bouchard set sail for the coast of California instead, and began ravaging the Spanish supply ships and coastal towns like Monterey, Morgan realized that he had indeed become a real pirate himself, just by being a minor member of the crew. That's when he decided to "jump ship" at the first chance, for he didn't relish being hanged when they would inevitably be caught.

Payeras was chanting on. Morgan came out of his reverie but he did not recognize any of the words that the priest was saying. The two Chumash men were also chanting along so Morgan decided that they were now saying the prayer in Chumash language. How long had they been walking? Morgan looked up at the sun. He judged that it was still fairly early morning, but they must have been walking several hours. Payeras looked back at Morgan. "We will begin the decade of the Rosary in English now". He obviously said this for Morgan's benefit but Morgan had no interest in the matter. Payeras began "Hail Mary, full of grace, hallowed be thy name". He looked back again. Morgan tried to ignore him, pretending to be interested in two condors in the tree top. But Payeras would not let him be inattentive to the prayer. "In this prayer, *Sharlezz*, we tell of the wonderful tribute paid to Mary, the Mother Of God, by repeating the salutation given her by Archangel Gabriel. When Padre Cambon was assigned to establish a new Mission at the joining of the trails running north from *San Diego* and where it meets with two trails from *Baja* California, he chose the name of Gabriel for the Mission. *San Gabriel Arcangel* had been chosen by *Dios*, God, to carry the message to Mary that she was to be the mother of our Savior *Jesuchristo*, Jesus Christ. So now, let us begin together. You can follow along as best you can. After only three or four sayings, you will know this powerful prayer as well as I do. Hail Mary, full of grace, Hallowed be thy name", Payeras continued. Morgan thought, I'll mumble along to keep him happy and then maybe he'll leave me to my own thoughts. Again Payeras started, "Hail Mary...". He listened for Morgan's collaboration. Upon hearing it, he continued. Not understanding English, the natives could not join in so it was up to Morgan to provide the verbal responses to Payeras. Because the prayer was spoken in English, Morgan was more aware of its repetitiveness. He finally asked Payeras, "How long does this blamed thing go on?" Suddenly he felt embarrassed that he had described Payeras' prayer as a cussed thing. Payeras only responded with patience, "Only three more *Ave Maria's* and we shall be finished with this decade".

Now what's a decade, Morgan wondered. He knew that a decade was ten years but surely Payeras doesn't mean we're going to pray for ten years! Payeras continued to pray, all the while holding a bead of the Rosary tightly between his forefinger and thumb and automatically advancing one bead with the completion of a prayer. Morgan began to realize that he could ascertain the status of the Rosary by looking at the number of beads remaining in the circle. The priest finished another group of the prayers in Spanish then began again in Chumash. It seemed to Morgan that no end was in sight, but finally Payeras blessed himself with the large crucifix at the end of the Rosary beads.

When Payeras had finished, he hung the large Rosary on the cincture around his portly waist and then announced that it was time for their first rest. They all sat, Payeras and Morgan on fallen logs, the Chumash men on the ground. "Ah, well, *Sharlezz,* we have done well to reach this point in only three hours. We should certainly reach *Mision San Luis Obispo de Tolosa* by nightfall. There Padre Luis Martinez will greet us and will offer us fine hospitality for the night." Fine, thought Morgan, but we still have eight hours of walking to do. It had been sometime since Morgan had walked so far and his leg muscles were already beginning to ache some. But how in tarnation can the priest walk with just those sandals? Not much support from them! Still, he seems to be doing well. And didn't he say that Padre Serra had walked from *San Diego* to *Monterey* many times even though he was a cripple? I guess priests are expected to suffer for their Lord.

One of the Chumash men spoke to Payeras. The priest replied with mild excitement and a pleased look. Morgan wondered what the interchange was about. After a few more words to the Chumash men, Payeras turned to Morgan and explained: "They were wondering if the swallows had returned to *Mision San Juan Capistrano*. For many years now these small birds have returned to nest at the Mission on this feast day of *San Jose'*, Saint Joseph, that is, who was the earthly foster father of *Jesuchristo*. Of course we will not know for several weeks, until a messenger may bring the news, but I am confident that the swallows have continued this tradition, because as I said at the beginning of our trek, today is *San Jose's recuerdo solemne*, how you would say, feastday."

Payeras was rising and the Chumash men took the cue, rising also. Morgan was a little slower to rise. Payeras chided him, "My, *Sharlezz,* you are not tired already are you?. We still have several days of walking ahead of us. But we'll take a few days respite when we reach *San Carlos* as I want you to spend a little time there to examine this beautiful Mission."

So the small procession started again and after walking several more hours Payeras called for a halt. He had been observing the sun and decided that it was midday. He announced, "We will now recite the *Angelus*". Then, remembering that the Chumash men would not know what he said, he spoke to them in their tongue. They immediately knelt, and awaited Payeras' lead. The priest began again *"Dios te salve Maria…"* Morgan waited to see if they were starting that Rosary thing all over again but Payeras did not remove the long string of beads from his waist rope. In fact, he recited only three of the prayers, then upon signal from the Padre, one of the natives produced some *tortillas* from an animal hide pouch that was slung on his shoulder. After eating, followed by a few gulps of lukewarm water from a leather bottle, they all rose and began walking again.

Now the priest began mumbling to himself. After a while Morgan realized that he was reciting private prayers and remembered that Payeras and Castellanos would always pace the plaza at the Mission at midday and mumble their prayers, unaware of each others presence. Payeras once explained to Morgan that it was called their *"oficio"*, prayers required of them to be said several times a day.

About in the middle of the afternoon, Payeras again removed the rosary beads from his cincture, grasped the Crucifix and signed himself again by touching the Cross to his forehead, belly, then the right and left shoulder. He began. *"Dios te salve Maria"*...and continued for the next hour or more in the same as early this morning. Morgan could not believe it!...Does this man do nothing but pray, pray, pray? When Payeras finished and replaced the Rosary to his cincture the natives spoke to him excitedly. It appeared that they had been anxiously awaiting the completion of the prayers so that they could address the priest. They both spoke at once, in urgent voices and with excited gestures. Payeras remained calm and appeared to try to be reassuring the men about something. "What's the matter? Is there trouble?", Morgan asked. "No, No", replied the priest. "These men remember the lore of the region and are worried about the bears". Bears? Although Morgan did not wish to show Payeras that he was overly concerned, he was a good deal nervous about bears. It had been a long time since he had seen one, back in Massachusetts, but here he had no musket, nor a brother George to bolster his confidence. Payeras explained, "We are nearing the region that is called *La Canada de los Osos*, The Valley Of The Bears. You see, more than thirty years ago a band of soldiers and missionaries, along with a few neophytes, got lost trying to get to *Monterey*. They were near starvation when they discovered that many bears populated the area. They did indeed kill a bear, but were almost killed themselves before subduing him. They did reach *Monterey* and after reporting about the numerous bears in the valley, a hunting party was sent back because the northern Missions were near starvation themselves. After giving praise to God for the success of their three months of hunting, they packed their mules and departed to *Monterey*. It was reported that they loaded their pack-mules with nine thousand pounds of bear meat. And in addition, they obtained twenty five loads of edible seeds as a result of bartering bear meat with the natives. Shortly after that, while on a journey from *Monterey* to *San Diego, Padre Presidente* Serra established *Mision San Luis Obispo,* his fifth, very near the Valley Of The Bears. That was seventeen hundred and seventy two." As an afterthought Payeras added, "The Mission is named for *San Luis,* Bishop of Toulouse, France".

My, my, what a story thought Morgan. I wonder if the bears still populate the place? That's what the natives are concerned about! "Should we be prepared for bears, priest? Are they still around?"

Morgan asked Payeras. "I don't believe that there is a large band of bears any longer, but I suppose that it is possible that there are some in the area. Why? Are you concerned for your safety, *Sharlezz?*" the priest asked. "Well, I just want to know what I might be up against, that's all", replied Morgan, trying to sound casual.

The small party continued walking, though a bit less carefree than earlier in the day. After another hour or so, with dusk settling in, the Chumash men suddenly stopped. "Padre!, Padre!" they exclaimed while pointing ahead on the trail. Payeras hurried forward. Two Native American men were standing on the trail about fifty feet ahead. Payeras called to them in Chumash. They responded in what seemed to be peaceful tones. "These men saw us walking and have been watching out for us a short time, to help if any bears did pick up our aromas, but they assure me that no bears have been seen for some weeks. They will escort us the rest of the way to *Mision San Luis Obispo*. We are only a half-hour from there." Morgan was relieved on both matters, the lack of evidence of bears and the proximity to the Mission.

As the weary travelers approached the Mission from the southwest they could see the full facade of the Mission, gleaming white in the sunset. The front of the church portion had three bells hung. Soon these started to ring to announce the travelers approach. To the left, but attached to the church was an extensive colonnade, having eleven pillars holding up an orange tiled roof. It was a far more impressive Mission than *La Purisima* from whence they had started many hours ago. Morgan thought about the tiles, and decided that they should be utilized at all the Missions, instead of the fire-vulnerable thatch that *La Purisima* had. Before they reached the Mission itself, a rotund Padre came out to meet them. He was as jovial as he was stout. He shouted to Payeras first. *"Buenas tarde, Mariano!"*. The two embraced and patted each others shoulders. Then Payeras introduced Morgan and the two Chumash men, as all entered into the Mission courtyard.

Following the well prepared evening meal, Padre Martinez escorted Payeras and Morgan around the Mission complex, while the two Indian guides socialized with friends that they knew who lived at the Mission. Padre Martinez was obviously proud of his Mission. He explained how it had prospered over the years, producing fine wine, olive oil, fruits and vegetables. And he was especially happy to show Payeras and Morgan his very large flock of poultry. This was Martinez's personal avocation. Of course, Payeras had seen the flock before and chided Martinez about the growth of the flock. "And does your flock of neophytes grow as abundantly?" he asked. Laughing lightly, Martinez and Payeras excused themselves so that they could go to say their vesper prayers. Payeras invited Morgan to join them, but he was ready to lie down and get some rest.

Early the next morning, following the celebration of Mass, the little band was on its way north again. Payeras explained that this evening would be spent at *Mision San Miguel Arcangel*, the next at *Mision San Antonio de Padua*, the following evening they would be at *Mision Nuestra Sonora de la Soledad*, and finally, only four days from now, at *Mision San Carlos Borromeo de Carmelo*. Morgan acknowledged that he understood the agenda and that he was anxious to see the Mission that had the same name as his. Again as they walked, just as the day before, Payeras took the Rosary from his waist cincture and began to intone the prayers. Morgan became annoyed by the repetition of the *Dios te salve Maria*, by the Hail Marys, even by the Chumash words that he did not understand, and by the *Ave Maria's*. He agonized when he thought about the repeated recitation by Payeras and the Chumash men. Again he drifted off into reverie and fantasized about his return to Sturbridge. This day was a repeat of the last, except there was no unnecessary fear of the bears.

Mision San Miguel Arcangel was situated in the an opening of a beautiful forest of oaks and other fine trees. Payeras referred to the area as *Los Robles*, which he explained meant "The Oaks". As they approached the Mission, they passed through a small village inhabited by natives, most of whom looked only casually at the arriving Padre and his small band. Morgan could not decide if this casualness was because of their disdain for the Padre and his followers, or because they were just lackadaisical people. Again, the Mission bell announced the arrival of the walkers and the Mission Padre came out to greet them. Payeras introduced Padre Juan Martin, but was not as jubilant as when he had met his old friend Martinez at San Luis Obispo. Still, the Padres were very cordial and Martin was obviously pleased to have the company of a fellow Spaniard, even if only for a few hours.

Morgan studied the building construction, especially the church, noting the rather crude roofs as compared to *Mision San Luis Obispo*. The roofs were of mud-sod patches. He asked Padre Martin if this was a temporary roof. Martin replied that he felt that the entire church was only of temporary construction, that he hoped one day to build a far more magnificent church. He explained that he was already beginning to manufacture adobe bricks and had constructed an oven to bake them well. "Are you using slave labor to do this?" Morgan asked.

Payeras showed embarrasment at this question while Martin stuttered in amazement. "Of course not," Martin replied. "We have the willing help of several thousand neophytes, who are very pleased to offer their labor to the glory of God. Further, we pay them well in the form of food and shelter. They are not in the least imposed upon!" Even though Morgan felt repressed by the Padre's reply, he was glad he had asked the question. He thought back to the many natives in the nearby village. He still wasn't sure if they looked servile, complacent or satisfied with their conditions. Later, Padre Payeras explained to Morgan that this Mission, perhaps more than any other, had the most willing neophyte workers, who welcomed the Padres when they first arrived five years earlier, and who worked diligently to establish the nearby village and to help construct the Mission buildings.

As Payeras continued on about the growth of the cattle herds, the wheat output and the spiritual accomplishments, Morgan just shrugged and ambled to a mat at the corner of the portico where he lay down for his second night's rest.

Again, as soon as the sun rose, all were ready for a hearty breakfast and the continuation of their journey. Morgan did have to agree that the Mission food was very delicious. Only the mid-day meal on the trail was somewhat distasteful but he could tolerate that by just thinking about the evening meal that was to come. He was beginning to feel unfaithful to Cimkonah and her fine cooking.

As they left the Mission area, Payeras took his rosary beads from his cincture but before making the sign of the cross he said to Morgan, "This morning we will walk between two beautiful lakes, *Nacimbiento y San Antonio*". "That's a mighty long name for a lake, ain't it?" Morgan asked. Payeras laughed lightly and explained, "That is two names, *Sharlezz*. *Nacimbiento* means the birth, or the spring. This lake is the beginning of the source of water for the area. The lake below it is *San Antonio*. I don't need to explain that do I? Anyway, we will walk in the morning among these beautiful lakes but in the afternoon the land will become less hospitable. We will walk in the foothills of the *Montana de Santa Lucia.* It too will be pleasing to the eye, but a bit more wearying to the body".

And so, on they walked with Payeras again droning on with the Rosary prayers in the several languages. And again Morgan tried to ignore the Padre's supplications to the Virgin Mary, while he absorbed the beauty of the terrain and engaged again in his reveries. Now he thought about his friends, Angelica and Juan Bautista, wondering if they were happy in the village of Juan's father. He wondered too what the natives of that village were like. Were they vibrant like the Chumash, or complacent like those he saw yesterday at *San Miguel*. Was the village pleasant and with abundant food, or were the natives eking out a food supply from the nuts, berries and a few birds.

Morgan's thoughts were especially pleasing when he thought about Angelica, but he immediately became pent up when he though about her raping by Rivera. He wondered, had Rivera been punished appropriately or only admonished. Did his *Comandante* feel that raping an native maiden was less of a crime than raping a Spanish maiden? Someday I have to find out what punishment was meted out to Rivera.

Payeras called for a rest. It was another beautiful day but a bit warmer than the two previous. In the distance they could see the two lakes that Payeras had mentioned. They were indeed beautiful, as was the mountain range in the distance. From here they could not see the ocean, but the easterly breezes brought some of its sweet smell to them.

Soon they were on their way again with Payeras continuing his Rosary. As he came to the English and Latin decades he looked to Morgan and with a slight upward nodding of his head, silently asked Morgan to join him in the prayers. Morgan pretended ignorance. After the noon-day *Angelus* prayers and the meager meal, they soon reached the mountain foothills. These were only gentle slopes but the weary travelers felt their legs rebelling against the additional labor in their steps. All were perspiring heavily, especially Padre Payeras in his heavy gray robe, when they saw the *Mison San Antonio de Padua* a mile or so ahead.

The sun had already disappeared behind *Montana Santa Lucia* when they reached the Mission.

They felt a bit better when the Mission bells rang and a few neophytes ran out to welcome them. Padre Bonaventura Sitjar met them at the front of the Mission church, where he greeted *"Bien tarde Mariano"*, Morgan and the Chumash men very warmly. He led them into a *lavandario* where they could wash away the day's perspiration and prepare for the evening meal.

During the meal Payeras explained that Sitjar had written a grammar, a book of vocabulary and a catechism in the language of the Native Americans of the area, the Salinan dialect. He had been at this Mission almost from its founding by *Padre Presidente* Serra and had accomplished a great deal in both the secular and clerical areas. Sitjar gave Payeras a report of the Mission status which Payeras proudly translated to Morgan. At this time there were over 15,000 head of cattle and other animals on the *rancho* around the Mission and almost 5000 baptisms had taken place since the Mission's founding thirty two years earlier. Sitjar had designed and built a water system, bringing abundant fresh water to the Mission from the *San Antonio* River (named by Padre Serra) by use of a dam and viaducts. The wheat, barley, corn, beans and *garbanzos* crops were also very productive.

To Morgan the buildings were even more impressive than *Mision San Luis Obispo*. The *campanario* and the two bell towers to each side were of burned brick instead of the usual white stucco, and again the orange tiled roof was impressive. Padre Sitjar seemed to be most proud of the waterway that had been constructed, having power enough to run the paddle wheel that drove a mill-stone. It was very reminiscent of the Sturbridge mill that Morgan used to visit, helping his father carry bags of their milled wheat back home.

After what seemed like a very short evening sleep, Morgan was awakened by one of the Chumash natives. He took breakfast with Sitjar and Payeras and all were on their way again. It was not long until Payeras withdrew the Rosary from his cincture, made the Sign Of The Cross and began the recitation of *Dios te salve Maria.* As if hypnotized and without even realizing it, Morgan joined right in with the Payeras and the Chumash men because now the Spanish prayer words had permeated his brain. He even mumbled along on the Chumash portion. When they came to the English decade, Payeras looked with pleased approval as Morgan verbalized the prayers without hesitation or embarrassment. When he suddenly realized what he was doing, Morgan asked himself, 'Does this make me a Catholic?' He hoped not, because he knew inwardly that if he were agree to let Payeras convert him, he would never get back to Massachusetts.

CHAPTER SIX
So close, but yet so far.

Although it seemed as if several weeks had passed since the little party had left *Mison La Purisima*, it was really only four days. Walking for nearly a week had tired Morgan a good deal, but he managed to keep up with the others. Perhaps it was the monotony of the days that had tired him more than the walking itself. Yes, they had received wonderful hospitality from the Padres at the several Missions where they rested for the night, but only Morgan's reveries of his boyhood and sea travels kept him from complete boredom. Occasionally he was intrigued by the landscape, the beauty of a mountain, a stream that they traversed, a lovely valley, some awe at the size of fields cultivated by the neophytes, even flocks of beautiful birds, or foliage that he had never seen before. These were but momentary distractions to a lad as young as Morgan. He had not yet lived enough years to fully appreciate the creations of nature.

What seemed to make the long walk even more boring was Payeras' constant praying. Morgan thought that even the Virgin Mary herself must be bored by the incessant droning of the Padre's prayers. Morgan wondered how a person could become so obsessed with one notion. Still, Morgan himself did occasionally begin to say the words of a prayer, completely unintentionally.

Finally, in the end of the afternoon of the fifth day, the small party of walkers could see *Mision San Carlos Borromeo* in the distance. Morgan was pleased, but not as excited as was Payeras or even the Chumash guides. Payeras, of course, was anxious to greet his old friend Padre Fermin Francisco de Lasuen, who had now been the *Padre Presidente* of the Missions for nearly eighteen years, since the death of Padre Junipero Serra. And Payeras was anxious to make his petition to Lasuen for the establishment of the new Mission between *Santa Barbara* and *La Purisima*. He now reminded Morgan that that was why they had made this arduous trek. Though he did not dare show it, Morgan became inwardly excited when he remembered that his hope was to make contact with a ship heading for Boston or New Bedford and begin his own journey home.

They were approaching the Mission complex and even from the distance of many hundreds of meters, Morgan could see that the bell-towers and the facade of the church were more "permanent" looking than those of some of the other missions, and certainly much more impressive than *La Purisima.* Now the bells began to toll and neophytes from the Mission came out to greet them. By the time they reached the proximity of the front of the mission, two Padres and many more neophytes were standing at the entrance, waiting to greet them like royalty.

Lasuen was the first to step forward, greeting Payeras like a long lost brother. They embraced, patted each other's shoulders and chatted excitedly. Morgan now remembered that Payeras had stated that he had not seen Lasuen for about two years, but previously they had served at several missions together in Mexico. That was before Lasuen had become *Presidente*, before he was so busy with the yoke of his office, and before Payeras had become virtually enslaved at keeping *La Purisima* in operation.

Payeras introduced Morgan to Lasuen and the other Padre. As they went inside the nave of the church, Payeras said, "Come *Sharlezz*, we will pray at the grave of *Padre Presidente* Junipero, for we owe so much to him for his great devotion to God and to the cause of the Missions, and to his wonderful leadership for so many years". Payeras, Lasuen, the other priest, and many of the neophytes, walked to a place near the sanctuary, knelt, and all made the Sign Of The Cross. Morgan did not immediately understand that Serra was buried there, below the floor of the church. He thought that all would be proceding to the traditional cemetery near the Mission. When he realized that he was at Serra's grave, he also knelt, somewhat automatically, but with reverence, because he had heard so much about the frail man who had walked many, many thousands of kilometers, though a cripple, for the glory of the God that inspired him. Somehow Morgan was impressed by the man's dedication to his cause and by the reverence that the others, even the neophytes, were displaying.

Lasuen led the prayers. Morgan was surprised that they did not all say the *Ave Maria's* that he had heard almost incessantly for five days. Instead, as much as Morgan could understand some of the Spanish words, the Padre was intoning Supplications for the deliverance of Serra's soul to heaven, thanks to God for the leadership and devotion of Serra, and finally an entreaty to God for them to also be recipients of God's graces and support for their remaining worldly days.

After nearly one hour of these prayers and supplications, all made the Sign of the Cross once more, rose and left the church. Now the mood became more jubilant again. Lasuen spoke to Payeras and the Chumash men. Payeras turned to Morgan and said, "Padre Lasuen has invited us to be his guests for as long as we like, to cleanse ourselves of the dust of our long journey, to take a short *siesta*, then to join him and the other Padre for supper." Morgan was happy thinking of each of the items mentioned. Again the Chumash men were escorted by other neophytes to the natives quarters, seeming to go happily. They apparently knew that the dinner invitation did not include them at the table of the Padres. Still, they seemed very pleased that they were being treated in an honorable way by their own.

When Morgan reached the cell of the Padre's quarters that was to be his, he found a basin of warm water, soap and towels to bathe himself. He even found that clean clothing was at hand. This time he would not have to enrobe himself in the liturgical garment as on his arrival at *La Purisima*. The clothes, he concluded, must belong to one of the Spanish craftsman assigned to the Mission.

The evening went well. Morgan did not understand the rapid Spanish dialogue among the Padres, but he occasionally recognized a word, and when Payeras felt that the matter being discussed would interest Morgan, he translated the dialogue for him. Once when the discussion centered on Yankee trader ships that embarked at Monterey, only a short distance from the Mission, Morgan became more interested than even Payeras realized. Soon Morgan excused himself, walked to the cell containing his cot, and retired for the night. He wanted to be up at daybreak to investigate which ships were in harbor or were due to arrive soon.

Early the next day Morgan thought that he had arisen early enough that he would evade Payeras. He started walking hurriedly along the cart trail that led to Monterey. A few neophytes looked at him curiously and as he approached Monterey, a few soldiers looked as though they might challenge him. None did, so he kept walking until he came to the port area. Two ships were moored, both Spanish. He spoke to a sailor in the best Spanish that he could muster. He asked if any *yanqui* ships were due into port. The sailor shrugged his shoulders, but Morgan could not determine if he meant this as a sign of not understanding his Spanish or not knowing of the arrival ships schedule. After attempting this method of communication with several more sailors, one responded in English.

"Oh, so you're are a yankee yourself." Morgan was dismayed. He quickly acknowledged his nationality. The other yankee sailor introduced himself, "I'm Benjamin Hopkins, originally from Baltimore". Morgan acknowledged "Ben" with a nod of the head and then explained to this new-found acquaintance how he happened to be there and what his plan was. The two retired to a corner of one of the nearby buildings and spent some time telling each other their stories. Ben told how he had arrived on a ship from Baltimore several weeks earlier, had gotten drunk the night before his ship sailed and how it left port without him. He remained in Monterey earning his food and drink by sketching pictures of the *soldados,* so they could send them home to their wives and loved ones. He offered to sketch a picture of Morgan, but Morgan explained that he had no money, food or drink with which to repay him. The sailor made the sketch anyway. It was a fair likeness. Then the sailor volunteered to check on the schedule of any arriving Yankee ships because he too, was attempting to get back to Baltimore, or at least to the east coast. They agreed to meet the next morning.

Morgan hurried back to the Mission, hoping to arrive before Payeras knew that he had been absent. When he was inside the Mission compound he saw Payeras walking in the garden, reading from the book that he always held when walking thus. As Morgan approached, Payeras looked up and gave the first acknowledgment. "*Sharlezz*, where have you been? It is not like you to miss breakfast! What has been so urgent that you were not with us for your morning meal?" Suddenly Morgan realized that he had broken a pattern that Payeras easily recognized. It was the first time in these many months that Morgan had not taken breakfast. "Oh, I guess that I was just so tired that I didn't wake up in time for breakfast. Do you think that Padre Lasuen's cook can fix me something?" He was being very polite, even callng Lasuen "father". "Oh I am sure that she can. Just go to the cooking room. She will feed you generously". 'Did I fool him?' Morgan wondered. But as Payeras was turning to return to his prayerful stroll, he said, "You are quite perspired, *Sharlezz*, for someone who has just arisen from a long slumber. Let us discuss this later in the day." Morgan did not yet know that Payeras had seen him walking away from the Mission compound while Payeras himself was walking to the church to celebrate his early morning Mass.

In the late morning, one of the Chumash men came to Morgan to say that Payeras wished him to go to the arbor area of the garden. When Morgan arrived he found Payeras sitting in the shade on one of several benches there. "Come, sit *mi amigo*", Payeras directed. Morgan obliged, not knowing what to expect from this man who was now his friend, father-figure and director. "Well, *Sharlezz*, what do you think of this beautiful *Mision San Carlos Borromeo?*, the *Mision* named in honor of the great saint whose name you bear. In life, San Carlos was the Cardinal-Archbishop of Milano, *Italia."*.

Morgan's reply was honest. "It is really very beautiful…and the construction seems so…permanent. I mean, the stones look so strong compared to the *adobe* and the stucco that all the other Missions have. How is it that this one is of stone?"

Payeras related the story of the Mission, how this was the seventh church building that was constructed here at Monterey and Carmel. The first church was a crude log building erected by Serra and a few soldiers in Monterey, almost 35 years earlier, in 1770. This was the second mission established by Serra, on the site where newly appointed Governor Don Gaspar de Portola had erected a cross one year earlier, after a long and almost disastrous trek from San Diego. After nearly missing the "beautiful protective bay" that the original discoverer had described, Portola's party had returned to San Diego almost starved, to report that the bay, first discovered more than one-hundred-and-fifty years earlier, and named by Sebastian Vizcaino, was not an ideal site to establish a new colony. Nevertheless, one year later, Portola and Serra and their party came, this time by ship, to the site. They found that the cross that had been erected one year earlier now had tokens of peace placed near it by the natives. There were meat, shellfish, a string of sardines, and arrows stuck in the ground. Serra immediately hung bells on a tree, ringing them joyfully and celebrated Mass, proclaiming this to be the site of the *Mision San Carlos Borromeo*.

Within a year Serra realized the site was not ideal, not having enough land to support the crops that he intended to grow to support the natives that were showing ready acceptance of the foreigners. Payeras related how Serra decided that it would be best if a better church and compound were built some distance from what was quickly growing to be a shipping port and *Presidio*, even a *pueblo,* Monterey. Serra was concerned about the effect of the many soldiers, sailors and newly arriving settlers on the morals of the neophytes. He had walked about ten kilometers into the valley of Carmel, deciding that that was the place to someday build a fine stone church, one with much tillable land all around it, for the neophytes to farm and to raise cattle for their sustenance. Serra knew that judging by the success of the mission efforts to that date, there would be many neophytes to feed, to house and to christianize.

Over the years, a series of churches had been built, but for various reasons, some because of inadequate construction or becoming too small for the fast growing congregation of neophytes, each was replaced by another. Although the sandstone blocks for the present church were being cut at Serra's orders, he did not live to see this magnificent edifice. He died on August 28, 1784, at age 71. He was buried near the altar of the then existing *adobe* church, alongside his long time friend and fellow seminarian, Padre Juan Crespi. When the stone church was started some years later, it was erected around the then existing church, and the two Padres remained in their original graves. The new stone church was one of a very few that was not designed by the first Padre assigned. For this church, architect Manuel Ruiz was brought from Spain. Morgan was greatly intrigued by the amazing story of the mission and its founder. He could understand why Payeras, Lasuen and the other Padres held Serra in such great respect.

"Well now, *Sharlezz*," Payeras changed the subject, "let us discuss the proposal that I shall make to *Padre Presidente* Lasuen later today." Not wanting to sound completely indifferent, Morgan replied, "Oh, I suppose that it's a good idea, if that's what you want." Payeras continued, "It will require much labor and we will not have the benefit of an architect such as Senor Ruiz. We will need the service of men who can direct the neophytes so that the structure will endure, not like some of the earlier churches here at Monterey. Padre Castellanos will not be of much assistance, I am afraid, and Lasuen has no other Padres to assign to help me. I need to assure him that I will have the assistance of a strong, experienced person." Morgan knew who he was referring to him. He now wanted to be sure that Payeras should not commit to his involvement. "Padre, I think you already know that I went to Monterey this morning to find a ship that will soon be sailing to

Boston or New Bedford. A yankee sailor told me that one would be arriving in port soon. I expect to be on it. I think I've served my time with you just as I said I would."

Payeras look disappointed but not completely subdued. "Well then, I shall only be able to tell Padre Lasuen that you must further consider your options, and will decide in the next few days". Not wanting to argue with Payeras, but knowing right now what his plans were, Morgan replied, "Yea, tell him that".

For the next several days Morgan went to Monterey port each morning to locate his new found yankee friend. Each day Ben said that he had no definite news of a yankee ship arriving, though others that claimed that they would be sailing to "America" had come into port. Both the yankee sailor and Morgan suspected that they were not truthful, but only wanted to obtain experienced seamen.

On the fifth morning neophytes began bringing cart loads of dried cow hides, tallow and other mission products to the port area. On that morning the yankee sailor also told Morgan that a ship, the "*Pride Of Gloucester*", would be in port by next morning, and would set sail the following day. Morgan was excited, he hurried back to the Mission to tell Payeras of his imminent departure.

As he approached the Mission, one of the Chumash men came running towards him. He waved his arms and spoke to Morgan, who could not understand the man's language, but certainly understood that the man was excited. All that Morgan could understand was "Padre Payeras", and the waving arms, obviously meaning that he should hurry into the Mission.

As Morgan entered the compound he looked all about but did not immediately see Payeras as he had expected. He began walking towards his cell, thinking of the words he will tell Payeras. Just then, Payeras came hurrying out of the church and waved joyously to Morgan. "*Sharlezz, Sharlezz!, Padre Presidente* has approved wholeheartedly of my proposal to build a new *Mision.* I have just spoken to the Lord, and promised Him to create another monument to His glory. *Padre Presidente* has allowed me to name the new *Mision* so I will dedicate it to *Santa Ines. Ines* was my own mother's name, and she honored her sainted namesake during her whole life, so it is appropriate that I choose this name."

Morgan could not help but to have mixed feelings, some joy for his friend Payeras, but even more so, a good bit of anguish about telling Payeras of his departure in two days. Nevertheless he blurted out his news of departure before he even remembered to congratulate Payeras. The priest suddenly looked very downfallen, his joy quickly turning to a very obvious look of great disappointment. Turning back toward the church, he said, "*Vaya con dios,* my son, I shall pray to our Heavenly Father for your safe journey home." Morgan followed a good bit behind. He saw Payeras go directly to the altar rail, slump in a kneeling position and make the Sign of the Cross. Morgan stood at the edge of the doorway. He too, said a prayer, in silence and with no outward sign, now realizing how much he respected, even loved Payeras, and how much Payeras had come to like and to depend on him.

The two days passed with Morgan and Payeras each having a good deal of inner conflict. They ate meals together, and they spoke gentlemanly to each other, but each knew that their relationship was now altogether different, just barely closer than that of total strangers. But neither spoke of the two great matters on their minds, the new Mission, and Morgan's departure.

The final morning dawned. Morgan saw Payeras go into the church. Should he depart now?, or should he wait for Payeras to finish his morning Mass, about an hour from now?. The evening before Morgan had asked the other priest if he could have a quill and some ink. He wanted to write a farewell note to Payeras, but he had not found the words, so the note was still unwritten. Now Morgan hurried back to his cell, took the sketch of himself that the sailor had made several days earlier, and wrote on the back. He then ran out of the Mission and to the port of Monterey. He found his sailor friend anxiously waiting. "My, you gave me a fright! I was afraid that you were going to miss our sailing". Morgan gave no explanation of his late arrival but gave the sketch with the note on the reverse to the sailor. "Promise me that you will get this to my family!" Morgan blurted loudly, then turned and ran back to the Mission. Ben hollered after him, but Morgan kept running away. "I must stay here a while longer", he called back to his sailor friend.

Payeras was just coming out of the church. Morgan shouted, "Padre Payeras!". Payeras looked up from his dejected demeanor, "Oh *Sharlezz*, I am happy that you came to say goodbye in person. Let me give you God's blessing for your travel." Payeras began to raise his right arm in the traditional Sign of the Cross when Morgan blurted "I have decided to stay with you and help build your new Mission!". Payeras fell hard to his knees and began to pray loudly "Oh Heavenly Father, this unworthy Padre thanks you for answering my fervent prayers! You have reached the heart of my son, *Sharlezz*! Praise be to You and Your Son, *Jesuchristo*!" Morgan too fell to his knees and the two men leaned on each others shoulders and embraced for some time.

Two mornings later, the La Purisima party left Mission San Carlos to return to their own home Mission. Payeras seemed jubilant during the entire five day trek. He spoke to Morgan much of the time, in between reciting the rosaries, about his ideas for the new Mission. Its location, its buildings, its garden, its rancheros; all were already fixed in Payeras' mind.

The party arrived at La Purisima to the excited welcome of Padre Castellanos, Cimkonah and the many, many neophytes. Payeras told all of Padre Presidente Lasuen's approval of the new Mission, and all showed their approval by cheering Payeras. The following weeks were filled with prayers of thanksgiving, of jubilation and of excitement, for even many of the neophytes looked forward to assisting with the establishment of this new honor to Santa Ines and to *Dios Todopoderoso*.

The summer passed with much activity at La Purisima. The new tile roofing, the additional stuccoing of the adobe walls, expansion of the water sources, the increase in the herds of cattle, all kept the mission inhabitants very busy. For Morgan, the time was passing quickly.

It was late August again. It had been a little more than a year since Morgan had swam ashore in his escape from Bouchard's pirate ship. As he worked away in the blacksmith shop or at doing some other chore that Padre Payeras would ask, Morgan would reminisce about the year. Had he made a mistake five months ago in not seizing that opportunity to sail out of Monterey with his new-made yankee friend? Will he get another such opportunity?

Each day of the past several months Payeras would tell Morgan that he was hoping that the next day would bring news of the imminent arrival of a Padre to begin the new Mission, *Santa Ines*. But the message had not come. Payeras was plainly concerned about the lapse of time. He was anxious that the new Mission would get its start before the cooler weather and the rains would set in. But he continued to express great confidence that the Padre would arrive soon, any day now. Morgan too, was hoping for that Padre's arrival so that he could fulfill his promise to Payeras to help with the construction of the Mission, then with a clear conscience, try to find passage home again.

Since April when they returned from *Mision San Carlos Borromeo de Carmelo,* both Payeras and Morgan were generally overseeing the neophytes as they busily applied stucco to the Mission walls. They had also started to afix some of the clay roof tiles that had been manufactured during the last six months, to the roof of the church. Both of these measures would help protect the Mission from the erosion that had occurred last winter and spring. But once given the instructions of how to apply these improvements, the neophytes were capable of performing their tasks without much supervision, leaving Morgan with little more to do than to keep pounding away in the blacksmith shop.

One thought that cropped up in Morgan's mind often was, what of Angelica and Juan Bautista? Were they alright? Were they happy in the village of Juan's father? Were they adjusting to the life of their own people? Was it difficult to subsist in the manner of their forebears, after having been indoctrinated into the white man's culture? Morgan wondered often, and wished that he could help his two friends in some way. He had thoughts again of trying to search them out. But surely that would lead to difficulties for the distraught couple. Nevertheless, he often thought that he should do something.

One early morning in late August the decision was made for him. Shortly after arising and stoking the fire in the shop, he was suddenly surprised by a sound from behind a nearby tree. At first he ignored it but then a voice, yes, he was sure it was a voice, was saying something in a loud whisper. As he looked about, a Chumash man stepped partially from behind the tree. He motioned for Morgan to come to him. After glancing about to see if others were nearby, Morgan did go to the vicinity of the tree. The native was trying to talk to Morgan. Yes, it was Chumash language, but Morgan was having trouble understanding the man's dialect. The native kept repeating, "Hooaan bawteestah, hooaan bawteestah". Finally Morgan realized that he was saying the name of his friend Juan. He quickly went to the native. "What of Juan Bautista?". Morgan was excited and eager to know why the man was here saying Juan's name. The native kept repeating Juan's name and then motioned for Morgan for follow him. After several such gestures, Morgan started walking toward him. The native turned and started walking quickly through a path into the wooded areas northeast of the Mission. Morgan followed quickly though he knew not where he was going or why. But surely this man must mean to take him to Juan.

They followed a foot path for nearly an hour, almost running some of the time. Through gasps of breath, Morgan would occasionally ask his guide, "What of Juan Bautista?", but the guide never answered, just kept walking quickly forward.

After another half-hour they came to a clear area and in the distance of a few hundred feet Morgan saw several Chumash huts. "Asuskwa", the Indian said. Morgan instinctively knew that he meant the name of the village. It consisted of a dozen or so round thatched huts, the traditional Chumash dwelling.

The man hurried to one of the huts, motioning for Morgan to enter. In the dark interior Morgan could hear low moanings of a female and the voice of Juan trying to sooth her. "Ohmygosh" Morgan gasped to himself as he saw Angelica lying on a *tule* mat, obviously heavy with child. There was also a squaw who was trying to help the baby to enter the world, but apparently with much difficulty.

The baby emerged finally, very dark blue, and without a cry. *"Oh! Santa Madre!",* Juan repeated several times. Although he had never seen a birth before, Morgan knew that the baby was dead. He looked at poor Angelica whose physical pain was very obvious, but he knew that she was now realizing the

116

baby's plight and emotional pain was now also added to her trauma.

Juan hugged the dead baby. Then Angelica asked for the baby. Upon taking the tiny lifeless body into her arms, and hugging it to her bosom, she now began to emit heavy sobs. Then both Angelica and Juan made the Sign of the Cross over the tiny blue body and prayed. Morgan recognized the words so he joined in also. Hearing his voice both Angelica and Juan turned towards him. It was the first time that they realized that he had entered the hut. Juan motioned for him to come closer. They all joined hands and repeated several "Ave Maria" prayers.

The native woman mid-wife stroked Angelica's forehead with a water soaked piece of animal skin. After a while Angelica appeared to be calmer, so the native woman left. The Chumash guide that had brought Morgan had remained in the background. Now Juan said to Morgan, "This is my father, the one who went to bring you here". The two bowed towards each other. The poor grandfather looked very sad. He too wanted to console the baby. He patted it lightly, then after patting his son's shoulder lightly, he left the hut. Morgan noted that he did not look towards Angelica at all.

After an hour of silence, Angelica drifted off to sleep. Juan left the baby by her side, then led Morgan out of the hut. Morgan was the first to speak. "Why did you not send for me sooner? Why did you not bring Angelica back to the Mission?" Juan explained to Morgan that he had often tried to convince Angelica to return to the Mission where Cimkonah could have helped her, but Angelica still continued to feel the shame of her "sin" of being raped, and would not return to her friends. Finally, when Juan realized that the baby's movements had stopped inside of Angelica's body, he knew that the birth would not be normal. He thought of carrying Angelica back to the Mission but then her pain became too severe and he knew that she could not survive the trek, even if carried.

Juan described how, when they arrived at his father's village, they were at first not welcomed. They had taken to the white man's God and the white man's ways, and were not considered to be Chumash people anymore. Gradually, as Angelica's condition became apparent, some of the native women became more friendly and eventually the local *wot,* chief, decreed that the couple were married and were to be accepted as Chumash again.

The Chumash culture embraced three levels of social strata. Juan's father was of the middle class, a simple hunter. For this reason he knew that Juan, whose native name was Strong Bear, would not gain much in life. Juan's mother had died shortly after his birth. Juan's father believed that by turning his son over to the Mission, Juan would receive better care, and because the Mission was closer to the ocean, Juan could someday become a canoe person, and thus become wealthier in life.

For the several months that he was at Asuskwa, Juan did hunt with his father and the other men, using bow and arrow. Although Juan had not been raised to have this skill, he adapted quite well and was able to occasionally shoot a rabbit or other small animal. Life in the Chumash culture was not disheartening to Juan, but as Angelica's pregnancy advanced, her distress became more apparent, and his anguish became stronger. He had often thought of sending for Cimkonah, but Angelica would not allow that either. Finally, as Angelica's baby's premature birth was imminent, Juan's father knew that Juan needed a friend to help him. So he had run to the Mission this morning, not even telling Juan of his plan.

The next morning Juan came to arouse Morgan at dawn. Morgan had slept on a *tule* mat out in the open, near a fire place. "Angelica is much worse! She is rolling in great pain and is very warm in the head!". The two ran to the hut. Angelica was now moaning loudly, rubbing her stomach fiercely and pleading for help. Juan held her hand and Morgan ran out, through the midst of the huts calling out for help. He knew that no one would know his English but his desperation was coming through in his calling. Several people came from their huts, including the mid-wife that Morgan saw yesterday. He motioned for her to come with him to Angelica's hut.

On entering, the native mid-wife looked very somber. Angelica was already showing signs of weakness. The mid-wife knelt beside her, holding Angelica's head on her lap. She looked at Juan. It was obvious to Morgan that the woman was telling Juan with her eyes that Angelica was dying. Juan suddenly realized the silent signal and grasped Angelica to his chest, hugging her as if to hold her from leaving in death. *"Santa Madre Mia. clementia! Por favor, clementia!"* he pleaded. With just a few more gasps, Angelica passed away.

119

As Juan hugged Angelica to himself, swaying and murmuring her name, Morgan went to Juan, placed his arm about Juan's shoulder and swayed with him. What else was he to do? How could he help his friend face the immensity of his loss. What could he do to ease Juan's pain, while at the same time admit to himself that dear Angelica would never again smile at him, or speak his name. Now he felt selfish. It was Juan that had lost his dear wife, and only one day after losing the baby son that she bore.

The village *wot* came to speak to Juan's father. When Juan sensed what the conversation was about, he arose showing anger. He argued with the chief and his father. He turned to Morgan suddenly. "They want Angelica and the baby to be buried here in the village burial ground. I will not permit it!". Pushing away from the two men, Juan reentered the hut. Morgan followed. Juan was wrapping Angelica in a blanket. He then did the same for the baby. Looking at Morgan with pleading in his eyes he said, *"Mi amigo,* will you help me carry Angelica and our son to the *Mision*? I want them buried there. I want Padre Payeras to pray over their bodies and their graves". *"Si, mi amado amigo",* Morgan softly replied.

Within the hour they were ready to depart the village. Juan bade a brief goodbye to his father, nodded his thanks to the mid-wife woman, and picking up Angelica's lifeless body, indicated to Morgan that he was ready. Morgan picked up the tiny baby and the two walked to the trail leading down to La Purisima.

After a while Morgan suggested to Juan that he should take a turn to carry Angelica, but Juan would not allow this. Nor would Juan, who was leading, slow his pace. After a while, as they walked, Juan began to speak, almost as much to himself as to Morgan. "It is the will of *Dios!* We must accept the will of *Dios!*. It is just as well that this poor infant was not born into the world, for surely he would have shown indication of his forced father's likeness and never would have been accepted by the people of my father's village." When Morgan grasped what Juan was saying he rather impolitely asked, "Are you sure that the baby would not resemble you?" "No", Juan replied, "he could not resemble me". Morgan pressed the matter. "Isn't there just as much a chance that you are the father, as well as the chance that Rivera is the father?" Juan showed irritation in his voice. "No, I said. That is not possible. Since Angelica and I have never had relations, it is not possible for me to be the father."

"You and Angelica have never had the relationship of a husband and wife?". Morgan seemed incredulous. Juan explained, "Because of what Angelica felt was her 'sin' of being raped, she would not permit herself to have relations with any man. I had to honor her wishes, because I loved her too much to attempt to persuade her otherwise."

Morgan was amazed, but even more so, he felt great pity for Juan. 'If it were me', he thought to himself, 'could I have controlled my emotions that well?' 'Probably not', he answered himself. Poor Juan. To be married to such a beautiful girl and yet not feel fulfilled in his love. What a predicament. What an emotional void!

It was late afternoon. They were nearing the Mission. As they emerged from the wooded section and entered the clearance between the trees and the

Mission, Morgan moved around Juan so as to enter the Mission area first. As soon as they were near enough he called out, "Cimkonah!. Someone call Cimkonah." A young neophyte lad saw the two and immediately ran towards Cimkonah's kitchen.

In just a few minutes, Cimkonah appeared. Upon seeing Juan carrying Angelica she ran to them. "Angelica, my poor child. What can I do to help you? What is the trouble that you are having?" As she came close enough to see Angelica's ashen face she burst out, "*Oh, Dios en cielo*, what is wrong?", She touched Angelica's face. *"Oh! Mia amado Dios, Angelica es muerto. Oh amado Dios!"*

Now Morgan came forward and unwrapped the baby's face. Cimkonah exclaimed again, *"Oh! carinoso Dios.* This *bebe* too!. *Oh! carinoso Dios!"* Cimkonah kept emoting with compassionate exclamations over both Angelica and the baby.

Payeras now appeared. The young lad had found him also and prompted him to come to the outskirts of the Mission. The Padre was now showing the same surprise and emotions as Cimkonah. *"Oh, mia Dios! mia Dios!".* The priest immediately made the Sign Of The Cross over both Angelica and her child. He began to pray. All the others, even Morgan, joined him in his memorial prayers. Then he said, "Quickly, take them to the Church. We will prepare to celebrate Mass immediately, and then the burial in the natives cemetery."

The sad procession walked solemnly to the Church. Within minutes Padre Castellanos joined them. The two priests garbed themselves for the celebration of Mass For The Dead. By now, the other neophytes and all of the Spanish craftsman, their families, and the constabulary *soldados* were beginning to fill the church. It seemed that within minutes, word of Angelica and her baby's death had spread throughout the *Mision La Purisima Concepcion* like a firestorm. Morgan remembered how crowded the church was during that now long ago Christmas morning Mass, and felt that every single person within the Mission must now be here.

After concluding the Mass and offering the necessary blessings over the two bodies, the two priests now led the procession to the cemetery of the natives. A shallow grave had already been dug. Angelica and her child were both lowered into it, the child on its mother's breast. Juan reverently placed a handful of dirt on them then moved back so that all of the others could do the same. Morgan was second, Cimkonah third, the two Padres next, followed by a long line of friends.

As evening fell, the burial was complete. The Padres had intoned the prayers to *Dios Todopoderoso*, and Angelica and the unnamed infant were no longer of this earth.

CHAPTER SEVEN
The Nineteenth Gem

Mision La Purisima Concepcion was a somber place for several months after the burial of Angelica and her tragically-born son. Their common grave was now adorned with the traditional Chumash colored pole, feathers and clay items made by her friends, and representing events in her short life. Many visited her grave daily, including of course Juan Bautista, who now remained at the Mission, and Morgan. Fathers Payeras and Castellanos also came often and prayed over the site. It seemed that no one would ever forget the lovely Native American girl and her ill-fortuned baby.

But the calendar was now showing late October and the priests were beginning to prepare for the coming Advent season. The days were now much shorter, and Mission harvests and other activities seemed to be in a lull. The abundant harvest had been finished, many cattle were slaughtered and the meat prepared for the long winter largesse, and many different kinds of vegetables were spiced and salted to keep them through the winter. All of the roof tiles that had been formed and baked were now installed and the stuccoing process had gone as far as the fall season would allow.

Even the blacksmithing needs had relented, so now often Padre Payeras, Morgan and Juan Bautista would walk to the site that Payeras had selected for *Mision Santa Ines*, about a six hour journey from *La Purisima*. Leaving immediately after Payeras' early morning Mass, they would journey to *Santa Ines'* location, discuss the probable arrangement of the buildings, the vineyard, the work shops, the *lavenderia*, and other required implements.

Payeras would make copious notes, then they would start their return journey, reaching *La Purisima* just about at sundown. Morgan did not especially like these long, all-day walks, but it was something to break what was again beginning to be a period of monotony for him. And now, more and more, he had been wondering if Ben Hopkins had gotten to the east coast and delivered Morgan's message to his family in Sturbridge.

After returning from one such journey to Santa Ines in early November, Morgan and Juan went to their quarters to clean up before taking a meal in Cimkonah's kitchen. As soon as they arrived in the kitchen, a young neophyte lad came to them, saying that Padre Payeras must see them at once. Upon entering Payeras' quarters, they found him in a highly elated mood. "Ah, come in *Sharlezz!, adelante* Juan! We have wonderful news to tell you. During the day a messenger arrived from *Santa Barbara* with a *comunicado,* ah, a letter, from the Superior General of the Franciscan Order for *Nuevo Espanola.* In this *comunicado* Superior Padre Ricardo Gomez has advised that two Padres, Francisco Javier de Uria and Juan Gutierrez, have been assigned to the new *Mision Santa Ines.* He further states that they are being transferred here from *Province de La Florida.* It seems that there, the great influx of English colonists, now called Americans, is negatively affecting the growth of our Missions among the natives of the area. Thus the two Padres are found to be available. They will begin the trek to California immediately. Following the path *El Camino Espanola*, how you would call, "The Spanish Trail", starting from *San Augustine*, they should reach us in only eight or nine months. Isn't that wonderful news! Oh *Gratias Dios!* Now let us all kneel and offer a prayer of gratitude to *Dios Todopoderoso* and *Jesuchristo* and to ask *al Espiritu Santo* to protect them on their journey, and to speed their arrival."

Looking at the document again Payeras rejoiced once more with an overly enthusiastic prediction. "Look, the *comunicado* is dated the fifteenth day of August, 1803, the feast of *Asuncion de Santa Virgen Maria.* Why! Padres de Uria and Gutierrez might be half of the way here by now! And *Santa Maria* will certainly protect them on this trek for the glory of *Dios Todopoderoso!*"

Payeras and Juan Bautista immediately knelt and made the Sign Of The Cross. Payeras then waited for Morgan to kneel. Feeling embarrassed and compelled to do so, Morgan knelt on the floor, while deliberately letting it be known that his knees were protesting the hardness of the floor.

Nevertheless, Payeras began the inevitable "Ave Maria", then continued with another fifteen minutes of prayers in both Latin and Spanish. Now realizing that Morgan had not joined in the prayers, Payeras changed to English and began "Our Father, which art in heaven…" He looked to Morgan, who was now picking up the words. They all concluded with a gusty "Amen", and as they all rose, Payeras gave both young men a great hug of joy.

By late November Payeras, Morgan and Juan had made two more jaunts to the *Santa Ines* site. On more than one such departure, Padre Castellanos had asked permission to join them. Morgan felt that the poor younger Padre felt left out of the excitement that Payeras was enjoying, but he explained to Castellanos that Payeras must approve of such a trek. By early December, however, both Padres started to give their full attention to matters of Advent and the coming *Navidad de Cristo*. Morgan, too, was changing his attention to the coming Christmas, because he remembered the enjoyment that he had last year at the many festivities.

He wanted to keep himself busy though, so he borrowed a few books from Padre Payeras library and began studying, as best he could, the subjects of water conduits, reservoirs and water supply. He tried to recall, then make sketches from memory, the water ducts that he had seen at some of the other Missions. Knowing that future water needs of *Santa Ines* would be crucial, he believed that it would not be practical to also draw water from the same stream and springs that *La Purisima* was using as its source. He decided to involve himself in this important development.

He went to seek approval from Padre Payeras to investigate additional water sources, before the festivities of *Navidad* would become more numerous. He asked permission for Juan and himself to leave the Mission compound for three or four days. Payeras agreed. He not only wanted to utilize Morgan's industriousness and ingenuity, but he also felt that it would be well for Juan to begin accepting Angelica's passing, by engaging his mind in other matters.

Thus, early the next morning, Juan and Morgan journeyed well into the valley between the coastal mountains and those to the east. They were following the stream that supplied the water to *La Purisima*, hoping to find another tributary that would flow toward the future *Santa Ines* site. After a day and a half of following the stream, instead of a tributary, they came to a large lake, the source of the water for the stream that they had been following. Morgan was even happier now, for he knew that the distance was not too far and that conduits could be installed that would bring water from this lake to *Santa Ines*, plenty of water. And he felt that he knew how to build and install the conduits, with laborious help from the neophytes, of course.

On the morning of the third day, Juan looked pensive. He told Morgan that he felt that he had been there before, but he could not remember when or why. They ate a breakfast of hardtack, then began their journey back to *La Purisima.* But instead of following the stream, Juan said he knew of a footpath that would lead more directly to La Purisima. Then Juan said, "I now remember that I was surely here, or how would I know of this footpath?" As they walked, Juan suddenly exclaimed, "Look, *Sharlezz,* I recognize that large rock formation! I know that I have been here before. Now I remember; my father and I had walked *to Mision Santa Barbara* one summer, when I was quite young. It was the just before he left me at *La Purisima.* And I recall that right over there, yes I'm sure, he showed me caves that have drawings on their walls. He told me that these drawings were made thousands of moons before, by our Chumash ancestors that lived in the area, long before the white man came."

Morgan was indeed intrigued by this story. He ordered Juan to take him to the cave entrance. After a few misdirected steps, Juan seemed to recall more readily where the entrances were. The first cave had a rather large opening and as they entered, the outdoor light illuminated a large portion of the first room of the cave. The walls were reddish stone and highly decorated with drawings of animals, constellations and other geometric patterns. Juan claimed that his father knew the meaning of many of the drawings. The colors too, had a meaning. Juan explained that the *shaman*, the high-priest of the tribe, would direct the painters and dictate their patterns. Morgan thought, 'someday I must find Juan's father and bring him back here. I'd love to know what these drawings mean, and how old they are'.

Morgan quickly sketched some of the drawings on the paper that he had been carrying to plot the river's course. After investigating several more smaller caves, they decided that they had better return to *La Purisima*, because if they did not return by nightfall tomorrow, Payeras would be worried and Morgan did not want to cause him any undue consternation.

Soon they arrived at another split in the trail. Juan concentrated for a few minutes then said to Morgan, "Here, *Sharlezz*, we must be careful to travel northward, so as to find the trail to *La Purisima.*" Morgan was now somewhat concerned that perhaps Juan had forgotten the correct trail to follow. After all, he has not been here in ten years or more. "Are you sure?", he asked of Juan. "Oh, yes. This is the proper trail to *La Purisima*. But someday, when we have the days of freedom that we would need, I will take you on *El Camino Refugio*, the trail to the great ocean waters. It is the trail followed by the *Mohave* tribesmen when they come to trade with our *tamol* people, what you call 'canoe people'. The *Mohave* bring many goods, but especially they bring a red stone material which is desired by our people for making the pigment for our decorations of dance, rock painting and *tamol* decorating." Morgan had heard of the Mahave people but was now amazed to learn that they travel so far across desert and mountains to barter their goods.

All the way back to the Mission, Morgan talked constantly to Juan about the caves and the paintings, the trails and the legends. He resolved to return there someday soon, hopefully with Juan and his father. Morgan was again excited about his California adventure.

Within a few days the traditional *posadas* activities started, so now everyday included excitement and enjoyment, making the days pass very quickly. Rosa Remirez' wonderful cooking, and the all-day aromas coming from both hers and Cimkonah's kitchen brought great anticipation of each meal. Not a person was dissatisfied with the taste, the companionship nor the festive feelings.

Morgan thoroughly enjoyed this *Navidad*, just as much as that of last year. Juan, however, while participating with the others, showed obvious sorrow that his beloved Angelica was not at his side. In addition to attending the morning Mass, he went often to the cemetery, and the church to pray alone. Morgan thought it best to let him have these moments of reverie, and to offer his prayers to *Dios Todopoderoso* for Angelica's salvation. In his own heart, Morgan prayed for Angelica too.

With the arrival of the spring of 1804, Payeras presented to Catellanos, Morgan and Juan, a long list of items that he felt must be accomplished to enrich the Mission and the life of the Chumash people. The number of Native Americans now wanting to move into the Mission was creating a problem of sustenance for all. Additional buildings would be needed as well as physical adornments for existing buildings, enlargement of the gardens of herbs and vegetables, additional expanded cattle grazing areas and an enlarged *fuente* and *lavenderia*. The newly arrived Chumash people began to build their own thatched-roof circular huts just beyond the Mission walls and it appeared that a full-fledged *pueblo* was being created.

This did not surprise Payeras, for after having visited the many other Missions last spring, he had recognized the pattern of the Native American's transition toward Mission life and he was trying to prepare for the expected migration. He also recognized the deficiencies of his own establishment and intended to re-create *La Purisima* into as fine a compound as the others that he had visited.

He announced that henceforth one-sixth of the Mission's neophytes would be allowed a two months furlough on a rotating basis. They could return to their native villages to visit relatives and friends, as well as to help retain their cultural connections. This would also create space for the incoming people. But, in actuality, not more than one-fourth in total chose to partake of this new policy. It appeared that most were now satisfied to live the white man's way of life.

The building improvements and expansions went forward, much of this under Morgan's supervision, with Juan's assistance. In fact, these two were becoming a well coordinated team. Again, Padre Castellanos expressed a desire to become more involved in the material side of the Mission's operation, but Payeras always counseled him with the necessity of concentrating on the neophyte's religious teachings. This function too, was expanding, and more and more Native Americans were being baptized into the Catholic Church.

With all this activity, the months were passing quickly. How quickly, Morgan had not even recognized. He was now almost 21 years of age and because of all the physical activity, he was in excellent condition. Juan too, was maturing and becoming a robust worker. Many times, as the two would pass through the courtyard, if they encountered young Castellanos, he would comment on their physiques and their manliness. Having only a slight physique, and being quite a bit shorter, he seemed envious. He also seemed sad and unfulfilled. Morgan could not help but wonder why Castellanos did not seem to be as inspired as Payeras in his work, or in his religion.

In late July Payeras received another *comunicado*. It was to advise that the two priests from *La Florida* had arrived at *Mision San Diego*, and after a few days of rest would be starting their trek to *Santa Barbara*, then on to *La Purisima*. With great excitement, Payeras predicted their arrival here by late

August, only a little more than a year since he was advised of their assignment to *Santa Ines.*

In a later communication from Padre Fermin Lasuen, *Presidente* of the Missions, Lasuen advised that he would not attend the future dedication of *Santa Ines* because of illness. He announced that Padre Estavan Tapis, acting as *Interino Presidente*, would dedicate the ground where the new Mission would be established.

While the news was exciting to Payeras, he was both disturbed to learn of Lasuen's illness, and very disappointed that Lasuen had not designated him to become acting *Presidente*. But knowing of Padre Tapis' fine work among the Chumash and his great religious devotion, Payeras acceded to the will of *Todopodeoso Dios,* and prayed for Tapis' success.

In early September 1804, a large band of travelers was seen on the *Camino Real*, southeast of *Mision La Purisima Concepcion*. Payeras quickly alerted all of the Mission's peoples, his associate Castellanos, Morgan, Juan, the *Soldados*, the Spanish craftsmen and their families, and the many, many neophyts, to be prepared to greet the distinguished visitors. All-in-all, almost one thousand people were on hand to extend a hardy welcome to the approaching Padres. *Capitan* Marco Hernadez, along with several of his *centinela*, and the several dozens of Native Americans were accompanying Padre Tapis and the two new priests. In addition to their travel pouches, the natives all carried a musical instrument of some kind. There were flutes, horns and drum like devises. Hernandez was pompously leading the line on his white horse, followed by the five *soldados*. One would believe that he was leading an army.

As they neared the *Mision La Purisima,* Payeras walked outward to meet them. Nodding to Hernandez, he quickly passed by him and greeted the Padres with great shouts of *saluder!, bien venido!* The three approaching Padres seemed well pleased with their reception, and returned the welcome salutes with shouts of their own. The greetings and joyful shouts between all parties lasted for many minutes, then all proceeded to crowd into the Mission compound, where a great celebration meal had been prepared by Cimkonah, the Spanish ladies and with the joyous help of many of the neophyte ladies and girls. Every niche of the compound was occupied by someone. The Padres first went to the church to pray, then went to Payeras' dining area and Morgan and Juan joined the Spanish families for the celebration *cena.*

The next day the two morning Masses were overflowing with attendees. Both were concelebrated by multiple priests. Each priest also presented his own sermon so that the entire morning was a continuous religious experience.

After lunch the five Padres discussed the new Mision *Santa Ines,* while Morgan and Juan were allowed to eavesdrop. Because of the rapidity of the Spanish language of the five priests Morgan did not discern much, but he decided that he would have his opportunity at a later time to present his thoughts on the Mission, especially the provisions for water supplies. Payeras displayed his many sketches, while the three visiting Padres looked at each other in bewilderment. Who was to be in charge of *Mision Santa Ines,* they wondered.

At the conclusion of this lively meeting, it was decided by Padre Tapis that on Sunday, three days hence, the dedication of the new *Mision Santa Ines* would take place. He allowed three days so that a proper altar could be erected to celebrate the Mass of dedication.

The next morning a column of Spanish craftsmen, neophytes, Padres, as well as Juan and Morgan all departed for the site of *Mision Santa Ines.* Hernandez too, with his men, proceeded to the site. The craftsmen and the neophytes carried the necessary tools and pieces of wood and fabric to assemble a suitable altar. Upon arrival at the site, Padre Tapis declared the location of the altar, facing toward the east. "As the sun rises on Sunday morning over yon mountains, we will dedicate this land to the glory of *Todoperosa Dios!*"

And so it was that on September 17, 1804, Padre Estevan Tapis, and the four other Padres, celebrated the Mass of dedication, for *Mision Santa Ines*, the nineteenth Mission of the chain which, 35 years earlier and 400 kilometers to the south, was begun by Junipero Serra, for the glory of God. The several Chumash musicians that had traveled from *Santa Barbara* and the choir of neophytes from *La Purisima*, which Castellanos had aptly trained, added great solemnity and reverence to the ceremony. Payeras knew in his heart that Padre Serra was pleased, as was Almighty God.

Each of the five priests gave brief sermons, all thanking God for the great honor of being involved with the establishment of one more gem in the long trail of gems. Payeras was especially laudatory, and described how he was honored by *Padre Presidente* Lasuen in being allowed to choose the name for the mission. He told of his mother's great devotion to Santa Ines, a maiden of the fourth century, who was martyred because she would not give up her virginity. Everyone was touched by his remarks and many of the neophytes were astonished at this incredulous story.

Each of the Padres spoke in glowing terms about their grand expectations for the future of *Mision Santa Ines,* but, had they been able to foretell that future, they would know that this Mission would never attain the prominence of many of the others in the chain.

Following the religious part of the dedication, *Capitan* Hernadez also spoke. He stated that he was honored to represent the Vice Governor of *Alta Califonia,* Juan Ortega, and he reminded all that while *Mision Santa Ines* was technically a part of the *Catolico Iglesia*, this land, and all in *Alta California* was the property of *Carlos IV, Rey de Espanola.* The importance of this Mission, like all the others, was to further establish the claim of the land for the Crown, he concluded.

During the Mass, although his soldiers had participated, Hernandez himself had sat in the shade of a tree, while his horse grazed nearby. After his comments, he returned to his shady spot.

Morgan decided to take advantage of this time to speak to Hernandez. He asked Juan to join him but Juan did not want to go near the man that he thought of as a *villano*. As Morgan approached, Hernandez rose, showing a bit of surprise that Morgan would want to speak with him. Morgan started, "*Capitan* Hernandez, I am *Senor* Charles Morgan, Perhaps you remember me." By now, Morgan's Spanish language skill was much improved.

"Oh, yes indeed, I do remember you", Hernadez replied. "And how are your priestly studies proceeding?", he taunted Morgan. But Morgan was prepared with a truthful answer. "Oh, I am not studying for the priesthood, only Payeras had aspirations for that. But I am earning my food and shelter by assisting Padre Payeras in maintaining *Mision La Purisima*, and I will be very much involved in the building of *Mision Santa Ines.*"

Hernandez seemed pleased that Morgan gave him an honest reply. "Well then, my government thanks you for the effort that you have exerted in helping to establish our claim to *Alta California*." Morgan nodded his acknowledgment, then promptly brought up the matter that he had wanted to know about, "Tell me if you can *Capitan,* what was the fate of *Cabo* Rivera? Was he court-martialed?"

Hernadez looked towards Juan who had drifted a little closer. He looked into Morgan's eyes and replied, "Since no one appeared to testify against him, *Cabo* Rivera was not court-martialed. He has, however, been re-assigned to duty in *Nuevo Espanola*, in *Baja California*, I believe."

Morgan called Juan to come closer. He then informed Hernandez, "The Chumash maiden that Rivera raped had his child, and both are now dead. This young brave was the husband of Angelica, the maiden. He married her so that her motherhood would be respectable, and of course, because he loved her very much." Juan stared at Hernandez with the look of disdain that he would have had for Rivera.

Hernandez seemed genuinely affected by Morgan's statements. He turned to Juan and offered his sincere condolences. "I am so very sorry for your lose young man. I did not know of this distressing impact, as a result of Rivera's reprehensible behavior. From the description of the assault as told me by Payeras, I did believe that he was guilty. I wish now that his punishment had been more severe, but as I said, without testimony against him…" Juan and Morgan both nodded that they accepted Hernandez' apology, and turned to leave.

As they did so, Hernandez caused them to stop and turn back. He stated, "*Senors*, Padre Payeras will soon receive an invitation to join Vice Governor Ortega and his wife Maria Consuela, at a *fiesta* at the *Presidio* in honor of the eighteenth birthday of their daughter Anna Maria Margarito. When Payeras receives this invitation, tell him that you are both also invited, as my guests."

Morgan and Juan were both stunned. Not so much at the invitation, but more by the fact that Hernandez had revealed himself as a person, not just a military puppet. Again they nodded satisfaction with the invitation and departed Hernadez' company.

After a few more days, Padre Tapis returned to his own Mission, *San Juan Bautista*, a days journey north of *San Carlos Boromeo de Carmelo*. The two Padres that were to staff the new Mission began immediately to delineate the design and construction of the new compound. Because Payeras had described how enthusiastically the Chumash natives in this area would welcome the new Mission, they decided that it should be even larger than Payeras had proposed.

Knowing that Padres de Uria and Gutierrez were excited to get started, Payeras reluctantly returned to *La Purisima*, but first expressing to the two that he was available at any time to consult with them. He hoped that they would not shut him out of this new project, but also recognized that they had been assigned to the development, not him. He suggested that Morgan and Juan would be of great assistance in communicating with the Chumash, so that they should remain at *Santa Ines.* The two new Padres agreed.

Morgan and Juan began immediately to direct the Chumash men in making boxes in which adobe bricks could be molded, and to construct a large oven in which to bake them. Others were assigned to obtain tall trees from the forest, which could be hewn into roof beams. Some had to be drawn from as far as thirty kilometers away. The Chumash women, of their own volition, began to furrow a large garden area for the future growth of vegetables, fruits and herbs.

Morgan described to the two Padres how he envisioned supplying water to the Mission. They immediately gave him permission to proceed. Morgan then hand picked a large group of native men, a team which he was to use to create conduits from hewn-out logs. Two halves of these logs were joined together and sealed with tar pitch and tied with rawhide laces to form a hollow pipe. The pipe sections were joined end to end and tarred to prevent leakage. Within a few weeks the aqueduct reached nearly half way to the lake, which was nearly ten kilometers away.

Two months had passed. The adobe bricks were being laid up to create walls and the compound was beginning to take shape. Morgan's viaduct was now almost complete and any day now water from the lake would be at hand for use by all. In the meantime, Morgan had had another group of Chumash men digging a large reservoir area a few hundred feet from what was to be the front entrance of the Mission. Morgan, and the Padres, were surprised and very pleased at the exertions of the Chumash people, many hundreds of whom had come down from the eastern foothills. They seemed genuinely pleased that they were to have their own Mission.

Late in October Payeras did receive the invitation of which Harnandez had spoken. Payeras, sometimes accompanied by Castellanos, would occasionally visit the new Mission site. Payeras brought the news of the *fiesta* to Morgan and Juan and they all set a departure date for their trek to *Presidio Santa Barbara*. Of course, they would also visit the *Mision Santa Barbara*, which was up the hillside a kilometer or so.

Several days before Anna Maria's party was to take place on November 16th, Payeras, Morgan, Juan, several Spanish craftsmen and their families, as well as several Chumash men and women all departed for Santa Barbara. Anna Maria Margarito was to have a grand presentation. Representatives from other Missions, both north and south of *La Purisima*, would also be attending. Each would bring an impressive gift and each would provide some kind of entertainment. Castellanos' choir was to sing, but Padre Manuel himself was not allowed to leave *La Purisima*, as someone had to remain in charge. Once more, a very great disappointment for the boy-priest.

For the gift to Anna Maria, the carpenter and a few of the Chumash men at *La Purisima* had constructed a wooden chest, which was highly decorated with delicate gold and silver filigree. On the top of the cover, one of the Chumash men had drawn a likeness of the Virgin Mary. Payeras had told the workers that Anna Maria would likely choose this chest as her favorite piece.

The *La Purisima* representation arrived the day before the party was to be held. All laved themselves and joined Payeras at a pre-appointed time. He led them in prayer on behalf of Anna Maria and her parents, the Vice Governor and his *Senora*.

The following day, the festivities began with a Mass, quickly followed by a sumptuous breakfast. Everyone was expectant of a wonderful day, including Morgan. He had been told of the beauty of *Senorita* Ortega so was naturally anxious to have the opportunity to see her. As he and Juan strolled through the *Mision Santa Barbara*, observing both its beauty and its construction features, they were hailed by a Spanish craftsman. He hurriedly came to them. He introduced himself, "*Buenas Dias Senor* Morgan. *Buenas Dias Senor* Juan Bautista. I am Roberto Mendez, the saddle maker here at the *Presidio*. It was my wife who sent clothing to you *Senor*, at the request of Padre Payeras." Morgan extended his hand, "Oh, thank you so much Roberto. And *mucho gracias* to your *Senora*, as well. The clothing was of the appropriate size, and I most certainly did need them."

Each man looked at the other, now realizing that they indeed were of about the same stature, for Mendez was much taller than the average Spanish man of that day. Juan just smiled at the situation, but stated that it would be nice if Morgan could meet *Senora* Mendez. "Oh, indeed, I would like that very much", Morgan added. "Yes, that will be arranged, this evening at the *fiesta*", Roberto replied.

Soon after they departed Roberto's company, they came upon *Capitan* Hernandez. He greeted them warmly also, and again urged them to attend the evening *fiesta.* Morgan and Juan were now feeling much more comfortable in their new surroundings.

In the early evening all of the *La Purisima* representatives again met with Payeras and participated in a lighter than usual *cena*, for they knew that at the later *fiesta* there would be much to eat. Payeras again led all in a prayer for the special guest and her parents, then all left for the *fiesta* locale, a large assembly hall at the *Presidio,* usually used for the assembly and inspection of the *soldados,* but now turned into a grand ballroom.

The atmosphere was joyous. The Vice Governor and his *Senora* were most gracious to all. When Padre Payeras introduced Morgan and Juan, both of Anna Maria's parents expressed genuine pleasure at meeting them. They complimented Morgan, and Juan. "Padre Payeras has related to us how helpful you have been to him, and how skilled you are at so many crafts", the Vice Governor commented to Morgan, with a large smile on his face. He looked to Juan and also complimented him on being such a great assistant to Morgan. The Vice

Governor continued, "When I spoke earlier to the new Padre de Uria, he also told me of your earnest attitude and your assistance to him and Padre Gutierrez. Both men are pleased that you are so cooperative." Morgan blushed, Payeras beamed, and Juan smiled broadly. Morgan stammered, "Pleased to make your acquaintance sir, and *Senora*."

The group moved away from the Vice Governor. Payeras quickly stated, "My, *Sharlezz*, you have impressed the Vice Governor with your talents. And everything that I told him was truthful. I am most thankful that the Good Lord has sent you to help me. Juan also." Morgan was very happy with himself, and surprised that he was so graciously accepted by the Vice Governor and the *Senora.*

Following a fanfare by several trumpeters, Vice Governor Ortega introduced his daughter Anna Maria Margarito, and all expressed their best wishes for her birthday. Following this, various presentations of gifts and musical offerings were made by groups from the several *Misions.* Anna Maria did indeed seem impressed by the wooden chest that was given her by the *La Purisima* representatives. Then a large group of uniformed musicians began to play. The Vice Governor and his wife were the first to dance, followed by many, many couples of *sodados* and craftsmen and their wives. The evening had started grand and it seemed to Morgan that it would go on for a long time. At least he hoped so.

Shortly thereafter, Roberto Mendez approached Morgan and Juan and introduced his *Senora, Margarito*. Morgan expressed his gratitude for the clothing, then added, "Perhaps someday Roberto and you, with your children too, would consider moving to our new *Mision Santa Ines* when it is finished. The countryside is beautiful and I believe that many new opportunities will be created." As soon as he had finished, he realized that he no authority to make such an offer, but he hoped that Padre de Uria would also encourage such a fine couple to become part of the new Mission's staff. Roberto and Margarito looked at each other and smiled their happiness at being invited to *Mision Santa Ines,* the new Mission that was expected to become a very important installation.

Soon after, Morgan noticed *Capitan* Hernandez and Anna Maria dancing. He thought 'What a lucky fellow he is. They look like a fine couple', but then added another thought, 'He is too old to be romantically involved with her'. Still they seemed to enjoy their dance and their lively conversation. As Morgan and Juan later stood observing the activities, Hernandez came to them and said, "*Senor* Morgan, *Senorita* Anna Maria Margarito would be most pleased to make your acquaintance." Morgan was genuinely surprised. "And I would be pleased to make her acquaintance, also." he replied. "It seems that you have an admirer, Sharlezz", Juan teased Morgan.

Hernandez gave a slight signal to Anna Maria, so that she would not accept the next dance invitation. The *Capitan* led Morgan and Juan to where Anna Maria was standing. "*Senorita* Anna Maria Magarito, I would like to present to you *Senor Sharlezz* Morgan, and his companion Juan Bautista," Hernadez bowed. Morgan and Juan both bowed to the young lady. Anna Maria extended her hand to Morgan. He seemed not to know what to do. Anna Maria smiled and extended her hand slightly further as she said, "Come *Senor* Morgan, invite me to dance."

Morgan was very red and very confused. He had never been in such a perplexing situation before. In fact, he had never touched a maiden such as Anna Maria, nor had he ever danced before. He offered his apologies, "I am very sorry *Senorita*, but I do not know how to dance." "Well come then", she insisted, "I will explain how to step as we try to do it together." Morgan eagerly, if not confidently, stepped onto the dance floor and placed his arm around the waist of this most beautiful young woman.

Though he stepped clumsily, Anna Maria was most gracious and explained how to step, even if he was not able to do so to the tempo of the music. As they finished, she was again most gracious to Morgan, "Well, we have done quite well together, did we not." For Morgan's part, he was glad the dance was done, but he wished that he could continue to hold the girl. Anna Maria withdrew with the comment, "It was a pleasure to meet you *Senor* Morgan. I hope that we will have another opportunity to meet again, even if not dancing." Morgan bowed to her, flushed again, and turned back to his friend Juan, who was smiling very broadly. Then he noticed that Padre Payeras was also smiling, and he thought that even Vice Governor Ortega and the *Senora* had a slight smile on their faces. He believed that it was because they could easily see that their daughter was enjoying her birthday *fiesta* very much.

At the end of the evening, as they made their departing wishes to Anna Maria, Morgan suggested to her, "Perhaps you would like to ride to the new *Mision*

Santa Ines someday soon, to see how it is progressing. The Padres would be most happy that you came to see the state of construction." Anna Maria smiled and replied, "And you *Sharlezz*, would you be happy if I came there?" Morgan was flabbergasted. He stammered, "Of course. It would be wonderful to see you again *Senorita*, ah, a great honor indeed."

The *La Purisima* group left early the next morning, immediately after Mass and *desayuno*. As they all walked along *El Camino Real* the subject of Anna Maria and Morgan's dance was the primary topic of conversation all the day long. Morgan himself was still in a state of shock to think that the daughter of the Vice Governor had even deigned to speak to him, much less dance with him. What he had no way of knowing was that the beautiful young girl was enthralled by the handsome *yanqui* that stood a head taller than most of the Spanish men, and was already the subject of much esteem by the Padres and the officials, because of his many accomplishments.

CHAPTER EIGHT
A welcome letter; a surprising note

Through the physical efforts of the many neophytes, Morgan and Juan, and even the Padres, the buildings of the *Santa Ines* compound were taking shape. The two Padres were especially happy to see the results of their design being fulfilled. Because the winter months were approaching, the new Mission had not had a chance to seed the needed crops into the ground, nor to start the raising of cattle. Padre Payeras' *Mision La Purisima* was required to supply the food that was necessary for the large numbers of Native Americans that had "joined" the *Mision Santa Ines*. Payeras was happy to assist the start of the new Mission in this way.

For Morgan's part, he felt that keeping busy was the best solution to his constant remembering of meeting the beautiful Anna Maria. In the back of his mind however, he was hopeful of finding a reason to have to visit Santa Barbara again. In fact, he had hoped to be there at the time of *navidad,* but this was not to be. Because *Santa Ines* had not advanced far enough, all of the neophytes and staff from there were invited to *La Purisima*. Morgan celebrated his third Christmas at *La Purisima*, as well as did Juan.

In mid-January though, Padre de Uria, who seemed to be the more aggressive of the two, sent Morgan and Juan to *Mision Santa Barbara*, with a letter asking Padre Narciso Duran if he could spare several craftsmen, especially carpenters and masons, to assist at *Mision Santa Ines*. Padre Duran informed

Morgan that he would require a few days to consider the request, and to determine which men would be willing to move to *Santa Ines*, while their families temporarily remained at *Santa Barbara*. Morgan was not unhappy with Padre Duran's delay. He hoped that by some chance he would again meet Anna Maria.

For her part, when Anna Maria learned that Morgan was at the Mission, she and her *duenna* were seen visiting the church more often than usual. Although Morgan was watching for her, it was not until late on the second day that they met. Before that, Morgan had been visited by Captain Hernandez.

Upon learning that Morgan was at the Mission, Hernandez rode from the *Presidio* to find him. "*Senor* Morgan", Hernandez called from across the plaza. "I must see you." Morgan and Juan turned from their studies of the Mission building. "Oh, *Buenas Dias*, *Capitan*", Morgan replied. "It is good to see you again. I hope that you have been well." The Captain nodded. "I am glad that you came to *Santa Barbara*. I was soon to send a messenger to you at *Santa Ines* with this letter that arrived for you on the trading vessel that came into port yesterday. The ship's Captain said that he was asked to deliver the letter here by a gentleman that sought him out in Boston."

Morgan was gleeful with excitement. Would this letter be from his brother George? As he opened the seal, he exclaimed to Juan and Hernandez. "Yes, it is from George. Oh, how wonderful that we have been able to reach each other from almost across the world. Please excuse me while I sit and read the news from home." Both gentleman nodded their approval to Morgan. Juan sat nearby while Hernandez gave a small wave of his hand and rode off without Morgan even realizing it.

Morgan began to read;

November 21, 1803.

My dear brother Charles;

It was so wonderful to learn that you are alive and well. We had wondered what might have been your fate. We hope that upon receiving this letter, that your circumstances are still well. Do the catholic priests that you call Padres treat you well? We so often hear of their strange beliefs, that we have great concern for you.

Your friend Ben Hopkins came walking into the village a few mornings ago. We were supremely surprised and pleased that he found us. He had walked from Worcester, after having received a ride on a farmer's wagon, who had taken his harvest to Boston to sell at the market. The drawing that Ben made of you was very comforting, to see you looking well, and so much more manly than we remembered. Ben left town the next day to return to Boston. We thanked him for his solicitous concern. He would accept no payment for this task, however.

My family is well. Since your departure now almost five years ago, I have married Harriet Beacham, and we have a darling daughter, Abigail. Do you recall Harriet? She is still as pretty as she ever was. 'Yes', Morgan thought, 'she was pretty, and a very serious girl. George has done well to take her for his wife.' The letter continued, **'Our dear sister Mary is well. She is still working at Mrs.**

Pennington's, who has expanded her boarding house into a full public house. Mary is so busy that she has found no time to find a suitor. I do hope that she will not become an old maid.

Unfortunately Charles, Papa and stepmother Anna have both passed away. Father in October of 1801 and Anna the following spring. They both had expressed sorrow that you had left home and both had hoped that you would return. Father died of poisoning of his blood due to a pitch-fork piercing his arm quite deeply. It was a most tragic accident, as another farm-hand threw the fork down from the top of the haystack, without realizing that Papa was there. I think that stepmama Anna died of a broken heart. Her son Harold, who is now in the third school grade is living with Harriet and I.'

Morgan now felt great pain in his heart that he had caused so much trouble to Papa and Stepmama Anna, and that he would never again see their face. Small tears rolled down his cheeks. He wiped them with his neckerchief. He continued to read,

'By the way, your friend Becky Reynolds is being courted by Nathaniel Aldrich. It is believed by everyone in Sturbridge that they will marry very soon. Nathaniel has finished Harvard and is now employed in his father's bank. He has stated his intention to seek the office of Selectman. He will most likely be successful in this attempt. I believe that he will use this office as a means to becoming elected to our General Court in Boston. He will do well.

Although I was still not eligible to vote, you must have heard that in the last election, our own John Adams was defeated by that Virginian Thomas Jefferson. It was a strange election, and in the end, Mr. Jefferson was actually elected by our House Of Representatives. While some believe that he will accomplish much for our new nation, there are others who are fearful of some of his ideas. In fact, it is rumored that Aaron Burr is trying to forge an alliance of New York and New England to separate from the new Union. I think that that would be a danger to us in New England and to our new country. Had I been eligible to vote, I would have voted for our John Adams, but I believe that Jefferson will also be a good leader for our 'infant' nation. Like many others, I do not trust Mr. Burr. And, by the way, Charles, by the time of the next election in November, I hope to have purchased a few acres of farm land, and if I can also afford to purchase a few cows, I will indeed be eligible to vote. Poor Papa, though he dreamed of having this privilege, he was never able to save enough money to buy the acreage and animals that he wanted and that would enabled him to vote.

While Mr. Adams was President he and Mrs. Adams moved into the new President's Residence in Washington, D.C. It is not quite finished, but we are told that it is a grandiose structure. One would believe that we have a monarch instead of a President.

While we do not have actual warfare with Great Britain, we still continue to have difficulties in dealing with them. They have threatened to blockade our ports, and Mr. Jefferson is very near deciding to close our ports to shipments to Europe. I believe that that will cause much unemployment among our shipping and mercantile industries. Mr. Jefferson is also trying to eliminate the payments that we are forced to make to those Tripoli pirates. When you were sailing with pirate Hippolyte Bouchard, did you encounter any American ships? I hope not.

You say that those Padre people are Spanish. Did you know that Mr. Jefferson has just purchased the former Spanish territory that the French had renamed Louisiana in honor of their king. The Spanish had only recently sold it to France, and they in turn sold it to us. My, how strange is this thing called politics. In any event, it will open vast new lands to our United States. I fear that many more of our Sturbridge farmers will migrate to those wild lands to homestead. The land is said to be very inexpensive.

How is the land in your California? Not very conducive to farming or growing of crops I would imagine. From what little we have learned of this Spanish territory, it is not very hospitable to humans. I certainly hope that you can find the necessary sustenance for your body. But please, Charles, try to extricate yourself from those Padre people and return to Sturbridge, where life is civil.

There is now a smell of snow in the air. I shall be taking the Springfield coach line to Boston,

**hopeful to find a ship that will be heading to Santa
Barbara or Monterey to post this letter, as you
directed.**

**With much love and with concern for your
safety, I am affectionately your brother, George.**

Morgan looked up from the missal and seemed
surprised that Hernandez was gone. He asked Juan
where he had gone to and Juan pointed down the hill to
the *Presidio*. "Oh" Morgan said, "of course". Then,
"Juan, I must find paper, a quill and some ink. I need
to write a return letter to my brother George. And I
need to do it *pronto* so I can give it to the ship's
Captain, to relay it to my brother." Juan nodded
agreement and rose to go with Morgan into the
Mission to seek a priest with the implements that
Morgan needed.

Upon obtaining them, Morgan spent about two
hours composing a letter of several pages. He advised
his brother that even though he had intended to return
to Sturbridge by finding a ship on which to become a
crewman, he has now decided to remain in California
for a few more years. He told George of his meeting
with Anna Maria, of how enthralled he was with her.
He also tried to allay George's fear of the Spanish, the
Padres and the Catholic practices. Then he described
the California lands, and said that someday he hoped to
be able to own some acreage there. If all of this should
become a reality, he might consider remaining in
California for good. He concluded by noting that he
would again write soon to advise George of his hoped
for success.

Morgan sealed the letter and quickly left the Mission to walk down to the port. Juan was accompanying him. They had only walked half-way across the plaza when they saw Anna Maria and her *duenna* exiting the church. Both ladies mounted their awaiting horses. Morgan and Juan paused to see their direction. Anna Maria and her companion rode directly to them. "Ah, *buenas tardas, Senorita* Ortega", Morgan spoke first. Anna Maria nodded and replied, "*Buenas tardas* to you, *Senor* Morgan. And to you *Senor* Juan. May I present to you my *duenna*, Carmelita Suarez, *mia tia*." Anna Maria's aunt hung back a little so that she would not appear to be too imposing, but she remained in hearing distance. She did not appear as old as one imagined an aunt to be, though Morgan had none. He wondered how he could speak his thoughts to Anna Maria without the chaperon becoming nettled.

"*Senorita*, I have a letter that I must deliver to the *Capitan* of a ship that is in harbor. I want to tell my brother George that I intend to remain in California, where I hope that my future be a fortunate one." Morgan hoped that this assurance to Anna Maria would be welcome news.

"Oh", Anna Maria lied, "I have heard that that ship may be leaving for Boston at any moment". She turned to her companion and ordered, "Carmelita, please let *Senor* Morgan borrow your horse for a short time. He has an urgent matter to which he must attend". Morgan was happy for the use of the horse, but he was elated when Anna Maria rode off side by side with him. He looked back to see the stunned faces of Carmelita and Juan. When they were out of earshot of the two he said, "You were quite skillful at evading your *tia*. Will you be in trouble with your parents when Carmelita reports that you parted her company, especially with a male *yanqui?*" "Oh, I think not", Anna Maria replied. "Carmelita is a friend as well as my *tia y duenna*. She understands my impudent nature. And my parents are understanding as well, so long as I do not place myself in an embarrassing or controversial position."

"Well, *Senorita*, I do not intend to place you in a position necessitating parental discipline, and I certainly do appreciate the use of this horse", Morgan replied. "Oh please, call me Anna Maria", she asked. Morgan was extremely happy with the way the situation was developing. He replied, "Yes, I will most happy to do so, if you call me Charles." Anna Maria giggled, "I will try to say it, *Sharlezz*, but we Spanish cannot pronounce it as in the English language."

They had reached the port area. Morgan looked about for the Yankee ship. He knew it by its name *"Emily Randolph"*. It seemed that Captains often named their ships for their loved one. He found it among two other ships flying the flags of Spain. 'My' he thought, 'this port is getting busier'.

He asked for Anna Maria's forgiveness as he parted from her. He went aboard the *"Emily Randolph"* and spent a few minutes with the Captain, giving him the letter to George. On returning to the pier he said to Anna Maria, "It will be best if we return to the Mission and return this horse to Carmelita". Looking disappointed Anna Maria said, "*Sharlezz,* I had hoped that we could spend a little more time together. Are you in such a great hurry to return to *Mision Santa*

Ines?" Morgan wanted very much to say 'I'll stay', but instead he replied, "As much as I would like to linger with you Anna Maria, we must not cause any difficulty for you or Carmelita. Hopefully we will have an opportunity to converse more at another time, a more appropriate time. I don't want to have your parents think badly of me, or they will refuse to allow us to meet again, and I want to do so very soon."

They rode back up the hill to the Mission and met Carmelita and Juan, who were sitting under a large oak tree. They were engaged in conversation as Morgan and Anna Maria rode up to them. Carmelita spoke first, "So, Anna Maria, you have returned. It is well for you that the time was not prolonged." She looked at Morgan to see if he understood the meaning. He did, and he blushed. Anna Maria laughed, "Do not fear *Tia* Carmelita, my purity is still in tact, and will remain so until my wedding day" Morgan reddened even more. Carmelita broke the embarrassment by stating, "Oh, Anna Maria, I don't know what we are to do with you. You are so impudent! When will you learn that a lady does not speak of such things among gentlemen." Now she laughed as she looked at Juan, who was also now very red.

As the ladies prepared to ride off Anna Maria said, *"Sharlezz,* I have not forgotten your invitation to visit the new *Mision Santz Ines.* I will do that soon". Then she teased Carmelita with, "And when I do I will not have anyone with me that will nag me about my conduct." They rode off toward the Vice Governor's *hacienda.*

Morgan and Juan looked at each other with amazement. Neither one had ever heard a lady speaking so candidly about matters of their personal conduct. Juan said to Morgan, "*Sharlezz*, I believe that that lady would like you to be her lover." Suddenly that realization came to Morgan. "My God, she is so frank in her statements. And I find that I like it!"

The next day Padre Duran told Morgan and Juan that he had spoken to two craftsmen who would be willing to move to *Santa Ines* for a few months. If they liked it there, they might move their families there and stay. Duran handed Morgan a letter, "Please deliver this to Padre de Uria. It explains all. The men will trek to *Santa Ines* in a few days."

Soon after, Morgan and Juan left *Santa Barbara* and walked back to *Santa Ines*. Arriving the morning of the second day, they were surprised to be met by Padre Manuel Castellanos. "*Buenas Dias Sharlezz. Buenas dias* Juan*", Castellanos was smiling to them. "Padre Payeras has acceded to my request to be transferred here. Padre Gutierrez has taken my place at *La Purisima Mision*. I am overjoyed that I can now be of a greater involvement in matters of the *Mision's* entire operation and to be closer to you"

"Well, that's great", Morgan replied, wondering to himself if it was to be great or not. The three went into the room of Padre de Uria. Morgan handed him the letter from Duran. He read it with a pleasurable smile. "Ah, now we can accelerate the construction of the buildings. Before next winter, we will have shelter for many more of the neophytes and quarters for more craftsmen and their families. Oh *gratias Dios*". As the three turned to leave, de Uria said, "Wait, I have another matter to discuss with you."

All three looked surprised and waited for de Uria to elaborate.

De Uria explained, "Padre Payeras and I have been discussing the matter of the transfers of Padres Castellanos and Gutierrez. We fear that we may have over stepped our authority. We both feel it advisable for Padre Castellanos to travel to *Mision San Carlos Borromeo*, to state his own reasons for wanting this transfer, and to obtain *Padre Presidente* Lasuen's permission." Castellanos tried to object, "Why is everything that I want to do is suspect? Why must I travel for five days to plead my case to Padre Lasuen? Can no one accept my eager wishes to perform more fulfilling tasks for *Dios Todopoderoso*?" Morgan tried to calm Castellanos, "Oh Padre Manuel, you will find your visit to *Mision Carlos Borromeo* to be most rewarding. Its magnificence is inspiring." De Uria then added, "Though I have not had the opportunity to visit *San Carlos Borromeo* myself, I understand that it is one of the most beautiful churches in *Alta California. Sharlezz,* since you have been there and know *El Camino Real,* Padre Payeras and I feel it advisable that you accompany Padre Castellanos to *Carmel.* I will need Juan to remain here, however, to help me understand the Chumash neophytes language."

Morgan had not expected this turn of events, but he had to admit to himself that Castellanos would probably benefit from his audience with Padre Lasuen, and indeed, he did know the way. Certainly Castellanos should not make the journey alone, even if accompanied by Chumash guides.

Deciding to sound supportive of Castellanos, Morgan accepted the assignment. "Yes, Padre Manuel, you will enjoy this trek, just as I did almost two years ago with Padre Payeras. I will be most happy to accompany you. And, if no one has told you so, you did a fine job of overseeing *Mision La Purisima* while the Padre and I were gone." From the look on Castellanos' face, it appeared that no one had told him that. Padre Manuel now appeared relieved and pleased. "Why, *mucho gracias, Sharlezz."* Castellanos wanted to add, 'Well, you're the only one who seems to think so.', but he kept silent.

Two mornings later Morgan and Castellanos were ready to walk to La Purisima where they would meet two Chumash guides, then proceed north on *El Camino Real.* De Uria and Juan came to bid them farewell. *"Adios, Sharlezz. Vaya con Dios. Par favor* use great care, do not get injured", Juan said to Morgan. "Oh, I don't expect that we will have any accidents", Morgan replied. Juan glanced towards Castellanos and said, "Oh, I do not mean physical injuries." Morgan looked knowingly into Juan's eyes and replied, "Do not worry, *mi amigo.* I will use great care that neither Padre Manuel nor I will meet with any difficulties."

When Morgan and Castellanos arrived at *La Purisima* they bade goodbye to Payeras and Gutierrez and were then joined by the same two Chumash men that had accompanied Payeras and Morgan north almost two years earlier. They greeted Morgan warmly. It was evident that they now trusted Morgan and had accepted him as a brother into their culture. Again, amid many wishes of *"Vaya con Dios",* the four walked out of the *La Purisima* compound. They had walked for several hours and Morgan noticed that the Chumash guides kept looking back at Castellanos, like they were expecting something to happen. After a few such glances, Morgan realized what they were anticipating. They thought that Castellanos should be leading them in the Rosary.

Morgan spoke to Castellanos, "Padre Manuel. Apparently it is customary during such treks as this, for the Padre to lead us all in reciting the Rosary. Are you prepared to do this?" Castellanos seemed have been awakened from a trance. "What? Oh, *si, si*. I will begin the prayers now." Morgan remembered his own periods of reverie when he made this same trip before.

Castellanos did begin the Rosary and recited the whole five decades in Spanish. The Chumash men seemed disappointed, although they did make their expected replies. Morgan had also joined them, so that they would not feel that they were isolated. It was plain to Morgan, however, that the men did not feel as included as when Payeras had recited some of the decades in their language.

Morgan looked up at the sun. He said, "Padre Manuel. It would seem to be about midday. Should we stop for a few minutes to partake of some food and water." Castellanos, again seeming to be withdrawing from a reverie said, "Oh yes. Tell the men to halt." The priest then began to nibble on a tortilla that one of the Chumash men had taken from his pouch. "Ah, *Senor Sharlezz*," the man said, seeming to be embarrassed. "Should we not recite the midday prayer?" Morgan then prompted Castellanos, "Padre, the men wish to recite the Angelus. Will you lead us?" Castellanos began the 'Dios te salve, Maria' prayer, and hurried through three of them. The men shrugged, sat, and ate their tortilla. It was evident to them that Castellanos had not the devotion of their beloved Padre Payeras.

Each day was a repeat of the previous. Morgan was dismayed that Castellanos was so negative and unspiritual. Compared to him, Morgan thought of himself as a saint.

They finished the march each day, met the Padres of the four Missions, were fed and slept. On the second night however, Morgan was awakened by Castellanos. *"Sharlezz"*, Castellanos whispered, "I am lonesome. Perhaps you would allow me to sleep closer to you." With this he placed his hand on Morgan's leg. "Padre Manuel", Morgan snarled, "I am very tired, and tomorrow we have another long day's trek. I think we should both say our nightly prayers and retire. I will pray for you to find the strength to maintain your vows, and you should perhaps pray that the weight of the priesthood is not beyond your ability to remain worthy." Castellanos realized that Morgan would not give in to this temptation. Now he felt shame and remorse for his attempted impropriety.

During the fourth day Castellanos seemed to want to again talk about his advances towards Morgan. "Tell me, *Sharlezz*, when you were on the sailing ships, did you not sometimes partake of affairs with other sailors. It is rumored that such events are commonplace on long voyages." Morgan was angered by the suggestion, but wanted to reply in a calm manner, hoping that Castellanos would recognize that he was again being impudent to Morgan. "No, Padre Manuel", Morgan rebutted, "I did no such thing. And, indeed, I did not see any other men acting improperly, 'though I also have heard such stories. For myself, I expect to remain virtuous until I am married. I hope that I will never be tempted beyond my strength." He hoped that that would cause Castellanos to conclude this matter.

At the end of the fifth day they entered *Mision San Carlos Borromeo* and met with *Padre Presidente* Lasuen. It was a cordial but polite meeting, nothing at all like the greeting that Payeras had received from Lasuen. The *Padre President* suggested that all should get cleaned, eat a good *cena* and retire. He seemed anxious to not discuss Castellanos' concerns on this evening.

After Mass the next morning, Lasuen invited Castellanos and Morgan onto his office. "Padre Manuel, I must admit that over the past several months I have received several letters from Padre Payeras in which he has described your concerns. And I can understand why many of these have, justifiably, caused you great anxiety. So it is my intention to correct these matters." Castellanos looked very relieved. Morgan was curious to know what the *Padre Presidente* believed was the solution to Castellanos' problems.

Lasuen continued, "I have arranged that you will return to *Nueva Espana* to attend our seminary there, for a few years of advanced studies. Upon completion you will be a far more learned theologian, and will be a great attribute to our Fransican Order." Lasuen seemed satisfied with his decision, but it became immediately obvious that Castellanos did not agree. "*Padre Presidente*", Castellanos complained rather loudly, "by that time I will be almost thirty years of age, and will have accomplished almost nothing in my life." His anger was apparent.

Lasuen seemed shocked that the young man would question his authority and his directive. "Manuel, my son, age is not a matter of the calendar. Age is a condition of spiritual and emotional development." With that, Castellanos became even more upset. "So, it is your opinion," Castellanos countered, "that I am immature, just as my father often accused. It seems that I am unable to attain any meaningful accomplishments. All because I am a child!" Lasuen was dismayed. He had never been spoken to like this by any priest, especially an underling. He tried to reply to the young priest, but was in stead looking at the rebellious priest's back as he stormed out of the *Padre Presidente's* office.

Morgan excused himself from Lasuen. "I'll go see if I can calm Padre Manuel. I'm sure that he did not mean to be disrespectful *Padre Presidente*. The feeling of a lack of self fulfillment has been on his mind for a long time, and it has now caused him to erupt in an improper manner." Padre Lasuen nodded agreement with Morgan and dismissed him with the hope that Morgan could indeed calm Castellanos' rebellious spirit.

When Morgan entered Padre Castelanos' cell, the young priest was still irate, muttering to himself and seeming to kick the air in exasperation. "Manuel", Morgan began, "please try to calm yourself and let us talk about your concerns. Padre Lasuen, and me too, are sympathetic to your situation. Lasuen thought that his solution was the best for you, but I'm sure that if you speak to him again, in a respectful way, he will listen to your reasoning." Castellanos had kept pacing while Morgan spoke. He did not reply to Morgan's suggestion. "No one, not even you *Sharlezz,* has any appreciation of the reasons for my exasperations. Oh, if my dear *Madre* were still alive, she would understand and would calm me, as she always did." With this, he quickly approached Morgan and threw his arms about Morgan's neck. "Please *Sharlezz*, hold me for a moment. I need someone to share my frustration. I cannot endure this alone."

Morgan was embarrassed. He hoped that no one was able to see the two of them in this embrace, but he did not want to repulse Castellanos either. He was honestly hopeful of helping this young man through his emotional distress. Castellanos held to Morgan for a few more minutes, then released him and sat on the edge of his cot. Morgan sat in the only chair in the cell. The two sat for several minutes, then Morgan again started the conversation. They talked for more than an hour. Morgan felt that he was bringing the young priest to understand his situation better. Castellanos seemed to be pondering the matter very deeply.

Then he said to Morgan, "*Sharlezz*, I want to pray." "Good", said Morgan, "let's do that together." Castellanos seemed pleased that Morgan would sympathize with his situation. "Thank you, *Sharlezz*. You are indeed a true friend. Now, as a friend, will you oblige me once more by agreeing to my next proposal." Morgan grew worried that this request might not be a proper one, but he still felt an obligation to listen to the priest's proposal before he denied it. "You see *Sharlezz*, I want to pray at the *Mision San Francisco de Asis,* and I want you to accompany me." Morgan was extremely surprised. He replied, "But

Manuel, that *Mision* is several days journey to the north. I don't think that Luseun will agree to let us travel there."

Castellanos quickly retorted, "I do not intend to seek his approval, *Sharlezz*. I want you to accompany me there, but whether you do or not, I plan to leave in the morning. I hope that you will be with me." Morgan was troubled, but he replied, "Yes, Manuel, I'll be with you. We can pray to *San Francisco* that you will find peace of mind in your priestly duties, whatever they are." Morgan hoped that this course would be the solution to ending the torment in Castellanos mind.

Early in the morning the two set out for San Francisco, which was developing into a very active seaport *pueblo,* one with much vice as well as holiness. The *Mision San Frasncisco de Asis* was within the *pueblo's* precincts, but as a seaport, the *pueblo* had attracted many undesirables. Morgan was very concerned that they had not notified *Padre Presidente* Lasuen, but he felt it imperative that he not disrupt Castellanos' own plan for his salvation, nor abandon him.

Three days later, upon reaching the *Mision San Francisco de Asis* they entered and prayed for an hour or so. That is, Castellanos prayed, but after a very short prayer, Morgan himself gazed about at every architectural feature of the church building. Then they entered the streets of the *pueblo*, seeking out some food. They found food and drink at a public tavern, then Castellanos rented a room for them, using money from his father that he had secreted.

During the night, Castellanos again made attempts to hug Morgan, who calmly repulsed them.

Finally, they fell off to sleep. In the morning Morgan awoke to find that he was alone in the room. Thinking that Castellanos was nearby outside, Morgan walked around the area, but found no sign of the young priest. Morgan returned to the room. He then saw a note that had been left by Castellanos.

'*Mi amado amigo, Sharlezz,* again I have humiliated you by my inappropriate advances. Please forgive me. I find that it is more and more difficult for me to withhold the demonstration of my love for you. I know that as long as I am in your company, this love will persist. I will not be able to maintain my vow of celibacy. I have decided therefore to leave now, hopefully to find peace of mind in new surroundings. I do not know what my future may be, but I know that Almighty God will always be your protector. Please pray that He will also be mine and will give me the strength to live according to His will. Do not worry about my destiny, but please pray for me. I hope that you do not feel badly about me. *Adios mi amigo*, Manuel.'

Morgan was flabbergasted! 'What has Manuel done? What difficulties does he now face? How can he remain a priest without living like one? I don't know what Catholics believe about this, but I always thought that if you took a vow, you had to stick with it.' Now Morgan envisioned Padre Manuel in a hovel of the *pueblo,* and with not a friend to turn to. 'And he is so immature, he will surely be duped into malicious conduct.'

But what was Morgan to do? Scour the *pueblo* in search of Manuel? There are so many ways in which Manuel could evade Morgan, he decided that it would be fruitless to wander around aimlessly. He must return to *Mision San Carlos,* and report Manuel's mutinous conduct to Lasuen. How he hated the thought of that encounter!

Morgan walked the 100 or so kilometers at a very quick pace. He was nourished at the two Missions on the way south and left very early each morning. He reached *Mission San Carlos* in the late afternoon of the third day. He was exhausted but he went immediately to the office of Lasuen. On being permitted to enter, he found Lasuen rising from his prayer kneeler. "Oh, *Senor* Morgan, come in. I am very surprised, but most pleased, to see that you have returned. And Padre Manuel, is he well? Is he completely exhausted from the many days of travel? We had wondered where the two of you had gone. I have just finished praying again for your welfare." Lasuen was obviously very anxious to hear Morgan's report.

Morgan began, "*Padre Presidente,* as you know, Padre Manuel and I left a week ago because Padre Manuel felt that he needed to find solace and peace of mind at *Mision San Francisco de Asis.* I accompanied him there because he was determined to go, and I was fearful that he could not manage to survive if he went alone." Lasuen answered, "Ah, that was very charitable of you *Senor.* Actually, we learned of your departure from the two Chumash men that had accompanied you here. They saw you leave very early in the morning, in the wrong direction they thought, so they followed you for some distance. But since you did not seem to want their assistance they returned and told me of the events. We thought that you were going to *Mision Santa Cruz* or *Mision Santa Clare.* I thought it best to allow Padre Castellanos to explore other *Misions*, to seek God's will in his travails. And I knew that under your protection, he would not be in danger."

"Well, Padre," Morgan spoke reluctantly, "Padre Manuel has not returned with me." Lasuen looked astonished. Morgan continued, "He has decided to stay at San Francisco, not the Mission, but the *pueblo*. I am sorry to report to you, sir, that Padre Manuel has apparently defected. "Oh, *Dios mia,*" Lasuen exclaimed, holding his chest, "what do you mean 'defected'?" Morgan felt nauseous at having to say it, "I mean that he may have renounced his priestly vows, and intends to pursue a different life." Lasuen moved to a chair, "Oh, *Dios sefia clementia mia,* what have I done? Oh, *Dios Todopoderoso*, forgive me. I have failed miserably in showing charity to the young man Manuel, and now I have driven him away from *Jesucristo*. Oh, may God have mercy on my soul*!"* Morgan purposely did not report the matter of the several advances that Castellanos had made or relate any facts of young Manuel's earlier life.

Morgan tried to ease Lasuen's sincere self-accusation. "Padre, it is I who have caused this friend to fall away. I was not as understanding of his plight as I should have been. I knew that he had a weakness and I failed to help him overcome this frailty." Morgan truly believed that he could have helped Castellanos, but did not concern himself strongly enough with the young priest's dilemma. Both Morgan and Lasuen were heart sick with the way that they had handled the delicate priest's emotional agony. Lasuen now seemed to be unaware of Morgan's presence. He walked to his kneeler, made the Sign Of The Cross and began to pray. That was his reaction to his own failings. Morgan returned to the cell that he was using, sat on the edge of the bed, feeling totally exasperated. That was his reaction to the same situation. But then he too said a little prayer in his heart for Manuel.

The next morning Morgan was prepared to return to *La Purisima*. The two Chumash guides were also ready. *Padre Presidente* Lasuen, looking very tired and sad, came to bid them farewell. He made the Sign Of The Cross over the three men saying "*Vaya con Dios, amigos.*" The hurt in his heart was still showing. Morgan shook his hand and by his eyes tried to express his sympathy for the old priest. They now shared a common burden for life.

As the three travelers walked along the *El Camino Real* the Chumash men could see that Morgan was sad and troubled. They asked what had happened. Without much elaboration, Morgan told them of the young Padre's decision to stay in San Francisco. They looked at each other with looks of understanding, but also of disappointment. Morgan also felt that they exchanged looks of knowing more than Morgan had related. Over the past two years they had recognized Padre Manuel's frustrations and his wrath at Payeras' seeming indifference. But since the matter was beyond any of their concern, they quickly dismissed the burden that was being felt by Morgan.

When they reached *La Purisima* many came forward to greet them. The greeters all looked somewhat dismayed at not seeing the young Padre also. The two Chumash men went amongst their people and whispered the tale of events at the northern Missions. The group of neophytes listened, then quickly disbanded as if knowing that Padre Payeras would not want them to be discussing this unholy saga.

Morgan went straight to Payeras quarters and told him the same story that he had related to Lasuen. Payeras' reaction was much the same as Lasuen, but with even more self-recrimination. Holding his chest, Payeras too, knelt and prayed. But quickly he realized that Morgan was now showing the signs of stress and remorse caused by Castellanos' defection. Payeras rose, placed his arm about Morgan's shoulder and tried to console him. This show of compassion now caused Morgan to completely break-down. He began to sob and to tell Payeras that the whole situation was his fault.

Payeras tried to explain that the matter of blame should be shared by all, since none had fully understood Castellanos' mental anguish. Payeras, too, prayed to God to forgive him for his own indifference.

Morgan said, "Well, Padre Payeras, poor Manuel's fate is now in his hands and those of God. I have worried in my heart how I would explain the matter to Padre Lasuen and to you. Now, I have done what I had to do, bringing you this very bad news." He seemed a little relieved to have the burden off his shoulders.

Payeras turned again to go kneel, but rubbed his heart again. Morgan quickly went to Cimkonah's cooking area and returned with a cup of *espina blanco* tea. Payeras looked up from his prayers and said, "Oh, *gratias Sharlezz*. I do need this. Go now and rest. Unfortunately, tomorrow we must go to *Santa Ines* and inform another person of Padre Manuel's departure." "Oh yes", Morgan replied, "I must report the matter to

Padre de Uria, as well." Payeras looked pained as he said, "And *Sharlezz,* also to Padre Manuel's sister Elena, who now awaits his return at *Mision Santa Ines.* " "Oh, my God,*"* Morgan gasped, "now I am to be the messenger of bad news to her as well. Whatever am I going to tell her?" Payeras replied, "We shall tell her the truth of our failure to be charitable and understanding." Morgan did not fail to note that Payeras stressed the "we".

CHAPTER NINE
Inevitable confrontations

The next morning Padre Payeras celebrated the early Mass then sought Morgan to join him for *desayuno.* By the tone of the conversation at breakfast it was apparent that Payeras planned to join Morgan in his return to *Mision Santa Ines.* Morgan said that he did not feel it necessary for Payeras to make the journey, that he should rest his heart for a few days. But Payeras insisted on accompanying Morgan. Payeras secured the company of two Chumash men to accompany them, and to travel with him on his later return to *La Purisima.*

They arrived at *Santa Ines* by late afternoon. They were greeted outside the unfinished compound by many neophytes, then as they neared the compound, by de Uria. "Welcome to *Mision Santa Ines* once more Padre. And welcome to you too, *Sharlezz."* He had no sooner uttered these words when a comely, finely dressed woman came out of the doorway of one of the hastily built quarters. She was almost running to them. Her arms were somewhat outstretched as if in anticipation of embracing someone. As she studied the group she suddenly stopped. "Where is Manuel? Is he not here with you? Did he remain at *Mision La Purisima*?" Then, as she looked at the faces of Padre Payeras and the unknown stranger, she sensed something worse. "Oh no, he is not Injured? Did he remain way up north at *Mision San Carlos Borromeo*, did he? Did he not know that I was here, anxiously awaiting him?"

De Uria spoke first, "*Senor* Morgan, may I present *Senorita* Elena Castellanos, sister to Padre Manuel." Morgan swallowed and said, "I am pleased to make your acquaintance, *Senorita* Castellanos." She bowed to him, then to Payeras, whom she had already met a few days earlier.

Morgan spoke next, "*Senorita*, I believe it would be best if we seek the shade of a tree, where we might confer for a time." Showing great anxiety the lady nodded agreement. The group went into the compound and sat on benches under a large oak tree. Elena persisted, "Where is Manuel? Why did he not return here? Tell me, please, what is his present situation."

Solemnly, Morgan related the fate of young Manuel. Elena was at first flabbergasted, then her demeanor showed a lack of composure. She first became indignant, then furious with Morgan and Payeras. She accused them of malice, then indifference and callousness. This was followed by shouts of retribution. "How dare you force my brother to abandon the priesthood that he loves so well. How dare you let him make such an irrational decision without stopping him. Do you not know that my father is a close friend of the Cardinal Archbishop of Madrid? Do you not know that my father is a Viceroy to King Carlos? You *Senor* Morgan, will be expelled from Alta California. And you Padre Payeras, will be severely disciplined by your Padre Superior General." She would have gone on further but she seemed out of breath. At one point Morgan was going to object to her assessment of the situation, but by his eyes Payeras told Morgan, 'let her vent her wrath'. And then

Morgan realized that some of what she said was true, that he and Payeras should have better understood the plight of the young priest.

Now Elena began to sob violently. None of the men dared to try to comfort her. She began to pace, wrenching her hands, continuing to sob. All that the three men could do was to sit and await for exhaustion to cause her to submit to reality.

Finally, Elena sat at the end of one of the benches, seeming to be alone in the world. Morgan motioned to the two priests. They quietly rose and left the immediate area. Now Morgan took a seat quietly beside Elena. He apologized for his involvement in all that had happened. He tried to explain his assessment of young Castellanos' emotional condition, which he admitted he had under-estimated. After more explanations by Morgan, Elena finally turned toward Morgan and indicated that she now better understood how alone her brother must have felt. That must have been the reason that he wrote her so often.

She confessed to Morgan that she was fearful of this possibility because she was not present to support him in his time of weakness. She stated that in Manuel's letters he had indicated his dissatisfaction with Payeras' treatment and his resentment at not being allowed a deeper involvement with the Mission's management. The reason that she had come to Alta California was to offer her support to Manuel. She said that she understood her brother, that he was always dependant on others to augment his slight courage. She explained his relationship with their mother and father, that due to the father's position, Manuel was usually afforded preferential treatment, and that his mother usually acceded to young Manuel's demands. She now realized that all-in-all, these conditions did not create in him the traits of character that were needed to be a strong person. She had hoped that in the priesthood he would have found serenity and spiritual fulfillment.

Morgan was finally allowed to speak. He explained Payeras' great responsibilities, and that Payeras did not feel that Manuel was yet mature enough to accept more intense duties. Morgan explained that he believed that if he himself had he not been present, that the elder Padre would have had to rely more on Manuel, so it was Morgan's fault, not Payeras', that caused the series of circumstances against Manuel.

Elena seemed to be slightly relieved. But it was obvious to Morgan that she believed that none of the difficulties were the fault of Manuel, that all were the result of circumstances beyond his control, and that God would understand all of this. Morgan assured her that her belief was true, and that God would indeed guide Manuel in his future decisions.

The two priests had been watching from a distance. They now saw Elena rise, take Morgan's hand, then with a slight bow, turn and walk slowly to her quarters. Morgan joined the priests and explained that he felt that Elena was now more understanding of the situation. Payeras smiled at Morgan and said, "*Sharlezz,* it was very kind of you to empathize with *Senorita* Castellanos. I knew from the beginning that you had the ability to counsel well. That is one of the chief responsibilities of a priest. I recognized from the beginning that you were a person of compassion. I continue to feel, as I always did, that you will someday make a fine priest." Morgan made no reply, for he knew that he was hoping to someday become the husband of Anna Maria Ortega.

Payeras returned to *La Purisima* and for the next several days, Morgan and Juan were busily overseeing the neophytes in their labor to complete the *deposito* for the Missions water supply, the *lavenderia* and the drinking water fountain. All of these implements were coming along fine. The viaduct was almost complete and soon the reservoir would begin to be filled.

Juan related to Morgan that while he had been gone with Padre Manuel, Anna Maria had ridden to *Santa Ines*, alone, and sought out Morgan. Juan had to explain to Anna Maria that *Sharlezz* had been sent to accompany Padre Castellanos to *Mision San Carlos Barromeo de Carmelo*, and would not return for several weeks. Anna Maria left *Santa Ines* without comment, but in Juan's opinion, very disappointed. Morgan, too, was disappointed that he had not seen Anna Maria. He was now trying to keep very busy so that he would not become more disappointed by thinking about this missed opportunity.

Almost a week after Morgan and Elena had discussed Padre Manuel's plight, she approached him. "*Senor* Morgan!", she began, "do you mind if I call you *Sharlezz,* as most others do?" "Not at all", he replied, "please do so. May I call you Elena?" She nodded acceptance. Then she said, "*Sharlezz*, I have heard marvelous comments about your creative ability. I understand that you have taken on the responsibility of building of a viaduct to draw water from a lake many kilometers from here. Is this true?" Morgan replied in the affirmative. Elena said, "I would like to see this viaduct and the lake. Would you accompany me there and show me your creation?" Again, Morgan replied in the affirmative, seeming to take pride that she would want to see his accomplishment.

On the next morning, Morgan had saddled two horses which the Padre had let him use for the day, since the lady could not walk through the rough pathway of the viaduct. Elena came out of her quarters wearing clothing much like a man's. Morgan was very surprised, and pleased by her apparel. She explained that it would not be comfortable to wear a dress on such a ride.

They departed mid-morning. It was, as usual, a beautiful sunny day. All along the path, Morgan explained the features of the viaduct's construction; how the neophytes had hewn out half logs, banded them together with raw-hide thongs and tarred them to minimize leakage, then joined the ten to twelve foot sections to each other. Though Elena expressed her approval of their efforts, she did not seem overly interested in the many details that Morgan wanted to explain.

Upon reaching the lake shore, she led them to a grassy area, suggested to Morgan that they allow the horses to graze and water themselves. She said that he should remove the saddles and place the blankets on the grassy shore, so that they might enjoy their luncheon. Morgan obligingly did all this. They ate and chatted pleasantly. Morgan was enjoying this relaxed day very much.

A short time after lunch, Elena said that she wanted to stroll about the grassy area a bit for some light exercise. Morgan continued to sit on the blanket as he watched her meander. As she left him, he admired her womanly shape, which was more obvious in the man-style breeches, shirt and vest.

After a time Elena called from behind some bushes and said that she was going to take a swim. Quickly she darted from the bushes and into the lake. Morgan was astounded when he caught a brief glimpse of her naked body. Never before had he seen a naked woman. More to his amazement, when she entered the water she waded only to her waist and turned towards Morgan, calling, "Come in, *Sharlezz*, the water is of a fine, refreshing temperature."

Upon seeing and hearing her, Morgan did not wait to consider if this was a proper manner of conduct, but immediately hurried behind a nearby bush himself. He undressed except for his underclothing, then ran into the water. Elena quickly waded towards him, chiding him that he had kept on his undergarment. She pulled at them, squirmed about him, touched him, and finally embraced him tightly, imparting a long kiss, one like Morgan had never experienced before. Morgan squirmed out of his undergarment and threw it to shore. After more frolicking, they left the water, reclined on the blankets, entwined, and basked in the sunshine.

The sun was much lower in the skies when Morgan awakened from a nap. Actually, Elena had awakened him, "Come *Sharlezz*, it is time to dress and return to the Mission." Morgan suddenly remembered that he was naked, though she was now fully dressed. He felt embarrassment as he ran behind the bush where his clothing was hung on the branches. Elena laughed as he ran.

Morgan re-saddled the horses and they departed. All the way back to the Mission Morgan was disturbed with his conduct, but he also acknowledged inwardly that he had just had a wonderful experience. His first such event.

At the Mission, Elena expressed how much she had enjoyed the day and then announced to him that she would be leaving the next morning for *Mision Santa Barbara*, then to San Diego, for her return trip to Spain. Morgan had not expected this announcement, but he also did not seem to mind that she was leaving. If she were not, would another such encounter ensue? Though he longed for another day like this one, he knew it to be best that she was departing.

Morgan unsaddled the two horse, wiped them down well, then returned them to their stalls. As he was returning to the Mission complex he encountered Padre de Uria. "*Sharlezz,* how did your day go? Was *Senorita* Castellanos impressed with your viaduct? Did you also show her the reservoir?" Morgan replied that yes, they had a fine day and that the *Senorita* was indeed impressed with all of *Mision Santa Ines*. De Uria then confided in Morgan, "Be careful *Sharlezz.* The lady has an unfortunate reputation of making herself available to many men. It is rumored that before coming here, that at *Santa Barbara Presidio* several of the officers were seen in her company."

Morgan thought to himself, 'it's too late for that warning Padre', then he said, "*Senorita* Castellanos has just advised me that she will be returning to *Santa Barbara* tomorrow, so we need not concern ourselves with her conduct any longer, need we." The Padre agreed, and Morgan wondered if the priest had now placed him in the category of the men that were 'seen in her company'.

For the next several weeks, although very busily involved in the many, many construction activities, he could not expel the memory of the day with Elena. He had much inner anxiety. He honestly admitted to himself that his encounter with the beautiful, older *Senorita,* was a joyous event, but he also could not completely free himself of the guilt that he felt. His puritanical New England upbringing reminded his inner self that it was a violation of one of the Commandments, which one he had forgotten. Then he would justify his action by reminding himself that in the four years he had spent as a sailor, nearly every one of his shipmates had already had many such encounters. And, since neither he nor Elena were married to anyone, was it really a sin? After all, he was not bound by the strict Catholic moral code that the Padres often sermonized about to the neophytes. But should he confide in Payeras, and relate the incident? Or admit to de Uria what had happened? Would that not be what they called 'confession', for which he was not obligated? But the most troubling aspect of the incident was, what would now be Anna Maria's opinion of Morgan.

Each time that he recalled the day with Elena, he would re-evaluate each of these aspects, but the question of Anna Maria's reaction to the knowledge of the event, was by far the most troubling. In the end, he decided that it would be best to never speak about the matter to her. He would not even tell his closest friend

Juan, although at times he suspected that Juan already had surmised what had occurred. One more shocking thought came to his mind; what if Elena spoke to others at *Santa Barbara* about her 'conquest'. Oh how terrible it would be if Anna Maria should hear of the matter in that way. Do ladies openly speak of such matters? No matter how he tried, or how busy he kept himself, these concerns remained in his troubled mind.

The construction of *Mision Santa Ines* was progressing well, in spite of some occasional disturbance by the Canalino Native Americans, who seemed to resent the Mission's establishment, and what they believed were the defection of their fellow natives of the peaceful Chumash tribe. Often visitors had to take a more distant path to reach *Santa Ines*, or risk harassment by the Canolinos. There were no assaults or killings, however.

The *Mision*'s rancheros were becoming quite filled with cattle. The population of these, plus horses, sheep, pigs, goats and chickens was expanding, and all appeared to be following the Padre's, and God's plan they believed, for the propagation of the Catholic Church, and the domestication of the natives in the name of *Rey Carlos IV*.

While Morgan was reminiscing often about his meeting with Anna Maria, and now only occasionally about the rendezvous with Elena Castellanos, Juan was somber and distant. Morgan would often ask if anything was wrong, did he have aches or pains, had Morgan treated him badly in some unknown way? Juan would always answer negatively, but did not explain to Morgan what was bothering him. One day in late August, Juan told Morgan that he had asked Padre de Uria for a few days leave to travel to *La Purisima.* Suddenly Morgan realized why Juan was so melancholy; it was one year since the death of his beloved Angelica and her baby. Of course, Juan would want to go to *La Puisima,* so that he could visit their grave.

So Morgan also sought the Padre's approval, and the two traveled to their former Mission together. Upon arrival, and as soon as they greeted Payeras, he joined them in a visit to the gravesite of Angelica. The Padre stated that the next morning's Mass would be offered to *Jesuchristo* for the repose of the souls of Angelica and her baby. Juan was very pleased that his former Padre wished to be so intimately involved. Morgan, too, was happy, for Juan's sake. He knew that Juan believed that prayer was a powerful and enriching solution to the discomforting feelings about those that are deceased. Morgan even began to feel that way about his Papa, Stepmama Anna and his dear brother Albert. He wasn't sure about the effect of prayer, but what could be wrong with giving it a try, he thought. As a favor to his friend, Morgan did attend the early morning Mass with Juan. Both Juan and Payeras, were very pleased that Morgan chose to do this. After Mass Juan and Morgan returned to *Mision Santa Ines.*

The rainy months would again be soon approaching. At *Santa Ines,* roofing tiles were being manufactured, as they had been at *La Purisima* and most of the other Missions, so that the thatched roofs of the buildings, especially the church, could be made more weather and fireproof. But enough tiles would not be ready to install, except on some of the smaller buildings. Because Padre de Uria and Gutierrez had laid out such a large rectangular compound, much more material was needed than could be produced, even by the hundreds of neophytes at hand. And some of these were becoming weary of the constant urging by the Padres and Spanish men, to produce more and more tiles, adobe bricks, application of stucco, and making of ironware fittings, hinges, latches and the like. These were being produced in the blacksmith shop that Morgan and Juan had established as one of their earliest *Santa Ines* efforts.

There was much being done, but as Morgan and Juan knew, there was much more to be done. But they, and especially the Padres, were generally satisfied that the Mission would one day be complete and would be considered by the Governor and *Padre Presidente* Tapis to be among the best of many.

As November approached, Morgan wondered about two things. Would he soon receive another letter from home, and would he be able to spend *natividad* at *Mision Santa Barbara*, where he could again see his beautiful Anna Maria. It had been a long time, a very long time, since he saw her. By now, some of the guilt of the affair with Elena Castellanos had faded. He could face Anna Maria with less trepidation and more confidence that he would someday become her husband.

To keep himself busy and productive, he began to design a grist mill that would start to be constructed next spring. Because the population of the Mission kept increasing, more and more meal was needed. Morgan remembered the grist mill in Sturbridge, and he had seen others that had been built at some of the Missions that he had visited. He was sure that he and

Juan could properly oversee the construction of a large and efficient mill.

Unlike the Padres and many neophytes, Morgan did not believe as strongly in the power of prayer, though he did offer a prayer in his heart at certain times and for certain things. Nowadays, one was said often for that hoped for visit to *Mision Santa Barbara*. Juan too, in his Christian heart and prayers, was praying for Morgan's prayer to be answered. And they were. A few days after the start of November Padre de Uria came to say that he had received a *comunicado* from Vice Governor Ortega, asking if the Padre would be able to excuse Morgan and his *amigo* Juan from their duties at *Mision Santa Ines* during *Estacion de Navidad,* so that they could assist his family in preparing their *hacienda* with the necessary decorations for the Vice Governor to properly officiate as the King's representative, and to welcome the many other officials and officers in the service of King Carlos IV.

"How should I reply?", de Uria asked. Morgan tried to hide his excitement. "Well, Padre, that's your decision. If you can spare Juan and me from your needs, we will be happy to accept the request of Vice Governor Ortega", Morgan answered with forced calmness. "But it is your decision, Padre." "Well", Padre de Uria replied, "I cannot possibly not accede to the request of the King's representative, especially for such a momentous event."

Morgan, and even Juan, wanted to jump with joy, but managed to sound indifferent. "Should we begin to pack for the journey?", Morgan asked nonchalantly. "Oh yes", the priest replied, "do so! And depart as soon as possible." The Padre started to leave, then turned back, and with a wide smile said," *Feliz Navidad* to you both. And *vaya con Dios* as well." Morgan looked at Juan and said, "Let's go Juan, let's pack quickly and leave tomorrow morning," Juan was surprised, "Why so soon, *amigo*, there are many weeks yet until *Navidad*." "Yes", Morgan replied, "but only a few days until the birthday of Anna Maria." Now Juan realized why Morgan was so anxious to get to *Santa Barbara.*

They arrived at *Santa Barbara Presidio* just one day before Anna Maria's birthday. Upon inquiring, they learned that there would be no large party for Anna Maria this year, just a family dinner. Morgan had hoped to have the chance to dance with Anna Maria. In that way he could again hold her in his arms.

When word of their arrival reached the Vice Governor's *hacienda,* Anna Maria persuaded her father to extend an invitation to Morgan to join the family celebration. Morgan was happy to accept, but disappointed that Juan was not also invited. Juan expressed understanding about the omission, but Morgan wondered about this discrimination, not knowing that the Vice Governor had a reason to invite Morgan alone.

The celebration dinner was a fine affair. The Vice Governor and his *senora* Maria Consuela seemed pleased to see Morgan again and were very pleasant to him. Anna Maria left no doubt that she was extremely happy that the handsome *yanqui* was present. It had been almost a full year since they had seen each other. Anna Maria was bubbly and almost giddy with excitement. With a slight glance towards her mother, and with an approving return glance by her, Anna Maria brought Morgan to the chair next to hers. *Tia* Carmelita sat across from the two. Morgan realized that he was being scrutinized by her and Anna Maria's parents.

The conversation at dinner focused largely on Morgan, although at first he did not realize this. The Vice Governor asked many questions about Morgan's early life, his years at sea, and his first years with Padre Payeras. *Senora* Ortega, and even *Tia* Carmelita, asked an occasional question also. Morgan began to notice that Anna Maria was keenly observing the reaction by the Vice Governor and the ladies by Morgan's answers. This is when he realized that he was being evaluated by Anna Maria's elders.

Soon the questions began to focus on religion. What, if any, was Morgan's religion? Was religion important to him? Did he believe in, and observe the Ten Commandments? (This one made him squirm a bit inwardly. Had he broken the Seventh Commandment?) Each of Morgan's replies to this point seemed satisfactory to the group. Anna Maria was smiling broadly. The Vice Governor now leaned a bit forward, engaging Morgan with what Morgan felt must be a question of paramount concern. "If you wished to marry a young lady that you believed would become a dutiful and loving wife," now the Vice Governor leaned even further forward, "would you become a member of the Catholic Church?" Before Morgan could answer, the Vice Governor added, "*Senora* Ortega and I would never allow our daughter to marry any man that is not of the Catholic faith." Morgan noticed the emphasis on the 'any man', realizing that

Don Ortega must mean him. Now Anna Maria also leaned towards Morgan, earnestly awaiting his answer.

"Why yes, I would", Morgan replied very matter of fact, then added, "Padre Payeras and I have had discussions towards that end." Now Morgan realized that he had stretched the truth a little in an effort to impress the Ortega family. And they were indeed impressed. Each of them smiled broadly, especially Anna Maria, who seemed to show pride that she had brought this handsome, intelligent and ethical, potential husband to the Ortega home. The conversation that followed, which was mostly by Anna Maria, became much lighter.

Following dinner they all adjourned to an extensive sitting room. Here, gifts were presented to Anna Maria. Morgan suddenly realized that he was extremely impolite, for he had not thought to bring a gift to Anna Maria. He felt very awkward, but the Vice Governor was very gracious, stating that Morgan's presence had given Anna Maria more joy than all of the gifts that she received. The Vice Governor and his wife both seemed very pleased to see their daughter so happy. After a while Anna Maria's parents, and her *duenna, Tia* Carmelita, withdrew from the room. Morgan let out a great sigh. Anna Maria also gave a sigh of relief and laughed, "That was quite an experience for you, was it not *Sharlezz?"* Morgan nodded agreement, as he remembered the stories of the young men in his village meeting a girl's parents for the first time, and how uncomfortable that experience was.

Now Morgan and Anna Maria chatted somewhat eagerly, then moved closer to each other.

Soon, Anna Maria made a quick move to Morgan's side and positioned herself so that he could easily kiss her. At first apprehensive, Morgan decided to risk Anna Maria's ire. He embraced her tightly and placed his lips on hers, first in a courteous manner, but soon in a passionate manner. Anna Maria was most receptive to this amorous conduct. They continued for some long time.

Anna Maria goaded Morgan, *"Sharlezz*, do you believe that a man should take a wife while they are both young? Young enough to have several children?"Morgan was at first a little surprised at these questions, but not unhappy that Anna Maria had raised the possibility of marriage. He replied, "Yes, I agree, Anna Maria, in fact, I believe that we should give some serious thought to the possibility of our marriage, for we seem to be very compatible." Then he added quickly, "and I love you very much Anna Maria." For her part, Anna Maria was ready for Morgan to propose. She practically drew him into the front of her and held his hand in such a manner that he felt compelled to kneel. Then he did propose, and of course she quickly accepted. They embraced and kissed for several more minutes.

Morgan, and most likely Anna Maria, would have liked to continue, but a gentle cough from outside of the room signaled that the others were about to reenter. Breaking away quickly, the amorous couple pretended that they had only been conversing, but the others surmised differently. After a few minutes the three ladies excused themselves and left. Morgan was now uncomfortable in the room alone with the Vice Governor. No one spoke for a while, then the Vice

Governor started the conversation, "Did you enjoy dinner, Sharlezz?" Morgan answered with a little too much enthusiasm, "Oh, indeed yes *Senor* Governor!"Then silence again. Now the father, seeming to want to come to a point asked, "Did you and Anna Maria find much to talk about?" The same reply came from Morgan, "Oh, yes indeed *Senor."* "Well, my son, is there any question that you would like to ask?", the father inquired.

Morgan had enough sense to realize that the father had given him the perfect opportunity to speak of marriage to his daughter. He wanted to speak but the only thought that came to mind was the story that his sister Mary had read to him when he was much younger, about a Pilgrim named John Alden and a girl named Pricilla. But Morgan recognized that this opportunity may not come again. He did indeed ask the Vice Governor for the privilege of marrying Anna Maria. The Vice Governor smilingly approved and called the ladies back into the room. *Senora* Ortega and *Tia* Camelita walked back in, but Anna Maria virtually flew into Morgan's arms. The Vice Governor then announced that he had given approval for the marriage of his daughter to the young man, *Sharlezz* Morgan. "Oh, *Sharlezz*, I am so happy. We shall be married on the first day of May, at *Mision Santa Barbara."* Suddenly Morgan felt that he was only a pawn in a chess game that had been arranged by the Ortega family. But he was nevertheless, very happy too.

When he returned to the quarters that he and Juan were sharing in an outbuilding of the *hacienda,* much to his surprise he found Juan awake. "How was your evening, *Sharlezz?"*, Juan asked. Showing much happiness Morgan described the evening's events, then announced that he and Anna Maria were to be married on the first day of May in 1806. Juan congratulated his friend and then asked. "And when will you begin taking lessons in the Catholic faith?"

Half laughing Morgan replied, "Why, how did you know that I said I would become a Catholic?" Now Juan laughed and said, "Oh I knew before you went to the dinner that Vice Governor Ortega would accept you as his son-in-law if you agreed to join our faith." Morgan felt a little foolish as he commented, "Am I the only person who did not know that I would propose to Anna Maria and agree to become Catholic?" Again having the feeling that he was a pawn in a game, he undressed and laid on the bed. As he blew out the candle Juan said, "Now *amigo*, don't forget to say your *Catolico* evening prayers. *Hasta manana.*"

CHAPTER TEN
Wedding Bells...

On November 16th, 1805, Anna Maria had turned 19 and on December 11th, Morgan turned 23 years of age. They were young and in love. Everything was perfect in their lives. Morgan and Juan, and the many servants of the Vice Governor, both Spanish and Chumash natives, had decorated the *hacienda* and the approach areas to the house with lavish, hand made Christmas decorations. *Senora* Ortega and Anna Maria had hand-drawn many of them for the wall and for hanging. The Chumash ladies and maidens had hand-painted them using berry juices and dyes made in the manner of the Chumash traditions.

The traditional Spanish procession of *posadas,* the search for an inn by Mary and Joseph on the nine days before Christmas, had once again pleased Morgan, but this year even more so, because Anna Maria was with him. Although Morgan missed Rosa Remirez' cooking and baking, Margarito Mendez' cooking was equally good. She was the wife of Roberto, who had donated his clothing to Morgan shortly after he had arrived at *La Purisima.* Roberto was one of the carpenters who had elected to move to *Mision Santa Ines,* at the urgings of Morgan. The Mendez family would be moving soon after Christmas.

At the Christmas morning Mass the church at *Mision Santa Barbara* was overflowing with the families of the Spanish craftsmen, the soldiers from the *presidio* and their families, as well as many visitors that had come to *Santa Barbara* at the invitation of the

Vice Governor, and of course the many native neophytes.

All too soon, however, the festivities of the season came to an end and much sooner than it had started, the Christmas season was over. Morgan felt the usual let-down, but because Anna Maria was at his side much of the time, he remained more joyous than in past years. But now the time had come for Morgan and Juan to return to *Mision Santa Ines.* He was saddened that he had to leave his beloved. Anna Maria, however, was not saddened, she was irate. She had expected that Morgan would remain at *Santa Barbara* to partake of his lessons in Catholicism, become baptized and begin preparations for their wedding. Although the marriage was several months away, Anna Maria acted as if it were to be tomorrow and was very eager to discuss plans for what was to be a very lavish affair.

Morgan explained to her that he and Juan had to return to *Santa Ines* to help Padre de Uria, especially now since Padre Manuel was gone. Anna Maria commented, "Oh, yes, that Padre Castellanos has betrayed his vows, hasn't he." Morgan made no reply to this, but he did not care for Anna Maria's attitude towards Castellanos. Morgan explained the urgency of the construction of the grist mill, the further completion of the Mission buildings, the need to train the Chumash natives in herding and husbandry of the animals, and the techniques in growing very large amounts of rye, wheat and corn, while using horse drawn plows which they had never done before. Morgan was continuing to add descriptions of developing the grape arbors, when Anna Maria cut him short, "Oh, I understand all of these needs, *Sharlezz*, but I did believe that you would consider our pending marriage to be more important to you. And you must immediately begin your studies of the Catechism."

Again, Morgan's reply did not please her. "I intend to study the Catechism and whatever else I need to learn at *La Purisima* with Padre Payeras. I will feel much closer to the lessons under his tutelage." Anna Maria showed much impatience. "*Sharlezz*, my parents and I thought that you would now remain here. Padre Amistoy will be most pleased to instruct and baptize you. He expects to do this for the future son-in-law of the Vice Governor."

It was obvious that they were not seeing the matter in the same view. Juan had been nearby during this discussion and began to offer a suggestion, "Why not partake…". Anna Maria cut him short, "This is none of your affair, Juan." Morgan did not like his friend to be spoken to in such a manner and he was beginning to become impatient with Anna Maria. "Anna Maria", he spoke firmly, "I want my friend Juan to be my witness at our wedding. I wish him to be heard." Anna Maria sulked. Morgan turned to Juan, "What is it Juan? Do you have a suggestion?" Looking embarrassed that he had caused consternation, he said, "I was going to propose that you take lessons from Padre Payeras, but perhaps every few weeks you could take the lesson here from Padre Amistoy. In that way you can accommodate both of your wishes." Morgan looked pleased, "What do you say to that idea, Anna Maria?" Although not too pleased, Anna Maria did accept the compromise so that she could see her beloved at least a few times before their marriage.

The two consulted with Padre Amistoy who said that he would be glad to accommodate them in any way they wished. He wrote a note to Payeras explaining the planned arrangement and gave it to Morgan to take to Payeras. Upon learning of this arrangement, knowing that Morgan and Juan would be returning often, *Don* Ortega provided horses and saddles for the two. Morgan and Juan were very happy to accept his generous offer.

The next morning, Morgan and Juan were ready to depart. Morgan and Anna Maria embraced and kissed lightly. Morgan, followed by Juan, left *Santa Barbara*, leaving behind a sullen bride-to-be. On the ride to *Mision Santa Ines*, Morgan spoke to Juan as much about the Mission's needs as he did about his impending marriage. Juan was not surprised by this, for was it not Morgan's dedication to his tasks that had impressed the Vice Governor that he would be a good son-in-law, and of course, a good husband to his beloved daughter.

During this very busy spring season, Morgan fulfilled his religious requirements as well as his secular duties. The arrangement of the two Padres sharing the instructions went well. It allowed Payeras to show much pride and happiness in his student and it gave to Amistoy the opportunity to recognize Morgan's fine character. In early April, when it was time for Morgan's acceptance into the Church and to be baptized, Payeras traveled to *Mision Santa Barbara* for the ceremony. The event was on a grand scale, with Vice Governor Ortega, *Senora* Ortega and *Tia* Carmelita, as well as several officials of the *Presidio,* including *Capitan* Hernandez, attending. Anna Maria and Juan were both close by. All were seen to be very happy, but the broadest smile was that of Padre Payeras, the first to have planted the seeds of the *Catholico* religion into Morgan's mind.

Previously, as a requirement for receiving his First Holy Communion, Morgan had to confess his sins to Padre Payeras. Payeras sat while Morgan knelt beside him. They were face to face, without a screen between them. The priest assisted Morgan in recalling the sins of his past life by bringing to mind the Ten Commandments. Morgan had no difficulty in replying negatively to the first six, though he had to admit to taking the name of The Lord Thy God in vain many, many times. But now Payeras came to the Seventh Commandment. Morgan faltered. Payeras seemed surprised. Finally Morgan confessed to his adulterous affair. He started to say the name of "El"—, but Payeras stopped him. "It is not necessary that you announce the co-sinner's name", the priest said. Although Payeras showed his uneasiness, he told Morgan to continue. Then, with revue of the eight, ninth and tenth Commandments, Morgan concluded his confession. Padre Payeras made the sign of the cross over Morgan, and with the words, "By the grace of Almighty God, and the power entrusted in me by *Jesuchristo*, I absolve you of your sins."

Morgan rose from the kneeler and as Payeras rose from his chair he commented, "*Sharlezz,* it will be best if you do not repeat any of your sins to anyone, not anyone. Do you understand? Now go, and remain in the good graces of The Lord." Morgan felt greatly relieved now that he had finally gotten the affair with Elena Castellanos off his conscience.

Along with all of this, Morgan was also very happy with the way things were progressing at the new *Mision*. The beginning of the grist mill construction was going well, as were the training of the neophytes. Some of the times that he had traveled to *Santa Barbara* Morgan had left Juan at *Santa Ines* to help oversee of the progress of the Mission. When Morgan would arrive at *Santa Barbara* alone, Anna Maria gave evidence of being ever more joyous. She commented that she hoped that after their marriage, Juan would not be so close at hand all of the time so as to interfere with their privacy. Morgan assured her that Juan knew that a married couple wished to be intimate at times, and that Juan would not invade their privacy. Anna Maria shrugged as if not believing.

By mid April, the *Mision* and *Presidio* at *Santa Barbara* were showing signs of the impending marriage of the important couple. Dignitaries, religious, civil and military were beginning to arrive in the *pueblo*. Each of the Spanish craftsmen was required to house a visitor or two. The Mission accommodated many, as did the *Presidio* quarters. The church, which was beautiful of itself, was now being given extra adornment. Chumash artists took great joy in repainting the *reredos*, the wall behind the altar, as well as the sidewalls and even the roof beams. Outside, the plaza was expanded to accommodate the anticipated crowds and new walkways and steps were added.

The Chumash neophytes rehearsed their singing and the musicians, under the tutelage of Padre Narcisco Duran, expanded their repertoire of hymns. The musical pipes, made of hollowed animal and bird bones, carved and joined together, created very melodious notes, as they had for generations, even before the Padres had arrived here.

Padres Payeras, Gutierrez and de Uria had come from their Missions as did Cimkonah and several of Morgan's old friends among the Spanish craftsmen and their families. It would appear that the occasion of this wedding would be as large a *fiesta* as any in the Spanish tradition.

Morgan's reception of his First Holy Communion and his Confirmation, adult acceptance of the laws of God and the Church, were to be administered on the day before the wedding by the Bishop of San Diego, Gilberto Rodriguez. Unfortunately, due to a minor uprising of the Ipai natives in the area of *Mision San Diego*, the *Comandante* of the *Presidio* there believed it to be too dangerous for the Bishop and the Governor to travel north. The administration of Confirmation, which had to be by a Bishop, but not being a prerequisite of marriage, was postponed. And to Padre Mariano Payeras befell the pleasure of administering First Holy Communion to his very good friend, *Sharlezz* Morgan.

There being no further impediments to the proper marriage of Charles Morgan and Anna Maria Margarito Ortega, the marriage took place, as planned, on May 1, 1806. Padres Payeras and Amistoy concelebrated the Mass and the marriage ceremony, and Juan and *Tia* Carmelita were the witnesses, as required by Church law.

The reception that followed was as grand as was possible in Alta California. The Vice Governor and *Senora* Ortega were proud to introduce their new son-in-law to the dignitaries that had arrived, especially those from the southern Missions, who were in greater contact with the Governor of *Nueva Espana* and the Bishop of Mexico City.

During the several days of *fiesta,* the newly married couple resided in a part of the *hacienda* that had privacy from the rest of the large house. Each morning it was obvious that the couple had enjoyed the benefits of marriage and that they were extremely compatible.

As the people began returning to their own Missions or *pueblos,* Juan sought out his friend, whom he had not seen since offering his congratulations immediately after the marriage ceremony. Morgan asked why he was leaving so soon. Juan said that he felt he should return to *Mision Santa Ines* to help Padre de Uria. While they were talking, Anna Maria kept some distance away. As Juan turned away, after he and Morgan had shaken hands, Anna Maria was seen to smile slightly.

On the third evening, as the newly married couple, her parents and *tia* were partaking of dinner, *Don* Ortega asked Morgan what were his plans. Morgan looked surprised, "Why, I plan to return to *Mision Santa Ines*, with Anna Maria of course, and continue to help Padre de Uria." Anna Maria showed her displeasure. The Vice Governor did not show disagreement, but looking very serious, said, "I believe that you must now begin to build a future for yourself and Anna Maria. I know that you have great concern for the continuing progress of *Mision Santa Ines*, but you must also consider that you need to secure an income that will allow you to offer Anna Maria, and your future children, a life of which they are worthy."

Morgan looked surprised. He had not thought about any more grand a life than that he had been living. He realized now that he had not given sufficient thought to the responsibilities of supporting his new wife and possible family. He addressed his father-in-law, "You are correct *Don* Ortega, I will have to obtain land and establish my own *rancho.* I know that if the Governor will grant me a parcel, I can do the necessary grooming and farming to make it a profitable enterprise." The Vice Governor was already ahead of Morgan. He offered, "Well, *Sharlezz*, the Governor has already granted me several tracts of land, and I plan to give one of them to both of you as a wedding gift." With this, Anna Maria jumped from her chair and throwing her arms around her father's neck shouted, "Oh, *Sharlezz*, isn't he wonderful. Now we can have our own land and our own *hacienda,* and we need not worry anymore about those Mission problems."

Now Morgan was confused and disturbed. Was he not to be allowed to assist the Padres in their efforts?. Was he going to be required to abandon them and their plans to educate the Chumash natives, to convert them from paganism to Catholicism, to instruct them in the traits of the white man, to insure their future livelihood? Morgan suddenly realized that he was now in support of the Padres, and had abandoned the early negative doubts that he had had regarding the natives well-being.

"What are you going to say to father, *Shalezz*". Morgan realized that Anna Maria was asking what he planned to do about their future. He had to accept the new responsibilities. He answered, "Oh, thank you *senor*. That is a most generous gesture, a fine gift. Anna Maria and I are extremely grateful."

The next day the Vice Governor had an aide bring a map of the area. It encompassed land for many, many kilometers to the south of *Santa Barbara*, as well as far north to *San Louis Obispo*. 'My God', Morgan thought, 'he owns all this land?' The Vice Governor pointed to two specific tracts and said, "*Sharlezz,* Anna Maria, you may have either of these tracts. You may decide, and then I will see to the proper change of the land grant. The Governor will sign, and you will be land-owners." Morgan studied the map carefully then said, "Tomorrow Sir, I'll take a ride to examine the tracts, and then let you know." Anna Maria quickly added, "And I'll go with you *Sharlezz.* " Morgan replied, "Of course, my love. We will agree on which *rancho* to select."

Early the next morning the two newlyweds and a Spanish soldier who was familiar with the territory, left on horseback to examine their potential land holdings. Anna Maria expressed a preference for a tract northeast of *Mision Santa Barbara*, the closest to her parent's *hacienda*. Morgan agreed to look there first because it was closer. They found the land, about 125,000 hectares, to contain great amounts of grazing areas, large wooded sections, streams of water flowing through, and a view of both the mountains to the east, and the ocean to the west. It was indeed an ideal landsite.

Next, they journeyed to an equally large tract, just southwest of *Mision Santa Ines*. It also contained open land, treed areas and ample water. It abutted the lake that was supplying the water to *Santa Ines*. Part of the land was in the foothills of the mountains and it also had a view of the sea and even included shore land of the ocean. Morgan favored this site because he knew that the largest share of their future income would be from selling cattle hides which were in great demand in the infant United States, as well as in Europe. Thus being closer to the ocean, would make it easier to transport the hides to the shore and the awaiting ships.

They returned to tell the Vice Governor of their selection. They had argued about their differences on the way back, but Morgan finally convinced Anna Maria to accept his choice. Another reason that he preferred this lower tract was its proximity to *Mision Santa Ines*, though he did not mention this to Anna Maria. He hoped that he might still have some time to devote to the Mission's development.

Within a month the Morgans had selected the site for their *hacienda* and several craftsmen came from all three Missions, *La Purisima, Santa Barbara* and *Santa Ines*, to help build the house for the beloved couple. Morgan arranged with the three Missions for the purchase of a few head of their cattle so that he could start his own herd, but the Missions donated the requested cattle, as repayment for services rendered by Morgan in the previous years.

During one of several trips to *Santa Barbara*, Morgan visited the *Presidio* to speak with *Capitan* Hernandez. Morgan had one other concern that he had not spoken to Anna Maria about. The land owner that adjoined their *rancho*, Humberto Ruiz, was known as a trouble maker, and had often ordered travelers to avoid his land, causing them to require several more days to reach the northern Missions. Morgan had heard Padre Payeras speak of this *molesto hombre* Ruiz and the trouble that he had caused. Capitan Hernandez had assured Morgan of the availability of his *soldatos,* should it be necessary.

By the approaching time of Christmas 1806, the *'Rancho del Sol',* as the Morgans named it because of its sunny pleasantness, was now the official residence of *Senor* and *Senora* Morgan. Juan Bautista had been hired by Morgan to be his assistant in managing the *rancho,* and a few of both Spanish and native men had been hired to maintain the land and the small but growing herd. The funds that were needed to support the cost of the *rancho* were loaned to Morgan by his father-in-law. Morgan was confident that he could repay these loans very soon.

One of the earliest projects of all the men of *Rancho del Sol* was to bring water from the lake to the *hacienda* and gardens. After having studied the aqueducts and the filtering system of *Mision Santa Barbara*, Morgan decided to use an open viaduct made of stones, rather than the wooden pipes as he had installed at *Mision Santa Ines.* The biggest difference in the two systems was that with the open stone viaduct, litter would flow into the reservoir. A large settling and filtering system, therefore, had to be constructed. With the much smaller number of men working on the project, it would be many months before its completion. In the meantime, water was brought from the lake in bags made of cattle hides, and transported by horses. Horses were becoming plentiful, breeding on their own. When needed, the wild young horses were captured and saddle broken.

The summer months, then the fall season had quickly passed and now winter was approaching. The Morgans celebrated their birthdays in a less than lavish manner. The realities of their new life, without the grand sponsorship of the Vice Governor, were now apparent. Anna Maria wanted to observe the Christmas festivities at *Santa Barbara,* but Morgan insisted that they do so at *Santa Ines*.

Although on a much smaller scale than that at *Santa Barbara*, the traditions were nevertheless carried out in a most enjoyable manner. The few Spanish families and the many neophytes that were residents of *Santa Ines* all wished to hold their own celebration of *Natividad,* for the first time at their own Mission. Padre de Uria, Morgan and Juan, and even Anna Maria, all helped to make their wish come true and to make the season enjoyable.

The day after Christmas, the couple traveled to *Santa Barbara* because Anna Maria and her husband wanted to announce to her parents in person, that she was with child. The Ortegas were overjoyed to hear that they would soon have an heir. *Tia* Carmelita returned to *Rancho del Sol* with the couple, so that Anna Maria would have proper care. On May 3rd, 1807, a daughter was born. They named her Maria Consuela, in honor of the child's mother and grandmother.

The stone viaduct which had been in construction for nearly a year was nearing completion, though no water was yet flowing in it. In early spring, as Morgan and Juan were inspecting the two kilometers of the aqueduct, they found a section that had obviously been dismantled. They immediately suspected Humberto Ruiz. The two rode to Ruiz' *hacienda.* There they met *Senor* Ruiz for the first time. Morgan explained the reason for their visit, though he did not directly accuse Ruiz of being the culprit. Ruiz quickly denied any knowledge of the matter, but also quickly added that he felt that Morgan's viaduct may be crossing into Ruiz' property. He said that he could not permit this condition. Then Ruiz made some comment to the effect that he had worked hard to develop his property, that it was not handed to him by an official of the government. Morgan understood the comment and assured Ruiz that he intended to work just as hard as Ruiz had and to operate a profitable ranch and to raise his family in a peaceful setting. He stressed the "peaceful".

Morgan also assured him that he had been careful when laying out the viaduct route, that it lay entirely within Morgan's *rancho.* They left Ruiz' home with each party feeling that they made themselves understood by the other, and had made clear the matter of property boundaries. As they rode away, Morgan and Juan both knew that they would be hearing more from *Senor* Ruiz.

While Morgan's ranch was slowly being developed, *Mision Santa Ines*, with its large pool of native laborers, was progressing ever more quickly. The *convento* wing now had accommodations for five priests, should they ever be assigned. The quarters for the craftsmen and their families were expanding, and, of course, the quarters for the *soldatos* had been completed as one of the earliest sections. Now Padre de Uria and his neophytes were working hard on completing the necessary shops for candle making, weaving, saddlery, and of course, rooms for instructions of the younger neophytes. Fire pits and vats had already been constructed, and the rendering of the animals was beginning to be a product of this Mission, as it was at all the others.

Morgan had instructed the natives on the method of sawing large tree trunks length-wise by use of a whipsaw. The saw was one of many tools that had been brought from Spain many years earlier, then used at several of the Missions. To use the saw, a deep pit was first dug so that a native in the pit could pull downward on the whipsaw, while another at the top of the pit pulled upward. It was a laborious method, but one that Morgan had seen as a young boy, when the local farmers made roof beams for their New England houses and barns.

Many beams had been made in this manner and then installed on the top of the church adobe walls. The beams would later be required to support the weight of the baked clay tiles so many of the beams were doubled. This was done by tethering them together with raw-hide thongs, which were applied wet. When the thongs dried they shrank very tightly around the beams.

Morgan was especially happy with the success of the grist-mill. It was now producing many bags of meal each day. The water works were also operating as planned and the fountains in the courtyard and in the *lavenderia* in the front of the Mission were functioning well. Some of the native artists were now painting colorful tiles to be attached around the adobe of the fountain well. The interior walls of the church were also being decorated. The Spanish craftsmen were busy making furniture, iron plows, hardware, and leather goods for the tethering and saddling of the horses.

Yes, the *Mision Santa Ines* was coming along well. After only two and one half years since its dedication, Santa *Ines* now had a herd of more than a thousand animals, including cattle, sheep, goats, swine, horses and mules. Its growing flock of chickens and ducks made for a lively, and noisy place.

Although Padre de Uria had labored alone for some time, he now had an associate, Padre Pedro Figueroa, who was a very dedicated man, both religiously as well as in temporal matters. He and de Uria were proud of the many dozens of baptisms that they had administered since the founding of the Mission, as well as the educational progress of the natives. Soon, they hoped, there would be no further sign of the native's paganism or rituals. God, the Padres believed, would be most happy with their work, in His name.

Morgan had sent Juan and one of the Spanish ranch hands to the *pueblo* at *Santa Barbara* to hire more hands. The herd at *Rancho del Sol* was quickly growing and more cereals were needed to feed them. They were to employ either Spanish men or natives. When the two returned they reported that no hands were obtainable, all were working at the *pueblo* near *Mision Santa Barbara*, building wooden and adobe houses for the many Chumash natives that had come to the Mission from the outlying areas. They reported that hundreds of houses were being built, and that it was reported that similar quantities of houses were being erected at many of the other Mission. It seemed that nearly all of the Chumash natives were happy to assimilate the white man's ways. But in a conversation with *Capitan* Hernadez, they learned that not all, had acquiesced to the intrusion of the white man, for there remained a few rebels among the natives.

Juan did bring good news however, because another letter had finally arrived from Morgan's brother. Morgan quickly opened the seal and began to read:

'February 23, 1806.

My Dearest brother Charles,

It is with great happiness that we learn of your good fortune and your impending marriage. In fact, by the time this letter may reach you, you will likely have already married. If that be the case, congratulations to you, and to your bride Anna Maria. My word, you certainly have become a notable gentleman, to become the husband of the Vice Governor's daughter. May much happiness abound in your union. I am so pleased also, to learn that those Padre people are not as devilish and as untrustworthy as we have heard. Still, one wonders, when realizing that they owe their allegiance to a man in distant Rome. What must their own King believe of their fidelity to him?

You may recall that I was hopeful of becoming an eligible voter. Indeed, I have. I was able to purchase a few acres and a few cattle, thus becoming eligible for the first time. In our national election of '04. Athough I favor the ideals of the

Federalists, I did indeed vote for the re-election of Mr. Jefferson, even though he is of the southern controlled Democrat-Republican party. I did so because I believe that he has many ideals that are compatible with mine. He favors the cause of small farm owners, and in the control our growing national government. He had opposed new taxes, most notably that on whiskey. Now, in many of the States where whiskey distilling is an important activity, they threaten to withdraw from our new Union. Many are speaking of a "whiskey rebellion". There seems to be no end to local concerns. I wonder if we can maintain our Union.

Mr. Jefferson has sent two fine men, Messrs Lewis and Clarke, to survey that new land that was purchased. It was formerly called the Louisiana Territory, but is now broken into several territories. Messrs Lewis and Clarke are traversing this huge tract all the way to the other side of our vast continent. Reports are reaching our news periodicals which describe their heroic exploits. They have an Indian maiden accompanying them and they state that she has been most helpful in preventing difficulties with the Indians tribes which they have encountered. Perhaps if they travel southward to California, you will meet them.

I am unable to determine what news you may be receiving about our Country. We are still at the mercy of England and France. They continue to do battle, (that man Emperor Bonaparte seems intent on controlling the whole of Europe) and in so doing they interfere with our free access to the ocean. Many fear that we will have to use force to maintain our freedom of the seas.

On a more pleasant note, our friends, Nathaniel Aldrich and his wife Becky have removed to Boston, as he has been elected as our Representative. I suppose that next he will try to become a member of our national Congress. I will vote for him, should he decide to do this, as I believe him to be an honorable man, and one with much persuasiveness. That is the kind of man that we need, if our New England concerns are to be promoted.

I am most pleased to report that my wife and child are well. In fact, in just a few more months, my dear wife Harriett expects to deliver to me a second child. How wonderful a woman is she. And our dear daughter Abigail is such a delight to her father. I certainly hope that your marriage will be enriched by children, as they are such a joy.

I hope that we will receive news in the near future of your circumstances. May they be well.

Your loving brother, George.

PS. Our dear sister Mary is well and has of late been pursued by a fine gentleman that has recently located to Sturbridge from Providence in Rhode Island. He had, for a time, attended Brown College there. He is employed by Mr. Putnam in his general store. Mr. Putnam is aging and was in need of a young man to assist him. Our dear Mrs. Pennington is well, though of late is much with deformation of her bones. PPS. Dear Reverend Dawson has been taken by his Maker into the land

of Elijah. We will miss his devout, even if loquacious, sermons.'

Morgan was misty eyed as he thought about his family and the lovely town where he had lived. But he realized, that was past, and now he must insure that his life in his newly adopted land was to be made pleasant for Anna Maria, his daughter and himself. He was sure that he had the power and determination to do just that.

CHAPTER ELEVEN
All is not well.

Although *Mision Santa Ines* was developing well, and *Mision La Purisima Concepcion* was now nearly complete, all was not well at all of the Missions.

Mision San Miguel Arcangel, located to the north, approximately half-way between *La Purisima* and *Carmel*, had had a devastating fire which destroyed not only many of the buildings, but also the entire lot of supplies of woven cloth, tallow, animal hides intended for sale, and the granaries containing many hundreds of bushels of precious wheat. The workshops and the food stocks, as well as needed income, were thus denied to the neophytes and the Spanish craftsmen's families and the Padres.

The more than one thousand residents of the Mission were destitute. It now became the duty of every Mission in the northern sector of the chain to supply food and materials, so that *Mision San Miguel* could survive. Joining with theMissions to the north, *La Purisima, Santa Ines* and *Santa Barbara* rallied to the need, providing much of their own treasuries of wheat, as well as supplying men and materials to begin the reconstruction of the burned-out Mission. Although the cattle herds at *San Miguel* had not been directly affected, there was great confusion about the ranges, with many of the non-Mission natives claiming ownership of much of the herds. There were also private ranch owners who claimed part of the herds as well. Actually, all of the herds had been started when soldiers, Padres and colonists from *Nueva Espanol* had driven the original cattle northward with them more than 25 years earlier.

Over the ensuing years many of the private ranchers had rustled enough cattle to start their own herds, and the non-Mission natives had done the same on a lesser scale. The Padres knew that these rustlers were again taking advantage of the confusion at the Mission and were attempting to steal more of the Mission's property. But the Padre's main concern was the feeding of the thousand Mission inhabitants and it was to be several years before the controversy about the cattle would be finally settled, with the Padres agreeing to relinquish their claim so long as no more rustling would occur. If it did continue, the *soldatos* at the *Presidio* would be called in on a larger scale to settle the matter.

Although *Mision San Francisco de Asis* was attempting to do its part in offering assistance to *Mision San Miguel,* it was having many difficulties of its own. At this Mission there were also over one thousand natives living on the Mission grounds, most assisting in the daily chores of the Mission. But some were less than cooperative. The latter fought amongst themselves as well as antagonized the neophytes about their new religion. It became necessary for the *soldatos* of the *Presidio* to often apprehend the trouble makers, usually inflicting severe floggings as punishment. Resentment among the natives was growing.

Actually, this resentment had manifested itself several years earlier at *San Miguel Arcangel* in the poisoning of three Padres, ostensibly by natives. As soon as it was realized that the cause of the Padre's illness was poison, many of the native women prepared antidotes in the form of natural herbs and medicinal plant concoctions. These treatments did bring about the recuperation of two of the Padres, but one, Padre Ernesto Medina, died a painful death a few days after the poison had been concealed in their evening meal. These three Padres, all relatively young, had only recently arrived at the Mission and were awaiting assignment of duties by Padre Martin. The only reason that Martin himself was not poisoned was that he had omitted supper, instead remaining in his study praying that the troubles of the Mission would come to an end.

When the *soldatos* determined which of the natives had committed the heinous offenses, they chased the culprits, overtaking them at the ocean's edge. One of the accused tried to flee by taking to the ocean and was drowned. The other two were captured and taken to the *Presidio* at Santa Barbara and were hanged. Their trial was very brief. The court officer decided that the fact that the three had fled the Mission immediately after the condition of the Padres was determined to have been caused by poisoning, was in itself proof of their guilt.

Adding further to the many difficulties of the Mission system, at about this time European diseases were beginning to afflict the previously immune natives. A measles epidemic broke out which infected over two hundred of the natives at *Mision San Francisco*, many being felled fatally. Through it all, the Padres were sure that *Todopderoso Dios* would provide the means to solve each problem and to inspire them to convert every native. They determined to overcome each and every obstacle that came their way, and they largely did so.

Edward G. Schultz

As news of each of these calamities would reach *Rancho del Sol*, Morgan would react with great concern and offer to do all that he and his small group of workers could do to alleviate the suffering of the neophytes. Anna Maria too, wished to assist in these humanitarian efforts, but she was more realistic. She was greatly concerned about the survival of their own ranch. Often she chided Morgan to let the Padres attend to their problems, and reminded him of their needs and of their future. Morgan would reluctantly agree that her assessment of the situation was correct, but he was always uncomfortable because he could not give more assistance to the Missions.

Meanwhile Anna Maria's *tia* Carmelita had been showing signs of gradually declining health and in the spring of 1808 she told Anna Maria and Morgan that she would like to return to *Nueva Espanol* where she had sisters and brothers living in *Ciudad de Mejico*. There she could also obtain medical attention, a necessity which was still virtually non-existent in *Alta California*. Reluctantly, they brought her to *Santa Barbara*, where they and her sister Consuela and her brother-in-law the Vice Governor, all bade her farewell. Placing her in a burro-drawn cart, two neophytes and two soldiers accompanied her as they began the long journey to Mexico City.

Anna Maria had previously hired a lovely native girl, one who had been given the name Martha at her Catholic baptism, in honor of she who had been a friend to Jesus. Martha was to be the new nursemaid for the child Maria Consuela, who was now a little more than one year old. Morgan and Anna Maria were pleased with the way that Martha coddled Maria

Consuela and were confident in her ability as a nursemaid and pleased by her love for their child.

A few months after *tia* Carmelita had left, word came from *Mision La Purisima* that Morgan's friend Cimkonah had suddenly passed away. Morgan was greatly saddened and said that he wanted to go to *La Purisima* for the funeral Mass and burial. Anna Maria agreed, and feeling confidence at leaving the baby with Martha, she accompanied her husband, as did Juan Bautista.

When they arrived they found Padre Payeras to be in great sorrow. Though Cimkonah had never accepted baptism, she had been his cook and housemaid for over twenty years, since shortly after the founding of *Mision La Purisima* in 1787. Padre Gutierrez, Morgan and many others, tried to comfort Payeras, but he seemed inconsolable. Nevertheless, on the morning of Cimkonah's funeral, Payeras was prepared to celebrate her funeral Mass, and to recite the burial prayers.

The church was again overflowing, for everyone wanted to make their last farewell to the lovely woman. Padre Payeras delivered a tearful eulogy, then the procession moved slowly to the native cemetery, where Cimkonah was buried nearby Angelica and her baby, who had died nearly five years earlier.

Morgan told Anna Maria that he wished to remain at *La Purisima* for another day or two, to visit and chat with the many friends that he had made while working there. She agreed and told him that they would stay as long as he would like. On the first morning after Cimkonah's burial, Morgan escorted

Anna Maria around the Mission, for she had never seen it before. As they ambled along, Morgan proudly identified the many items that he had made in the blacksmith shop, as if they were the most important features of the many buildings. Anna Maria smilingly agreed that without these necessities, the Mission would indeed be only a frontier site, instead of the busy *pueblo*-like establishment that it was. As Morgan walked along the colonnaded plaza he reminisced about the events that had occurred many years ago. He showed Anna Maria the storage bin where he had spent his first night, the schoolroom where the children were given their Spanish language lessons and where they learned their Catechism by rote, under the tutelage of the wives of the Spanish craftsmen. He recalled vividly, though he did not mention it to Anna Maria, the first day that he saw Angelica in that semi-dark schoolroom, squatting as she recited her lessons along with the other neophyte children.

During their strolls, as they met Padre Payeras who paced as he read his *officio* prayers, they smiled and hoped that he was adjusting to the cooking of a new housekeeper. He appeared to have finally accepted Cimkonah's death, and they knew that he was no doubt offering prayers to Almighty God for the repose of her soul in heaven.

During the afternoon, Anna Maria stayed by herself. She had already seen that the people of this Mission had great respect for her husband and she was proud and happy at this. As Morgan continued to wandered freely about the Mission, renewing more old friendships, Anna Maria sat on a bench under the arbor, reading and enjoying the solitude. Late in the second afternoon Morgan joined her. They were discussing their planned departure the next morning, when they were suddenly and greatly surprised.

"Sharlezz, Sharlezz", some one was calling. Morgan turned and exclaimed, "My God, is that you Manuel? I can't believe that it's you. Where did you come from?" "Yes, it is I". Padre Castellanos replied, "I am so happy to see you again *mi amigo Sharlezz*." Morgan was astonished. He didn't know if he could believe his eyes. "Manuel", he said, "how long has it been since we parted in San Francisco, two years?"

The priest replied, "Yes *Sharlezz*, about two years. But I only recently learned of your marriage and I sought permission to come here to see you and your bride and to offer my congratulations, and my blessing if you will allow me. But on my journey here I learned of the death of dear Cimkonah. Alas, I arrived too late for her funeral. May her soul rest in peace." Morgan had caught the word 'permission'. He asked, "When you say that you sought permission, does that mean that you are still a priest, Manuel? You are still in good standing? I notice that you are still wearing your Franciscan robe. I was about to ask you about that." "Yes", the young Padre replied, "I am still a member of the Orders Of Friars Minor. Let me tell you the amazing story. Oh, *Sharlezz*, I am so happy. How wonderous is the plan of *Dios Todopoderoso*. He has granted every wish that I sought, and more."

The young priest was speaking hurriedly and excitedly, but when he stopped to draw a breath, Anna Maria interrupted. She had been sitting close by impatiently, but finally broke in, *"Sharlezz,* are you not going to introduce your spouse to Padre Castellanos?"

Morgan rose, as did Castellanos. "Oh, I am so sorry Anna Maria. I became so engrossed in Padre Manuel's explanation that I inexcusably forgot your presence here. Padre Manuel, this is my beloved wife, Anna Maria." Castellanos bowed and offered, "*Buenos Tardas*, *Senora* Morgan, I am most happy to make your acquaintance." Morgan said to Anna Maria, "Our old and dear friend Padre Manuel Castellanos has come to visit us and to offer his congratulations and his blessing on our marriage." Anna Marie, looking doubtful, replied, "Oh, so we are to be blessed by one who has been defective in his duties? Will that help our marriage more than the blessing of Padre Payeras at the time of the making of our vows." Morgan was shocked. "Anna Maria!, Padre Manuel has come here in good graces, to express his best wishes for our happy marriage. He is fully competent in the eyes of the Church, to grant us his blessing. He is a priest of the Church."

With this, Anna Marie appeared to be a little less indignant about the matter, but was still cool to the young priest's presence. Castellanos bowed slightly, saying, "*Senora* Morgan, I am very happy that you and *Sharlezz* have received the Sacrament of Matrimony within the cannons of the Church. It is not my intention to demean your bond of matrimony. Your husband has been a very good friend to me. I hope that our friendship will continue, and that you and I will also become friends. I am also informed that you have a beautiful girl child. I hope that before my return to San Francisco I will have an opportunity to see this wonderful blessing." Coolly, Anna Maria replied, "*Si*, that would be lovely", but she withdrew a little more as if to make it obvious that she still did not fully accept Castellanos' friendship.

At Morgan's insistence, Castellanos now continued to relate his story. After he had left Morgan in San Francisco he ambled throughout the *pueblo*, wondering what he would do with his life. As he roamed, people seeing his priestly robe, sought his advise, and in many cases forgiveness, through the sacrament of confession. The young priest was amazed at how many individuals felt that they were in need of counseling, or wished to be advised on how to amend their sinful practices and find a new purpose in life. Most, he felt, were truly repentant, but could not bring themselves to enter the Mission compound to seek forgiveness in a formal Confessional box. The young priest suddenly became aware of the good that he could do outside of the Mission compound.

After several weeks of such activity, Castellanos realized that he must report his presence and his new found ministry to the Padre Pastor at *Mision San Francisco de Asis.* Padre Francisco Palou proved to be a very understanding man. He allowed Padre Castellanos to continue his work among the downcast, but only until Palou would write to Padre *Presidente* Lasuen to apprise him of the situation and to determine if Castellanos would be granted permission from the*Padre Presidente* for this outside ministry. He urged Castellanos to return to the Mission compound each night so as to perform his necessary Vesper prayers and readings. He also was to celebrate Mass each morning before venturing into the *pueblo.* Castellanos gladly accepted these conditions.

Upon learning of Castellanos' return to the *Mision San Francisco de Asis,* Lasuen himself traveled there to apologize to Castellanos for his earlier lack of understanding of Padre Castellanos' concerns. He assured the young Padre that he was very pleased that Castellanos had remained true to his vows. And Padre Lasuen did grant his permission for Castellanos to continue in this new ministry, for the time being.

"Sharlezz, since that time I have had many, many wonderful experiences." The young Padre was elated. "I truly believe that I am fulfilling the will of God by being allowed to minister to those souls that had fallen away from the Church, or who have never before felt the need for God in their lives. Oh, this ministry is so fulfilling to me. I am exhilarated with my priestly responsibilities as I have never been before. I am exceedingly grateful to God, to Padres Lasuen and Palou, and to you too, *mi amigo.* You were so very understanding of my dilemma. And now, since my return here, Padre Payeras and I have spoken and are supportive of each other's role."

Morgan was almost speechless. He shook his head several times, trying to absorb the sudden turn of events, and trying to find the words to express to Castellanos his joy that the priest was finally experiencing the fulfillment that had evaded him for so many years.

Juan had joined the group shortly after Castellanos approached Morgan, so he heard most of the priest's narration. But Castellanos continued, *"Sharlezz,* Juan, had you heard of the epidemic of measles that had broken out last year at *Mision San Francisco?"* The two replied, *"Si",* that they had heard.

The priest elaborated, "We realized what the disease was, because many of we Spaniards, including myself, had had this ailment when we were young. We recognized the symptoms, and because we were previously afflicted we knew that we were now immune, so we worked among the sick, attempting to ease their pain and fever. While we could not of course, cure the disease, we did treat them using concoctions made by many native women, from plants and berries. It did indeed relieve the high body temperature, and the lotion they prepared eased the itching of the skin. We would not let those not afflicted go near those who were, so we Padres were the ones that labored among the sick. Unfortunately, many neophytes did die in spite of our efforts. Did you know that some of the *Misions* have established infirmaries and have sought to bring nurses from *Nueva Espana* to staff them? I am urging Padre Palou to build one at our *Mision*."

Morgan and Juan were fascinated by the experiences of their friend. Castellanos then offered "Let us renew the friendship that we three enjoyed in our days together at *Mision La Purisima*." The three continued talking for a long time, unintentionally excluding Anna Maria. Then Castellanos raised another matter, that of his sister's visit. "I understand, *Sharlezz*, that my sister Elena visited *Mision Santa Ines*, but returned to Santa Barbara. Can you tell me anything of her visit?" With this, Anna Maria looked up sharply, while Morgan looked a little embarrassed. He hoped that this embarrassment was not recognized by Castellanos. "Yes", Morgan replied, "Elena did visit *Santa Ines* for a few days, but returned to Santa

Barbara, and I am quite sure that she departed soon after to San Diego and a return voyage to Spain."

Castellanos looked disappointed. "*Sharlezz,* I am greatly disappointed that I was not here to meet her. But I am even more disappointed that she left thinking that I had disowned my vows. For surely you must have told her of our experiences at *Mision San Carlos Borromeo* and in San Francisco." Morgan reluctantly agreed, "Yes, Manuel, I did relate to her our meeting with *Padre Presidente* Lasuen, and of our short time in San Francisco *pueblo.* I'm afraid that she did leave very disappointed. I think now, Manuel, that you should write her immediately, explaining your new circumstances. I'm sure that she will be most pleased." "*Si, si, Sharlezz*, I will indeed write her and hope that a messenger will carry this letter to Santa Barbara immediately. I know that Elena must be distressed and that she will be joyous to learn of my fidelity. I'm afraid that she, like many others, had doubts about my fortitude."

Anna Maria was very attentive throughout this part of the discussion. At one point Morgan was sure that she would inject her own thoughts about Elena, but fortunately Anna Maria remained silent. Perhaps that was because of a glance or two that Morgan had given her during the dialogue.

Soon Castellanos reluctantly ended the discussion by stating, "I wish to again converse with Padre Payeras and then I will depart for *Mision Santa Ines* to confer with Padre de Uria. Following this I will be returning to *Mision San Francisco*, where my services are needed among the neophytes and others. But before I depart the area, I would be very happy to visit your *hacienda* and to see the blessed child that God has given you." Morgan smiled his agreement, but showing obvious relief, Anna Maria said, "Oh, then you are not remaining in this area? Well, may God be with you in your journey and in your missionary efforts. I will bid you *adios* now in case you do not find the time to visit our *ranchero.*" Castellanos gave Morgan and Juan a warm handshake, and with a bow to Anna Maria, left the arbor.

The next day Morgan, Anna Maria and Juan all attended the morning Mass, following which they bade farewell to Padre Payeras, expressing assurances to each other that they would visit more often. On their return journey to *Rancho del Sol,* the matter of Padre Manuel's integrity and Elena's conduct was discussed by Morgan and Anna Maria. She remained convinced that the young priest was not sincere. For Morgan's part, he felt it necessary to criticize Anna Maria's ungraciousness towards Manuel. It was not an enjoyable journey. Juan Bautista rode along behind them, not daring to intrude.

Later that evening Morgan and Anna Maria had more words on the matter of Castellanos. She stated that she was surprised that he would want to remain friendly with a man that had disgraced his priesthood. She repeated her suspicions as to his conduct when outside the Mission walls. She reminded Morgan that it was common knowledge that Castellanos' father had secured his ordination under strange circumstances. Morgan was very upset with her. He tried to convince her that Castellanos was a dedicated priest, no matter what the past. At bedtime they had not reconciled. It was the first night since their marriage that they did not share the same bed.

As Morgan thought about the matter during the next few days he wondered if Anna Maria was truly indignant about Castellanos' unorthodox duties and his past, or was she actually jealous that Morgan was befriending him. Now he thought about small comments that she had also made in the past about Juan. He was now beginning to see Anna Maria in her haughty socialite, and jealous personality. He had never noticed this in her before.

When the party of three had returned from *La Purisima* one of Morgan's Spanish cattle-tenders told him of an incident involving neighboring rancher Humberto Ruiz. It seems that several Padres and other Spaniards from *Nueva Espanol,* who were trekking northward on *El Camino Real,* had been threatened by Ruiz and a few of his men. They had ordered the group of travelers off his land. *El Camino Real* traversed both Ruiz' and Morgan's property, but the trail was considered to be available for use by all. In this incident, the Padres in the group insisted that they had a right to pass on the trail. One of Ruiz' men had fired his musket over their heads in warning, but the Padres and the people in attendance with them, continued to follow *El Camino Real*, since it was "the King's Road". In the end, Ruiz relented and returned to his *hacienda.*

Hearing this, Morgan was very upset. He and Juan once more rode to Ruiz' home. Morgan stated that he would never close the portion of *El Camino Real* that traversed his property, that Ruiz should not do so either, and that, if necessary, he would see to it that *soldatos* from the *Presidio* would enforce the freedom of the trail. Ruiz snorted something to the effect that Morgan was using the office of his father-in-law as a threat, but when slamming the door in Morgan and Juan's face, it was obvious by Ruiz's facial expression that he wanted no trouble with the officials.

A few days later Padre Manuel rode up to the *hacienda* and was greeted warmly by Morgan. "I have come hoping that I might see your child. Will Anna Maria permit me to do so?", the priest asked. "Why, certainly, Manuel. We are honored that you came so far to visit us." He called to Anna Maria. "Anna Maria!, Padre Manuel is here. He wishes to give his blessing to our family. Do bring Maria Consuela." Anna Maria came to the door, quickly followed by Martha carrying the baby. Morgan was pensive about the meeting but Anna Maria remained pleasant.

They all sat on the *veranda* cooing at the baby and laughing each time that the baby smiled. Soon Padre Manuel rose and said that he must be on his way. Anna Maria took the baby in her arms and held it out to the priest. Padre Manuel smiled broadly, then blessed the child with the customary sign of the cross over the babe's head. Morgan was exceedingly pleased. Then he was completely surprised when Anna Maria knelt before the priest and motioned for Morgan to join her. With tears in his eyes, the young priest offered his blessing to the two of them, then also to Juan and Martha, and left without another word. Once again, a baby had brought reconciliation. Morgan squeezed Anna Maria's hand gently and nodded his thanks to her. The women then took the baby into the *hacienda* and the men left for the yard.

A few days later, in the morning as was his custom, Juan went into the kitchen of the Morgan's *hacienda* to receive his cup of coffee from Martha. As he sat and began to sip, he suddenly realized that Martha was smiling coyly. "What is so *gustoso*?" he asked. "Oh", she replied smugly, "last evening only one bed was used." Juan stood quickly, gave Martha a hug, and said, "Oh! That is *maravilloso!* Now perhaps we can converse with them without receiving dogbarks in return." "*Si!,* Martha replied, "this morning they are both smiling broadly. It has been nearly two weeks of *infierno* for us"

No sooner had they finished their comments when Morgan entered the kitchen to secure his customary cup of coffee. He realized that both Martha and Juan were smiling broadly at him. He blushed, "Well, I suppose that you now know that *Senora* Morgan and I slept in our bed together. *Si!,* we have reconciled All is *bueno*. We have mutually agreed that each of us is too stubborn, but now we are one again. Now Juan, let's get to work."

Some time later, one of Morgan's ranch-hands stated that he believed that Ruiz' men had rustled some of Morgan's cattle. Having no way to prove this theft, Morgan decided that he needed a future means to insure against this kind of thievery. Since his cattle herd was only a few hundred head at this time, he ordered that all of his cattle to be branded. He fashioned a branding iron with the symbol of the sun and its rays, as his mark. It was the first time that it was found necessary to brand cattle in *Alta California*.

Due to the size of the extensive Mission herds however, often in the tens of thousands, it was not feasible for them to be branded. The Padres were required, however, to report their holdings to the *Padre Presidente* on an annual basis. These annual reports, which also had to include the number of other animals, quantities of field produce, and of course, the number of baptized neophytes, were required by the Viceroy of *Nuevo Espana*, who then forwarded the information to King Ferdinand VII. Thus was the bureaucracy of the extensive Spanish domain.

At this time, however, King Ferdinand had much more to worry about than the holdings of the far away Catholic Missions in *Nuevo Espana* and Alta California. When the soldiers that were accompanying *tia* Carmelita to Mexico City arrived there, they found the city to be in great confusion. Word had just arrived that Napoleon Bonaparte had captured Spain, forcing Ferdinand to abdicate his recently acquired throne. Napoleon then appointed his brother Joseph Bonaparte as King of Spain. This was the culmination of many decades of war between England and Spain, in which Napoleon Bonaparte had at first allied France with Spain, but now turned against her.

In *Nuevo Espana* unrest had also been growing, but having nothing to do directly with the mother country's difficulties. For more than two centuries now, New Spain had been governed by a Viceroy, the King's representative. But during the latter several decades, a gradual desire for independence had been growing. Demands for changes in the methods of governing this far-away province of Spain were being promoted by many.

Several classes of social distinction had developed. Those who were born in Spain, the most influential in governing and in cultural matters, were called *peninsulars,* and were the highest of the several classes. Those who were of Spanish heritage, but born in *Nueva Espana*, were called *creoles,* and were restricted to only lower positions which they could hold in government or in the Church. Lowest of all were Spaniards who had married natives. These and the children of their marriages were called *mestizos.* The latter, and the black slaves that had been imported from Africa, were the servants and laborers for the wealthy, or forced to work as farm-hands in the extensive fields of wealthy landowners.

When news of the King's abdication was received in Mexico City, many of the *creoles* and *mestizos* began to speak of independence from Spain. But the army still remained loyal to the King's Viceroy and enforced his rule over the country. The underlying unrest, however, could not be eliminated, and it continued to foment.

As the news of the situation in Spain and of the unrest in *Nuevo Espana* reached the *Misions* and the *Presidios* in Alta California, it caused great concern in these pilgrim lands. Morgan's father-in-law was not immune from this consternation. He, being a *peninsular,* was worried about what his future might be, should the *creole* elements in New Spain gain control. While he had much wealth in personal land holdings in Alta California, any change in the government in Mexico City could possibly eliminate his land grants and his power.

To Morgan, however, this all seemed to be a far-away matter, having little if anything to do with his life, his land, or "his" Missions. The future would, of course, prove him wrong in this unrealistic attitude. Being somewhat remote from the main seat of government in Mexico City did have its advantages. One such advantage was in not knowing every intimate detail of the intrigues that were taking place there. But it would be several more years before any effective revolt would change the country's controlling element. The years, however, were slipping away quickly. Morgan was just too busy developing his *rancho* and his livestock herd to realize this fact.

He kept very busy working at expanding his herd. He diligently made sure that every heifer was sired as soon as she became mature enough, and every cow reimpregnated as soon as was possible. Every bull was utilized fully and more and more calves were gamboling on the ranch.

In between his ranching activities he would occasionally receive a summons from either Padre Payeras or Padre de Uria to supervise the repair of a water duct, a break in a dam, to expand the reservoirs, or assist in mending a building or a roof. Morgan would gladly oblige these requests and then offer to do more.

Each of the Missions continued to enlarge their compounds. More and more of the native populous were coming into the Missions for their sustenance. Almost daily, natives from the eastern hills or from the areas to the north would walk into one of the Missions, seeking food and shelter. They were of the belief that their traditional methods of survival were more arduous than the work at the Missions, for it was not easy to hunt in the hills for deer meat, or to combat bears, or to grow the produce in the crude ways as their forebears had done. But after being indoctrinated into the servile tasks as assigned by the Mission padres, they realized that the foraging methods developed by the many generations that had preceded them, might have been less invasive to their accustomed life skills. Although they realized this fact belatedly, most nevertheless remained at the Missions, subservient to the padres.

At *Rancho del Sol,* by 1810 Morgan felt that he could now slaughter some of his herd, which had grown to nearly one thousand head, and to offer the hides to the American merchants that were now patrolling the coastal areas in search of such hides. More and more often, American vessels were sighted off the coast and more of their agents were plying the *pueblos* and *ranchos* in search of hides to purchase. Now too, he was able to sell his meat products to some of the Missions as well as to cure much of it for sale in the *pueblos* of San Francisco or Santa Barbara. Other products could also be sold; the tallow for candle-making and the casein for making cheeses were always in demand.

After the slaughter, however, the hides had to be stretched and dried. This was an arduous task requiring much labor and much space as well, for each hide had to be tied to stakes and suspended in air to dry in the sun. Prior to this stretching, however, there was much scraping of meat residue and soaking of the hides in order to insure their proper preservation.

The stretching also made the hides flat so that they could be stowed below decks in the cargo vessels, in preparation for their long voyage to the eastern coast of the United States, or even to Europe. The increasing populations of both America and Europe required more and more leather for boot making, more saddles, more ladies purses and even more clothing made of leather.

After the slaughter and the drying operations, which took several months in the dry summer weather, the hides had to be stored and protected from the rainy season. Morgan, like other ranchers, had to build large barn-like structures in which the hides could be piled. Morgan's remembrance of the New England barns was useful, but the available material in *Alta California* was different. Nevertheless, he instructed his laborers in which material to gather. Large pine trees to be used as vertical corner posts had to felled first, followed by smaller trees for the roof beams. The sides and the roof were not of wood, but rather of tules that were gathered along the coast, and pine tree branches that were plentiful in nearby forests. Morgan had decided to construct his barn near the coast, at the top of a cliff-like projection. Morgan had conceived of a method to get the hides to the shore without much effort. His idea was yet to be tested.

The hides would need to be loaded into the Yankees dinghies, from where they would then be ferried to the larger craft in the deep water. If the larger vessel were to be loaded too close to shore it would likely become mired in the sandy ocean bottom and unable to sail.

One day, when the barn was very near completion, three horsemen were seen approaching.

231

Soon it was able to be discerned that one was Ruiz, Morgan's irascible neighbor. Morgan bristled, expecting trouble of some kind. But Ruiz only came to chide Morgan.

"So, you think you are going to be able to trade with the *Yanquis*?", Ruiz taunted. "*Si,* I expect so", was Morgan's unruffled reply. "Why do you think that it is not possible? They need the hides, and I have many to offer. Are you not also intending to trade with the yankees?"

Ruiz only sneered in contempt, "Oh, I got plenty of hides to sell. Many more than you, but the agents only want to trade with the Missions, 'cause there they got hides by the many thousands. Why, a ship can be filled with just one trade. Why would the agents want to deal with a small-timer like you?" But Morgan's reply indicated his lack of concern with Ruiz' reasoning. "Oh, agents will seek me out, I am sure. And I can get a good price for my fine hides. I have no doubt."

Again Ruiz' reply was intended to demean Morgan. "Oh yes, if I had a father-in-law that was a Vice Governor, I could demand that *yanqui* agents buy up my load too!" To this Morgan made no reply. Then Ruiz added, "Besides, you have a long way to tote those hides to the beach so's the *yanquis* can load them on their dories. The only way to get down there is by that long wagon road to the north, 'cause I ain't gonna let ya use the shorter trail across my property." Morgan again offered a reply without showing any concern, "Oh, I'm gonna get them down to the beach below real easy, and I don't need to cross over your property either." Then Morgan turned his back to Ruiz and continued to work on the barn structure. As he did so he thought to himself, "I'd better get a good price for these hides, because I sure want to make some pay-back to Vice Governor Ortega after all these years." Although he knew that Ortega did not need or expect the payment, Morgan's self-esteem required him make such a payment.

CHAPTER TWELVE
Is the world coming to an end?

Following the two weeks or so in 1808 when Morgan and Anna Maria had had their short marital difficulty, their conjugal relations had been very fine. Morgan's management of their land and herds had led to income by sales to *yanquis*, the Mexican Army and to a few northern ranchers. Some of the transactions were by barter but nevertheless, they profited the overall operation of *Rancho del Sol.* Anna Maria was very proud of her husband's industriousness, and his skill in ranching and farming. She was also pleased that her father expressed his pride in the fine young man that *he* had selected for her, and in his conscientious obligation to repay the Vice Governor for the loan that Morgan had received following his marriage to Anna Maria.

All seemed to be going as planned, or at least, going quite well. By early 1809 Anna Maria was again pregnant. Their daughter Maria Consuela was now almost two years old and was a happy child, showing good intelligence, good health and was a joy to both parents and to Martha, her *ninera*. Juan Bautisita too, enjoyed playing with the child and as young as she was, he often gave her a ride, while carefully holding her, on the back of a pony. As the child giggled and tried to spur the pony to more speed, Juan would laugh and call to Morgan so that he would not miss seeing the child's early skill at horsemanship.

On the 12th of September in that year, Carlos Mariano was born, being named for his father and

Padre Mariano Payeras. Anna Maria agreed to the names, but at the baptism, performed by Payeras, and in the Spanish tradition, she had the Padre include the name Juan, ahead of Mariano, to honor her father as well. In fact, the Vice-Governor and his *Senora* had traveled to *La Paurisima* for the rite. Payeras and all of the Mission's residents were honored that the Vice-Governor had traveled the distance from Santa Barbara to attend this baptism. Due to the Vice Governor's presence. many special events were held in his honor and an atmosphere of *fiesta* pervaded the Mission for several days.

La Purisima, as well as all of the Channel Missions, were enjoying great success in their work of converting the Chumash natives to the Catholic faith. The extent of their land holdings and the resultant expansion of cattle herds and other animals were flourishing. The annual reports reaching the Padre *Presidente* were very exciting to the entire Franciscan Order. Even the Governor of *Nueva Espana* was most pleased, not only because the Missions were flourishing, but more importantly, because he recognized the monetary value of "his" kingdom.

The fall harvest of wheat and its stockpiling went on without any weather problems and the Missions were preparing for their winter activities. Morgan and his ranch hands were doing the same. During the more relaxed winter months Morgan thought that he should be planning the next phase of his expansion. He had sold his first lot of hides to the *yanqui* traders at a good price. Why not? They were very good hides and had been treated and stretched well. And his plan to get the hides to the beach worked very well. When Ruiz had chided him about the long wagon road to the north to reach the beach down below, Morgan already knew how he would overcome that obstacle. He simply had his men fling the hides over the edge of the precipice and let them sail down to the sand. As the wind caused the hides to float to and fro, the *yanqui* sailors laughed and chased them as they fell to earth. It took several days for the loading of the dories and transfer of the hides to their brig. When these same brigs had arrived from the eastern part of the continent they were loaded with items that those in the west would want or need. The Spanish ladies of the Missions and *pueblos* were especially anxious to obtain material with which to make new clothing, needles and thread, feathers for decorating their hats and clothing, and if they were wealthy enough, they bought the clothing and the latest hats already made. These were from the new United States. As trade with these brigs increased, more news from the United States would be brought to the Missions and *pueblos* by the *yanqui* sailors.

For his part, Morgan was always on the watch for a brig that would be returning to Boston or New Bedford. In the late fall of 1812 he learned of such a ship in Monterey, the *Paul Revere.* He already had prepared a letter to his brother George to announce the birth of Carlos Juan Mariano, explaining the boy's name, and providing a report of his success as a rancher. He also mentioned the reports from *Nueva España* regarding the political intrigues there, and expressed hope that *Alta California* would not be drawn into any possible conflict between Spain and its territorial government in what was being referred to more and more often as *Mejico*, instead of *Nueva Espana*.

Morgan did not feel that he could leave *Rancho del Sol* himself to bring the letter to Monterey, nor did he trust one his ranch-hands with such an important document, so he sent Juan, instructing him to find a trustworthy sailor to deliver the letter to his brother George at Sturbridge. On the outside of the letter he wrote a note promising that whoever delivered the letter would be rewarded by George with payment of two dollars. Though the payment was expensive, he knew that his brother would honor the promise.

After Juan Bautista had left on foot for the northern sea-port, Anna Maria told Morgan that he was foolish to have entrusted such an important matter to Juan, suggesting that Juan would likely seize the opportunity to drink and become involved with a woman. Morgan was dismayed that Anna Maria would say such a thing. "Has he ever given us reason to believe that he would conduct himself in such a manner?", Morgan asked. "Perhaps not", she replied, "but you know how a person can betray themselves when tempted. He just has not yet seen such allurement." Morgan then remembered his own seducement by Elena Castellanos, and his fall from grace, but he replied, "I do not feel that we need concern ourselves about Juan's loyalty. He will not fail me." Now he was again thinking of Anna Maria's sometimes earlier derogatory comments regarding Juan and wondering why she felt so. Anna Maria confirmed his fears. She replied, "I do not like the man. He is always about when we should have our privacy. Why must he always be like a shadow to you? Can we not discuss our affairs without him being within hearing distance?"

Morgan thought a minute, then admitting to himself that what she said might be true, he said, "Now that you bring this to my attention, you are correct. I had not realized how much I consider Juan to be my brother. But even a brother has no need to know everything of his brothers marriage and personal business. I'm sorry that you feel that he is an intruder, Anna Maria, I'll talk to Juan when he returns, to clarify our relationship." As Anna Maria turned to leave the room, she replied, "If he returns!" Now Morgan was even more agitated by her remarks. He thought, 'she not only doesn't like Juan's nearness, she seems to dislike him in total. Why would she feel like this? Has he ever given her reason to form such an opinion about a person that I see as a very fine person, one with good morals.'

One person that seemed to trust Juan and enjoy his presence was the child Maria Consuela. She had learned to speak a few words and one of the earliest was "'wan". Perhaps she had spoken this word before saying "*madre*". Perhaps Anna Maria was jealous because Maria Consuela showed this love for Juan.

As Morgan sat one evening with Maria Consuela on his lap and playing with her fingers, he began to wonder about Juan. It had been a considerable time since he had left for Monterey. Let's see, was it now five, or six weeks since his departure? Did he find the ship *Paul Revere*? Did he locate a seaman that seemed trustworthy and willing to take the responsibility of the delivery to the inland town? Twice before Morgan had been lucky enough to find such a seaman. Would Juan find one like those earlier couriers? Morgan wondered if his decision to send Juan on his journey on foot was a wise one. He had felt that every available horse was needed at the ranch for its many daily activities. Of course walking to Monterey would take three or four times longer than riding there. He had given Anna Maria more reason to question Juan's timing. And Anna Maria seemed to be looking for opportunities to criticize Juan Bautista. Morgan was getting annoyed by her often petty comments. He now realized that upon Juan's return, he must somehow arbitrate the matter.

On the evening of December 19, 1812, Morgan sat bouncing Maria Consuela on his knees, when there seemed to be some movement of his chair, more than he was caused by his joyful leg action. At first he ignored it, but very soon another movement occurred, this time stronger and of longer duration. He quickly raised Maria Consuela to his chest, holding her tightly and shouting, "Anna Maria!, Martha!, did you feel something?" From two other rooms came simultaneous and excited replies, "Yes! What is it? Why is the *hacienda* shaking?" The two women ran to where Morgan was. Martha was holding Carlos Juan close to her. "*Sharlezz!* What is it. What is happening?". Anna Maria spoke with great alarm, "What could be causing the *casa* to shake so?" The group gathered together in the center of the large sitting room. With great concern in his voice, Morgan said loudly, "I think it's an earthquake! Quick! Take cover under the *grande tablon!* Protect the babies under your bodies! Take care not to smother them! If this tremor continues

239

some of the ceiling may fall, even the roof! Remain under the table until the shaking stops!"

Morgan himself ran outside to see if he could determine the extent of any damage. He surveyed the sides of the *hacienda,* then the outbuildings. All had obvious damage, though not severe. Many of the ranch hands were also standing outside peering. He called to them, "Go back inside! Take cover under the strongest part of the roof, under the beams!". Just as he turned to return inside the house a tremor that was many more times severe than the first two struck, shaking down one wall of the hacienda and its adjacent corners, leaving a part of the roof overhanging by rafters that were connected to the remainder of the roof. "Oh my God", thought Morgan as he ran inside. Finding that the women had done exactly as he had ordered, he joined them on the floor, trying to use his body to shield all of them. "We can only wait and hope that the tremors will end *pronto!"* he told them. Anna Maria began to pray, *"Oh Todopoderoso Dios, clemencia! clemencia! Santo Maria, protectionismo!"* Martha also began to pray, joining Anna Maria by repeating each utterance. Morgan prayed too, but silently, with the hope that the earthquake would end soon, and without any more damage to his home and buildings. Then he wondered, 'How widespread is this thing? Are the Missions going to feel it also?'

At *Mision* La Purisima and *Mision* Santa Ines, it was the fourth evening of the *posados.* Nearly everyone at both Missions were outside in the courtyards, making the slow procession from one craftsmen's home to the next. Every Spanish man and woman, their children, and almost all of the neophyte population were taking part in the traditional Christmas procession, with the Padres nearby, watching and enjoying the *jubilo*. When the tremors started, panic ensued among the many hundreds, all running back to their abode. The Padres also ran to their quarters, shouting as they ran, "Take cover! Take cover! *Proteccionismo!*"

After what seemed like an hour, but what was in fact only about ten or twelve minutes of severe intermittent tremors, much of the Mission buildings were greatly damaged. The inhabitants shuddered all through the night, wondering if the world was coming to an end. But the next morning, as everyone emerged, still alive, the extent of the damage could be ascertained by daylight. Seeing the terrible amount of damage, some of the Spanish craftsmen told the Padres that repair was not possible, that the damage was far too extensive for them to correct. The neophytes, too, stood by shaking their heads, thus indicating that they did not believe that repair was possible. But the Padres, having retrieved their sacred vessels from the destroyed church, celebrated a Mass in the open courtyard, which was attended by almost every inhabitant of the Missions. They gave thanks to *Todopoderoso Dios* that no one was killed and that only a few minor injuries had occurred, miraculously they believed. When Morgan arrived the morning after the tremors had occurred, he found the Padres conferring among themselves, already deciding what would be the best plan of restoration. At both Missions, the two-man team of Padres spent several days determining the best plan. Morgan had ridden to both Missions the first day after the earthquake to survey the damage. He told both teams of Padres that he would return soon.

The devastation at *La Purisima* was far more severe than at *Santa Ines*. The *Mision* compound was subject to three distinct tremors, and following the third, a torrent of water rushed through the compound from the dammed-up water higher in the hills.

On the second morning, after instructing his own laborers about the methods of repair to his *hacienda* and other buildings, Morgan rode first to *La Purisima*. He had formulated his plan for restoration, assigning mental priorities to the many tasks that needed to be accomplished. When he arrived at *La Purisima,* he went to what remained of the Padres quarters. There he found Payeras and his associate, Padre Gutierrez, having an avid discussion. Morgan immediately began to describe his plan, but Payeres interrupted him. "We thank you *Sharlezz* for your great concern, and for your thoughtfulness, but we have decided to start the entire *Mision* over." Morgan looked confused. Then Payeras added, "at a new location". Morgan was even more confused, "What do you mean Mariano? At a new location? After twenty-five years, you would relocate the *Mision?*" Payeras continued, "*Si,* from the earliest days of this *Mision* I had felt that it should have been established further inland, for reasons of water access, closer to our grazing lands and closer to *El Camino Real. Si,* on higher ground and further inland will be best. And since it appears to be generally agreed that this *Mision* is beyond repair, what better time to take advantage of the desire of *Todopodero Dios?"*

Morgan could offer no intelligible rebuttal. He simply shrugged and said, "Mariano, you always seem to know what is best. If I can be of service, please tell me. And my very best wishes to you both as you carry out God's wishes." With a few more words and an *"adios"*, Morgan then rode to *Mision* Santa Ines, where he again offered his help to Padre de Uria. Here too, the Padres had celebrated a Mass of thanksgiving that no one was killed. DeUria was more willing to let Morgan describe his plan for restoration of the Mission on the same ground. The two Padres, Morgan, and many Spanish craftsmen conferred, deciding on what items were repairable and the priority of the repairs. First among them was the repairs to the viaduct so that water would once more be readily available to the inhabitants. Morgan agreed to lead a group of the neophytes to accomplish this task. Within a few weeks, the viaducts, the reservoir walls, and the *lavenderio* fountain were all in good repair. Many other tasks were also going forward and within a few months, many walls, roofs, and porticos were well on their way to looking new again. But it would take many more years before the Mission was fullyrestored to its pre-earthquake condition. And the work did not stop there because prior to the earthquake, not all of the planned buildings and shops had ever been finished. So the work continued for many more years. In all of this time the herds of animals and the population of neophytes kept growing.

A few days after the earthquakes, however, Juan Bautista had returned to *Rancho del Sol*. He had not experienced the tremors because the Missions to the north were not affected by the earthquake. He reported to Morgan that he had indeed contacted a sailor on the *Paul Revere* that agreed to deliver the letter all the way to Sturbridge. Morgan was much relieved. Then Juan reported that he had met another sailor, one Tomas Doak, from Boston. "He is at *Mision San Juan Bautista*, just north of Mision San Francisco. He is employed by the Padres there to decorate the *iglesia*. His art is wonderful! I have seen it!" Morgan expressed surprise, "You went to *Mision San Juan Bautista*? You have spoken with this Tomas Doak?" "*Si, si*", replied Juan excitedly, "I have spoken with him. He stated that he is the first *Americano* to settle here in *Alta California*. But I told him that you have been here almost ten years already. He did not believe me." "Well, I shall have to meet him", Morgan replied, "after we have settled the matters of reconstruction here at *Rancho del Sol* and at *Mision Santa Ines*".

It was many months before the repairs to the Morgan *hacienda* and the other buildings of *Rancho del Sol* were completed, and several years before the *Mision Santa Ines* was reconstructed and expanded. And the work went on continuously after that, Including Morgan's periodic assistance, until the full quadrangle compound of the *Mision* was finalized.

But after more than a half-year had passed since the earthquake had occurred, another disaster occurred in the life of Morgan and Anna Maria. This was a very personal disaster, one that would affect their lives forever.

On a beautiful sunny June morning, Juan Bautista and now six year old Maria Consuela had ridden off for a short horseback ride. By now Maria was quite expert at riding the pony that her parents had given her for her sixth birthday one month earlier. She and Juan had taken such a morning gallop almost daily. But after a few hours, longer than usual, Juan Bautista came riding back, appearing to be alone.

When Morgan saw him in the distance, alone, he rose quickly from his bench on the *portico*, sensing that something was wrong. As Juan came closer, Morgan could see that he was holding Maria Consuela in his arms, with her pony meandering along behind. Morgan began to run toward Juan. "Juan!, what has happened? Is Maria alright?" Juan did not immediately answer, giving rise to even more concern by Morgan. He repeated, "What has happened to Maria? Is she injured? Why does she not cry?" By now Juan was dismounting from his horse, still holding Maria in his arms. When Morgan neared Juan, he could see Maria's head, dangling in an unnatural position. He took his child into his arms, immediately realizing that Maria was dead. "My God, what has happened? What has happened to my darling little girl? Oh my God, why have you let this happen?" He looked at Juan for answers, but Juan was speechless, standing with his head hanging in despair.

The two walked towards the *hacienda*. Just then Anna Maria came out the door and seeing the two men carrying her child, began to run forward. "Sharlezz!, what has happened? Is Maria injured? Here, Let me help her!" Reaching for her daughter, she now recognized the broken neck of Maria, and that she was dead. "Oh *Mia Dios*!", she screamed. "What has happened?" She was now beginning to be delirious with the realization of her loss. She turned to Juan and screamed, "What have you done to my baby? What have you done, you demon!" Juan did not reply. He just stood mute with his head hanging. Then Maria began to beat him with her fists, sobbing uncontrollably. Juan still stood motionless, accepting the blows as if it was his just punishment. Morgan also stood motionless, in severe shock.

The next morning Morgan and Anna Maria rode to Santa Barbara, with Morgan holding the lifeless body of Maria Consuela. Anna Maria cried all the way, though not as delirious as the day earlier. They met with Maria Consuela's Grandparents, who were also dismayed and heartbroken when they fully absorbed the tragic situation. All then attended a funeral Mass celebrated by Padre Amistoy, after which they buried Maria Consuela in the cemetery beside the Mission.

Returning to *Rancho del Sol*, it was several days before anyone dared speak of the tragic death of Maria, though young Carlos often asked where was his *hermana*, his sister. Finally, Morgan did ask Juan what had happened on that fateful day. Juan explained, "I was not watchful enough! It is my fault, *senor* Sharlezz". Juan was unusually respectful of Morgan. "Well, tell me all that happened before you place the blame on yourself", Morgan replied. Juan explained, "As we rode on our usual path, Little Maria was in front of me. I should not have let that occur." "Go on Juan, tell me what happened", Morgan began to show impatience. "As Maria was galloping along, a *serpiente*, you know, what you call a snake, suddenly appeared on the trail. Maria's pony became frightened and reared high on his hind legs, throwing Maria to the ground. She struck her head on the side of a large boulder. I heard her little neck snap. When I hurried to her, I could see that the force of the blow was fatal. Oh, I am so sorry, *senor* Sharlezz! May *Todopoderoso Dios* have mercy on her, and on me, a poor sinner!"

Morgan sat pensive for a few minutes with Juan looking anxiously for a reply. Finally Morgan said, "No, Juan, it is not your fault. The pony was young and became alarmed. It is unfortunate, but it is no one's fault. It is God's will, which we very often do not understand."

Juan rose, almost crying and looking perplexed, saying, "I am so sorry, *Senor* Sharlezz, I am *mucho afligido*". Morgan shrugged, "I understand, Juan. But please, do not believe it to be your fault. Do not feel guilty. Just pray for Maria, please". As he left the room, Juan replied, "*Si, Senor* Sharlezz, that I will do for the rest of my life."

Now Morgan sat wondering how he would explain the incident to Anna Maria. He knew that she would not be so forgiving of Juan. When Morgan did tell Anna Maria of the details, all that she replied was, "I want him out of my *casa*. I do not ever want to see Juan Bautista, the *demonio*, again." Morgan tried to absolve Juan, but Anna Maria only became more determined. "I want him out, and furthermore, I think that you should also discharge him and banish him from our *rancho*." Morgan thought for only a short time then replied, "No, Anna Maria. I will not discharge nor banish him. I do not believe that he was directly responsible for poor Maria's accident, therefore I will not hold him guilty. It was truly an accident, not a malicious act by Juan."

Sobbing loudly, Anna Maria left the room, shouting to Morgan, "Oh! I cannot believe this! I cannot believe that you can so easily forget the tragic death of our baby!" Inwardly, Morgan wondered if perhaps he was being too charitable.

Anna Maria kept to her room for the next several days. She ordered Morgan to move his clothing into a different bedroom, and the two hardly spoke at all. Anna Maria would not even give much time to young Carlos. Martha became much more of a surrogate mother to Carlos. Morgan tried to devote more time to the young boy so that he would not feel the loss of his mother and sister so much.

Several weeks passed with this distant demeanor continuing between Morgan and Anna Maria. It was a great strain on everyone, especially Martha, who seemed to have the responsibility of tending to Carlos every minute of the day and night. When Carlos would cry for his mother, Martha would expect Anna Maria to emerge from her room and hold the boy, but such did not happen. Anna Maria was in a very depressed mood. Morgan now wondered what he should do about it. He decided that one of the Padres might help counsel her. But he knew that neither Payeras nor de Uria would be accepted by Anna Maria. Morgan therefore sent for Padre Amistoy at Santa Barbara, asking him to come to visit Anna Maria at *Rancho del Sol.* Amistoy of course agreed and came soon to speak with Anna Maria. After several days, however, Amistoy told Morgan that there was nothing more that he could do, that only God and time would heal Anna Maria's depression. After Padre Amistoy left, Morgan could hear Anna Maria sobbing even more loudly, many hours of the day and night. Morgan himself often cried, and prayed, silently in the privacy of his own room.

Not much changed during the next several weeks. Morgan knew that he must now accept the fact that Anna Maria may never return to normalcy, and that he and Martha would have to raise Carlos into boyhood. In the meantime, Juan Bautista kept well away from the *casa,* not daring to be seen by Anna Maria, lest she engage in more of a tirade against him and all in the household. Life was not pleasant at *Rancho del Sol* anymore.

After another several weeks, Ignacio Remirez, Morgan's carpenter friend arrived from *La Purisima,* bearing a letter for Morgan. He explained that a rider had brought the letter to *La Purisima*. It had first arrived at Monterey, being brought there by a sailor that had just arrived. The letter was then brought to the Mission at *Carmel,* and then to *La Purisima* by another rider. Morgan thanked his friend Remirez for his kindness, then anxiously began to read the letter. It was dated 21 June, 1813. Morgan thought about the timing. He had sent his letter in the fall of 1812, and George must not have received it for more than six months. Now it has taken another seven months for this letter to reach Morgan. He thought of all of the events that had occurred, events that George had no way of knowing about.

21 June, 1813

My dearest brother Charles,
       It is with great pleasure that I acknowledge receiving your letter of October, last, but It is

disconcerting to realize that it has been almost three years since we have last heard from you. As in our lives, many events must have occurred in yours.

Harriet and I are so very pleased to learn that our Abigail has another cousin. We hope that your new son Carlos Mariano is well, as also your daughter Maria Consuela and your dear wife Anna Maria. My, your family certainly is growing!

Our family has also grown. Harriet has delivered to me a fine son. We have named him Charles, in honor of you, just as his cousin, your son Carlos.

We are also pleased to learn of your success as a rancher. It seems that you learned your lessons well when you were a boy here on Papa's farm in Sturbridge. I learned my lessons well also, for our farm is prospering well. We expect to be able to buy additional acreage from our neighbor Ezekial Thomas. He had hoped that his son Jeremiah would take over their farm, but Jeremiah has left to seek his fortune in Illinois Territory. Several other young men from the village have done the same. I hope that they do not find the savages there to be too vengeful.

(Morgan thought again of the last letter that he had sent. My! All that has happened since then, and unfortunately so very tragic!)

I am able report additional good news, that of our beloved sister Mary. Last May she was married to Seth Stebbins, that fine young man from Providence. He has now purchased Mr. Putnam's

General Store and is providing a very comfortable living for Mary and himself. We are hoping to learn if Mary might be expecting a child, but no news to that effect as yet.

I don't know how much news you are able to learn about our country. Perhaps you know that Mr. James Madison was elected our President. Almost from the time of his inauguration he has had to confront the matter of great Britain's inflammatory actions on the high seas. She has taken American seamen and conscripted them into her service, claiming that they were British deserters. How absurd! But we here in New England are suffering the effects of embargoes against the British that have been enacted by our Congress, in an ill-fated attempt to force the British to desist from her policies. Our meager armies have attempted to invade Canada, with each incursion being thwarted by the superior British armies. This is not a war of our liking, nor does it seem to be accomplishing its intended ends. Oh when will the Congress stop being duped by those "War Hawks" of the southern states and the western territories. I fear that if we do not soon win some battles, or gain some prizes on the seas, our country will be lost. There has even been some talk of secession from the union by the New England states, who bear the brunt of these foolish policies of our Congress, and Mr. Madison himself. I suppose that every event has some good within it. The good of this war is that we are becoming a much more independent nation, one that is developing its own manufacturing capabilities, now that we can no longer import from

England or France. And New England is the leader in this industrial expansion.

Well Charles, I could go on for a much longer time concerning the difficulties of our still young country, but I will not. Hopefully, your new country, you call it Alta California, Is not experiencing the kinds of political quandaries that we are embroiled in here.

While speaking of things political, I should advise you that Nathaniel Aldrich, who has been our Representative to the Legislature for the past four years, has now been elected our Congressman in Washington. He and Becky and their two children will soon be moving to Washington as he will be beginning his term.

Well Charles, dear brother, we send to you our sincerest wishes for your personal good fortune, and as well for your lovely wife Anna Maria and your family. May the Almighty confer His blessings on your efforts. We trust that the same Almighty to which you now pray is as gracious as is our Almighty, who has shown His great mercies towards us.

With great concern for your continued welfare, I am,

> your loving brother, George.

P S. We are hearing that the United States is expressing interest in purchasing the territory Know as Florida from Spain. We understand that there are many Catholic Padres there, pursuing the conversion of the natives, just as in Alta California. One wonders if we need that additional territory to

govern, with its Holy Roman control. I hope that you do not take offense when I say that, should we adopt Florida, I feel that we should immediately expel the Spanish and the Padres, leaving us a free hand to deal with the native tribes in our own way.

Morgan sat pensive for several minutes, then thinking of the sad news that he must relay to George in his next letter, he began to weep. Juan came and sat beside him, placing his arm around Morgan's shoulder, and embracing him tightly. Ignacio Ramirez, not understanding the cause of Morgan's sadness, started to ride off with an *"Adios, amigos"*. Morgan looked up and shouted "*Muchos gratias*, Ignatio!", then hung his head low again.

CHAPTER THIRTEEN
Disaster everywhere…
of Morgan's own making.

"Anna Maria,—Anna Maria". Morgan was calling softly from the outside of the door to Anna Maria's bedroom. Receiving no reply he called again, while at the same time tapping softly. "Anna Maria, I must speak with you." Morgan waited for a reply. Receiving none, he quietly and slowly opened the door. He was pleased, and somewhat surprised to find that it was not locked. Peering into the room he could see that all of the draperies were pulled closed. It was quite dark, in spite of the bright sunny day outside. He could see Anna Maria reclining on the bed, with the *manta* pulled up to her eyes. As his eyes became accustomed to the darkness he could see more clearly, that Anna Maria's large brown eyes were peering towards him.

"Anna Maria, I have come to tell you that I must leave for a few weeks." He waited for a reaction. "You are leaving, *Sharlezz?*" Anna Maria's voice was barely audible. "Yes, Anna Maria. I must leave for a few weeks", Morgan repeated. Again Anna Maria's voice was barely audible, "*Sharlezz*, you will return?" Now Morgan became pleased that Anna Maria seemed to care. "*Si*, Anna Maria, but I must leave for a few weeks. Juan and I are first going to Monterey to try to locate some *yanqui* sailors, then to *Mision San Juan Bautista* to speak with an *Americano* sailor who is working there for the Padres." He wondered if he should have mentioned Juan Bautista's name.

Anna Maria's soft reply ignored the mention of Juan. But her reply pleased Morgan again. All that she said was "Carlos?" Now Morgan knew that she cared about their young son. "Martha is tending to Carlos very well. He will be fine in her care, but he does miss you Anna Maria, very much."

Morgan thought back on the events of the past six or seven months. How he had taken Anna Maria to Santa Barbara on the monthly anniversary of Maria Consuela's death, to the grave of their daughter, hoping that Anna Maria might finally accept that their daughter was now with her Maker. He had hoped that visits to her parents and additional counseling by Padre Amistoy might bring her to accept the truth of the tragic event. Morgan also had to bring the sad truth to Carlos' grandparents, that Anna Maria was not showing her young son the motherly love that he wanted. At first Vice Governor and *senora* Ortega did not believe Morgan, but on later trips to Santa Barbara, Morgan had brought Carlos along, with his nurse Martha, to visit the grandparents. Now Anna Maria's parents could see for themselves that she seldom heeded the child, nor appeared to want to embrace him. "Why has she forsaken him?", *senora* Ortega asked Morgan. The only rationale that Morgan could offer was, "I am unable to understand myself, but apparently for some reason, she fears that acceptance of Carlos will be a denial of Maria Consuela." The grandparents and Padre Amistoy all tried, by gentle counseling, to make Anna Maria understand that Carlos needed his mother, just as Maria Consuela had needed her at that age. But some barrier had entered Anna Maria's mind, one that she could not mentally breach. Morgan also wondered if he had tried hard enough to bring Anna Maria to an understanding of her motherly role. He did, after all, have to continue to manage his *rancho,* to supervise the many activities involved in enlarging his herd and overseeing his now many ranch-hands. But perhaps, he thought, I should not have spent quite so much time at *Mision Santa Ines,* assisting with its growth. He had also visited *Mision La Purisima* often to keep abreast of its reconstruction and to offer help if needed. He felt that he needed this mental diversion from his family problems.

Morgan's reverie was interrupted. He suddenly remembered that he was continuing his explanation for the trip. Morgan said, "I must go to find these sailors to learn more about my family. It seems that there is another war being waged between the United States and Great Britain. I am greatly concerned about the welfare of my family."

"Oh, my", Anna Maria spoke a little more audibly. "*Si*, I understand, *Sharlezz.* Go with God. I will pray for your safe return, and for your family's welfare as well." Morgan showed his pleasure at her recognition of the matter. "*Muchos gratias*, darling". He moved towards the bed, but Anna Maria lowered herself deeper behind the blanket. Morgan stopped immediately, then bade AnnaMaria goodbye with a kiss waved into the air. He left the room feeling greatly relieved that Anna Maria might be on her way to recovery. He would not feel quite so guilty now about taking this trip. While he naturally wished to let his eastern family know what had occurred in his life here, he found that he was also very anxious to know of the conduct of the war. Strange, he reflected, 'I thought lately that my country was now Spain, no longer the United States, but I guess that I cannot detach myself from the land of my birth".

After giving instructions to his ranch hands, Morgan and Juan Bautista saddled their horses and set our for Monterey. Since it was on their way, they first stopped at *Mision Santa Ines*. Padre de Uria was pleased to see them and to report the improvements that had been accomplished since Morgan's last visit, one of many visits following the damage caused by the earthquake more than a year ago. Morgan could see that the repairs were well done and also that the *portico* had been elongated, with more buildings added to the compound. As he gazed about he was surprised at the number of new dormitory buildings that had been added to house the neophytes. When he mentioned these to Padre de Uria, the Padre smiled and with great pleasure showing, said, "Si, Sharlezz, we are gaining new converts daily. We now have many hundreds. And more come from the mountains almost daily." Morgan promised Padre de Uria that he would return in the near future to assist the Padre in any way that he could.

Morgan and Juan rode on to the new site of *La Purisima*. Here, of course, the compound showed much less completion, though the structures were coming along well. Padre Payeras welcomed them very gregariously. He urged Morgan and Juan Bautista to remain overnight, which they agreed to do. At the evening's dinner Morgan explained to Payeras and Gutierrez his concern about his family in

Massachusetts. They were surprised to learn of the war going on between the very young United States and the centuries old, and far superior Great Britain. They said that they understood Morgan's concerns. Then, when Morgan mentioned the possibility of the United States purchasing Florida, they were flabbergasted. "What shall become of our *Misions* and our Padres? And the neophytes?" Both Padres were astounded at this disclosure. Later the conversation turned to the exchange of memories of their days past in the original *Mision La Purisima.* But all agreed that the new location, and the progress of the building program was pleasing to *Todopoderoso Dios.*

Early the next morning the duo left for the first leg of their journey to Monterey. They promised Payeras that they would stop at *Mision San Carlos Borromeo.* Payeras expressed concern that Padre Tapis was advancing in age, while his duties as the successor to Padre Lasuen and the expansion of the *Mision* system, still required a great deal of energy. He asked Morgan to report on his return, his opinion of the good Padre's health. Morgan promised Payeras that he would do so. Three days later, the two were indeed at *Mision San Carlos,* where they found Padre Tapis to be in good health, even if more frail than when Morgan had seen him many years earlier. Padre Tapis said that he remembered the tall *yanqui* that he had first met at the dedication of *Mision Santa Ines*. The *Carmel* locale brought back memories to Morgan of his friend Castellanos, and the disagreement between he and Padre Lasuen. But Tapis stated that he was aware of Castellanos' assignment and was pleased with the work that Castellanos was now doing in San Francisco *pueblo* and said that he was sure that it was pleasing to *Todopoderoso Dios*. Morgan decided then and there that he would also visit San Francisco to seek out his friend Padre Manuel.

They rode to Monterey but upon arrival learned that a *yanqui* ship had left port just the day before, and it was expected to be a week or more before another would arrive. Morgan and Juan decided that they would ride to *Mision San Juan Bautista*, and that after discussions with Tomas Doak, they would look for Padre Manuel Castellanos in San Francisco.

Late on the next day they arrived at *Mision San Juan Bautista* and sought out Tomas Doak, the American. Though it was late in the afternoon, they found him painting the walls of the church with brilliant colors that he had concocted with the help of natives of the Miwok tribe, natives to the area. Doak seemed talkative, but stated that he was tired from this day's work and would join them in the morning. Morgan and Juan then went to find the Padre in charge, to introduce themselves. Padre Filipe del Arroyo de la Cuesta greeted them warmly. Morgan explained that he too, like Doak, was *Americano*, and that he had helped build *Misions La Purisima* and *Santa Ines*. Padre de la Cuesta was obviously happy to meet them and to learn of their loyalty to the Church. When Morgan stated that he was married to the daughter of the Vice Governor, de la Cuesta was even more pleased. "Perhaps you can help persuade your father-in-law to attend the dedication of our new church. We are hopeful that it will be completed by early next year. Our small original church was severely damaged by earthquakes that had lasted for twenty days. That was in the year 1801. We started our new, much larger church soon after. Fortunately, we were not affected by the earthquakes that you had to endure last year." Morgan said the he would speak to his father-in-law, though he knew not of his schedule.

In the morning Morgan and Juan met with Doak who stated that he had not much time to "palabber" because the Padres were pressing him to complete the church decorations within a few months, a task that Doak felt was not possible. He explained how he had arrived at the Mission after deserting his Philadelphia based ship, due to an altercation with the "rapscalian" captain. He walked to this Mission because he felt that no one would pursue him this far inland from either Monterey or San Francisco. When he arrived he found that the Padres had just dismissed a Spanish painter that had come here to decorate the church and other buildings. The Spaniard wanted a raise in salary to seventy-five *centavos* a week. The Padres said that they could not afford that payment, as they had no money themselves, only the annual stipend received from the Spanish Government, most of which was used to pay the soldiers assigned to the Mission. The Padres believed that providing room and board to the painter was enough pay while doing work for *Todopoderoso Dios.* The Spaniard left and Doak volunteered to do the decorations, accepting the room and board as payment. The Padres agreed readily. Doak had been here almost two years so he knew little of the war with Britain. He was surprised to learn that Morgan had preceded his own settlement in California by several years. He thought that he was the first American settler. Following a few more words of amiable conversation, Morgan and Juan left for San Francisco.

They rode to the *Mision San Francisco de Asis,* another days journey to the north. After introducing themselves to the Padre in charge they inquired of Padre Castellanos. They were told that he would soon return from the *pueblo,* that he spent most of the day in the village that had grown nearby the Mission.

Morgan and Juan roamed throughout the Mission compound, noting the expansion from the times when either had been there before. They spoke with several of the neophytes, inquiring about their health since the outbreak of measles that had occurred some years before. They were told that the Padres were looking after their health, that a new infirmary was staffed by dedicated Spanish ladies who treated them well. But they stated that there was nevertheless, resentment by some neophytes about the way that the Spanish soldiers treated them. Morgan wondered if the Padres knew of this matter, or sensed that there was such resentment.

Morgan and Juan were invited to partake of the evening *cena* with the Padres. They readily accepted. Halfway through the meal, Padre Manuel entered, looking tired and disheveled, his cassock soiled and covered with dust. Morgan immediately rose, hurried to his friend and gave him a great hug. Manuel was greatly surprised and very pleased to see Morgan. He was overjoyed at receiving such a warm welcome from his long-time friend. Juan too, rose and shook the hand of Padre Manuel vigorously. He sat, taking a sip of wine and nibbled at a *fajita.* "Padre Manuel", another Padre spoke, "you seem to have had a busy day." "*Si*, I did indeed", he replied, "more than the usual number of drunken sailors accosted me." Morgan was shocked, "You mean that every day you are abused. Why do you place yourself in this position?" Manuel replied philosophically, "Oh, sometimes there are incidents, but most of the time I am welcomed and appreciated by the people of the *pueblo*. The seaport village is growing quickly and now receiving immigrants from many parts of the world. We have Portuguese, French, American, British, Russian and Chinese sailors entering regularly, and they do not always agree with each other, or with me either, sometimes. But I feel that I am able to accomplish a lot of good, for those people who do need help, and especially those who need God."

Everyone at the table nodded agreement with Padre Manuel's missionary work. "God is needed everywhere, not just here in our Missions", the head Padre concluded. The group left the table, with Morgan, Juan and Padre Manuel reconvening outside. After more discussion of events that had transpired since last they met, and more comment about Padre Manuel's work, suddenly Manuel said, "Oh, *Sharlezz,* you may be pleased to learn that I have received a letter from my sister Elena, and she is planning to come back to *Nueva Espana*, and to visit me here. She, too, is pleased that I am so excited about my new special Mission, and that I am so strongly supported by my superiors. She also mentioned that she hopes to see you as well while here." Morgan became giddy at the news, "Really, Manuel, she wants to see me?" He blushed a little. He was glad they were in the darkened light. Juan was not so elated to hear the news.

The next morning the two left for Monterey once again. An American ship had indeed arrived in port. It's homeport was New York and it was to depart in four days. That would give Morgan an opportunity to find the trustworthy sailor that he wanted to deliver another letter to his brother George, although getting to Sturbridge, Massachusetts, from New York City, would be more difficult than from Boston or New Bedford. While seeking out the desired sailor, Morgan was composing a long letter to his brother. In it he described the earthquake of December 1812, the tragic death of his daughter Maria Consuela, and his wife's resultant mental depression. He included comments about Carlos' growth and other news of his *rancho* and of the Missions.

While wandering about the port and speaking with several American sailors, Morgan learned of the burning of the city of Washington by the British and of land battles that had taken place along the Canadian border in New York and Illinois Territory. Now he was even more concerned about his family. Would the British also burn other cities? New York, Philadelphia, or especially Boston. He felt that the British would hold resentment for that city, due to it being the place of the start of the Revolution. Morgan tried to reassure himself. Even if the British captured and burned Boston, why would they march all the way inland to Sturbridge? Would they want to take the arsenal at Springfield? Would they sack the towns along the way? As he would write a sentence into the letter, he would offer a silent prayer that his family would be safe. He also prayed that his own California family,

Anna Maria and Carlos, and that the padres and Juan and all his friends, would see no harm of any kind.

On the last day before sailing, Morgan contacted a sailor that said he might consider taking the letter to Morgan's brother in Sturbridge, but he would want five dollars to do so. Morgan stated that his brother would pay two dollars upon delivery, but not five. Morgan offered three. The sailor said he would accept four, but wanted it now. Morgan explained that he had only *pesos*, not dollars. The sailor reluctantly agreed to wait for payment in Sturbridge. Morgan was inwardly concerned that this sailor might not be as trustworthy as the last two. But in further conversation about the parallels in their lives, that is, leaving home for the seas at a young age, Morgan learned that the sailor's home port, as a novice whaler, was New London, Connecticut. He also learned that the sailor originally came from Putnam, Connecticut, which was only a few miles from the Massachusetts border, and that he planned to visit his mother when next in New York port. Morgan felt more at ease now, feeling that this sailor would indeed travel the extra twenty five or so miles to receive the four dollars payment.

Having accomplished their several goals, Morgan and Juan rode back to *Rancho del Sol,* making the necessary stops for overnight accommodations. They were always well received by the Padres at these stops. Nearing home though, they made a point to stop at *La Purisima* to report to Padre Payeras what they had learned. They told of Tapis' health, of Padre Manuel's activities, and of the state of war in the east. Upon learning of the burning of Washington, the new nation's capitol, Payeras wondered aloud about how far the war might ensue. Was Florida and the Missions there in danger?

As Morgan and Juan approached the *hacienda* of *Rancho del Sol*, Morgan waved to Juan, a signal that he must return to the ranch-hand's *cabana,* without being seen by Anna Maria. Juan did as he was told, turning his horse off the trail. When Morgan arrived at his *hacienda* he was hopeful to find Anna Maria recovered. Although she was in the living room when he arrived, she did not greet him very warmly. She was in the large room, standing with Carlos and Martha nearby. Carlos jumped up to greet and hug his father and Martha offered a warm *"buenas dias"*. Anna Maria looked about. Morgan knew that she was trying to determine if Juan Bautista was near the house. Not seeing him, she seemed somewhat relieved, though not joyous.

Morgan approached Anna Maria to see if she would accept a hug. She did not, instead moved a few feet in another direction. Morgan thought, 'Oh, I'm so disappointed. She has not improved greatly.' Nevertheless, Morgan tried to act as nothing were wrong. He narrated the events of their journey, of their success in finding a sailor that would deliver a letter to George, of the news of the war, and of their meeting with Padre Manuel. At this latter comment, Morgan could notice the displeased look on Anna Maria's face. Morgan tried to ennoble Manuel's activities by explaining the good work that he is doing for God. Anna Maria showed no acceptance of Morgan's spirited description. Then Morgan made a statement that he thought would be of interest to Anna Maria, but he would later regret forever. He commented casually that Padre Manuel's sister Elena was planning to return to *Nueva Espana*.

"And of what concern is that to me?, or for that matter, to you?", Anna Maria spoke with anger in her voice. "That *cochina,* that *puta,* how you Americanos say 'whore', of what interest is her visit to you *Sharlezz?"* Morgan was shocked at the vengeance in Anna Maria's voice. He foolishly added more fuel to her fire by commenting, "Oh, she is not such a bad woman as you seem to think, Anna Maria. She has great love and concern for her brother's welfare, and she is a popular figure wherever she travels." "Oh!, I cannot believe that you do not recognize the deceit in her", Anna Maria was fuming. "Her popularity, as you call it, is her ready involvement with any man that will be willing to demean his own character for a few hours of intimacy with her. To me, that is the description of a whore!"

Morgan looked sheepish and reddened. Seeing this, Anna Maria looked accusingly at Morgan, "When she visited *Santa Ines,* you were there *Sharlezz,* were you not?" Morgan dared not look up. He mumbled, "Yea, I was there. And she was very nice to me, even after she first blamed me for Padre Manuel's so called defection." "Oh, so she was nice to you", Anna Maria pursued the point, "how nice was she?" Morgan began to feel that Anna Maria suspected his involvement with Elena. "Anna Maria, there is something that I must tell you". Morgan motioned for Martha to take Carlos and leave the room. Martha seemed intrigued by the conversation and obviously did not want to leave. She did so very slowly, hoping to hear more of the conversation.

"Anna Maria", Morgan began, "it is true that Elena was very nice to me. In fact, one day we took a ride into the hills. She was very alluring, and I could not resist her temptation. I have had this on my mind for a long time. Now I want you to know how sorry I am for this terrible sin." "Oh!, *mia Dios*! What are you saying *Sharlezz*? That you were not an unblemished groom when we married? Oh!, *mia Dios!*". Anna Maria was devastated. She slumped into a chair. "And there were others?", she demanded to know. "No!, I swear by God there were no others", Morgan defended himself, "and I had confessed this sin before our marriage. God has forgiven me. Can't you do so also?"

Now Anna Maria became more incensed. "God has forgiven you? How did God forgive you?" Morgan explained, "In the confessional. Padre Payeras told me that God has forgiven me." "Oh! *Mia Dios*. Padre Payeras knows! And how many more know of this?" "No one! And Padre Payeras told me to tell no one", Morgan explained. Anna Maria was irrationally incensed. "And how many has Padre Payeras told of this incident. Are we to believe that he did not speak of this, or have fantasies himself, of this tryst?" Morgan was flabbergasted beyond belief, "You believe that a good padre reveals the contents of confessions that he has heard. That he has fantasies of sexual involvement? My God, Anna Maria, what of your Catholic upbringing? Don't you know that a Padre cannot speak or retain the information of such actions. They are forgiven by God and forgotten by the Padres."

"Yes, that is the teaching. But how are we to know what occurs in the minds of the Padres? They are men too", Anna Maria continued, "and speaking of beliefs, I was taught that one must be a virgin until marriage. Women and men both!" Then speaking decidedly, she said, "Since you have defiled me, I cannot ever again be intimate with you."

As she left the room, Morgan was aghast. 'Never again to hold my lovely Anna Maria? What meaning is there to life now?' Now he slumped into a chair. Martha had been eavesdropping at the door to the kitchen. She too, was aghast at the admission, and at the reaction by Anna Maria. 'Oh, the poor *senorita*! And then she thought, 'oh, the poor *senor*!' All the while, Carlos continued to play on the floor with the small wooden figures that the ranch-hands had carved for him, oblivious of all adult tribulations.

CHAPTER FOURTEEN
The weeks drag on…the years fly by.

Carlos was no longer playing with his wooden toy figures. He was now riding his own horse, just as capably as any of the ranch hands. Morgan found it hard to realize that ten years had elapsed, that Carlos was now twelve years of age, approaching manhood.

So much had happened, Morgan reminisced. But all so quickly. And yet, some events seemed to prolong themselves continuously. Anna Maria continued to show resentment towards Morgan. She made it obvious that she never again intended to be his wife. She still had not accepted her daughter's death, nor forgiven Juan Bautista and Morgan for causing it, and still did not accept her role as a mother. Morgan had reared Carlos into early manhood and Martha had been Carlos' teacher and substitute mother.

Although Carlos had adjusted to these conditions, Morgan had not. Some days he held great resentment towards Anna Maria, then would have to convince himself of the inevitable, that he would be a bachelor the rest of his life. He was married in appearances only. The Church and society offered no alternative.

The incident that had caused the great separation, Elena Castellanos' Future visit, never occurred. Although she had visited her brother in San Francisco, she returned to Spain within a few months, never attempting to meet with Morgan. But the damage had been done. Anna Maria was unforgiving of

Morgan's pre-marital offence. Their lives were never to be as husband and wife again.

Elena had actually come to *Alta California* to convince her brother to request that his Superior reassign him, allowing him to return to Spain. Manuel would hear none of this. He was happy, he said, doing God's work in a ministry that was needed for the good of many souls. Manuel was enraged when he learned that Elena had even gone to Padre Tapis secretly, requesting that Tapis write to the Superior General of the Franciscan Order in *Nueva Espana,* to order a transfer of her brother. Tapis would not of course, pursue this direction without Padre Manuel's agreement. Manuel and Elena had harsh controversy between themselves when Manuel learned of his sister's deceit. Elena returned to Spain angered that she could not control the destiny of her "little" brother. 'Finally', Manuel felt, 'I am free of her domination.'

Through Morgan's years of solitude, he had often confided in his friend Juan, in Padre Payeras or de Uria, sought out the counsel of his in-laws, and when in Santa Barbara, sought out Padre Amistoy. All were understanding, and somewhat helpful, but life without his wife's companionship was very difficult. Often, when he journeyed to Santa Barbara, he endeavored to interest Anna Maria to join him, but she would not. Very occasionally, however, Anna Maria would herself ride to Santa Barbara, bringing Martha and Carlos with her to visit his grandparents. Morgan could not help but believe that she did so maliciously, to appear to be a respectable mother. He held rancor in his heart.

Once, during the first year of separation he had gone to San Francisco alone, not being sure himself if he would give in to the temptation of the flesh, as there were now many prostitutes in the *pueblo*, serving the many sailors that came to port. But first he found his friend Manuel Castellanos, who strongly supported Morgan, convincing him not to become involved with these women.

"Once when I was tempted not to remain chaste, you supported me and convinced me to remain true to my vows. Now I urge you to do the same", Manuel advised Morgan. "We can pray together that Anna Maria will someday adhere to her vows and once again accept the will of God in a proper marital state." So the two prayed. After consoling his sobbing friend, Manuel urged Morgan to return home, asking God to restore their marriage and to inspire Anna Maria to recognize her motherly duties towards Carlos.

During the long, lonely ride back to *Rancho del Sol,* Morgan hoped and prayed that Anna Maria would someday become his wife again, but he also realized that if there were any chance that that would happen, it would never be so if Anna Maria learned of another unfaithfulness by him. He resolved to be strong when these temptations arose, and as many of the Padres had suggested, immediately put his mind on other matters.

And there were certainly many other matters to occupy Morgan's mind. He had to be sure that his crops and herds were expanding because the yankee traders were coming to the west coast more often, and so too, the Chinese, French, Portuguese and the English. All of the nations had an insatiable appetite for hides and tallow, as well as wheat, barley corn, peas and other crops.

The Missions, too, needed his help. Although Payeras and de Uria often told Morgan that they were prospering well enough, Morgan felt that his hand, in some of the construction matters especially, was necessary. Indeed, his recommendations were usually accepted by the Padres, and the neophytes were confident in Morgan's leadership, so the cooperation among all was productive.

At both Missions, many utility buildings had been constructed for storage of the hides, tallow, wheat, and processing of these many products of the Missions. Additional water works were added, and an infirmary was established at *La Purisima.* The combined herds of the two Missions numbered in the thirty thousands, as did the acres of crops. Crafts such as saddlery and silversmithing were being developed by the Spanish craftsmen and these products too were In great demand by the many traders. The herds of formerly wild horses, descendents of those brought to the New World by the Spanish invaders in the 1500's, were now being trained to accept riders, making a greater demand for the need for leather goods. Indeed, it seemed that almost no one walked anywhere now, not even many of he neophytes.

. Overall the Mission system was both successful in the harvest of souls and profitable in its temporal performance. But there were also some difficult times during the past ten years. In the years of 1818 and 1819, droughts had occurred, leading to the death of many animals, and in 1818 a major fire at *La Purisima* had wiped out the homes of many of the neophytes. Each of these adversities was eventually overcome by prayer and hard work, the prayers by the padres, the hard work by the neophytes. The number of dormitory buildings to house the neophytes had increased at both Missions and while some of these new Christians seemed happy with their new lives and their new religion, many were not.

More and more often, when Morgan would visit *La Purisima* or *Santa Ines,* the padres would tell of the "desertion" of many neophytes. To prevent the loss of these "souls" from the Church, the *soldatos* would be dispatched to hunt for and return the natives who had rebelled against the Mission's well established rules and regulations. Each week it seemed that more and more of the natives wished to return to their former life of nature and freedom.

And far to the south of the Missions, in *Nueva Espana,* political matters were not going smoothly for the King's representative either. For many years now, a group consisting of some independent thinking padres, Mexican born Spaniards, those known as *creoles*, and many *mestizos*, those of mixed Mexican and native blood, were becoming exasperated with the excesses of the Viceroy and the Spanish army. At first small insurrections had occurred and been quickly crushed. But gradually and consistently, the demand for independence from Spain was growing. These attempts at independence had begun ten years earlier, led by a man named Miguel Hidalgo y Castillo. These early insurrections were always suppressed by the army, but the fire for independence from Spain was never completely extinguished. In 1820 the mother country itself was facing an internal revolt, as well as defending itself from English and French forces. The Viceroy in *Nueva Espana* could expect no help from King Ferdinand VII. So the Viceroy ordered his military leader, Augustin de Iturbide, to crush the revolutionary movement. But in February 1821, Iturbide and an insurgent leader, Vicente Guerrero, jointly negotiated the establishment a new government. *Nueva Espana* was now to be known as Mexico and governed by Iturbide, who declared himself Emporer Augustin I.

News of this event did not reach the northern Missions for several weeks. When the messenger did reach Santa Barbara, Vice Governor and *senora* Ortega were in panic. Morgan rode to Santa Barbara to advise them to remain calm, that it might be dangerous for them to return to Mexico City, and to stand fast and hope that their land holdings would remain in tact. He hoped the same for his land as well.

During the previous tumultuous ten year period in *Nueva Espana*, Morgan had written several letters to his brother George, advising him of the situation, including the possibility of Morgan losing his land and fortune. George had each time replied with a plea for his brother Charles to return to Massachusetts, where life was now quite prosperous. Morgan never entertained this possibility. He and his family belonged in California, and here they would stay. Inwardly he felt that the political situation would eventually calm itself, and he hoped and prayed that all would be resolved without any serious effect on his land, his family, or "his" Missions. Had he been able to foresee the events of the next ten years, he might well have returned to Sturbridge.

One serious result of the Mexican revolution was that the new government refused to pay for the support of the constabulary soldiers stationed at the Missions and Presidios. After two years of non-payment, the troops were belligerent. The Padres managed to maintain some order by providing for the upkeep of the families of the soldiers and craftsmen, but the Missions too, without any government support, were finding it harder and harder to trade with the visiting ships.

In May of 1823, while trying to resolve a dispute between a soldier and several neophytes, Padre Payeras suddenly grasped his chest. A neophyte maiden ran to the kitchen to fetch some *espina blanco* tea, but by the time that she returned, Payeras was on the ground, gasping for air. Padre Gutierrez had been summoned. When he arrived, seeing his beloved Pastor's color, and upon checking his heart beat, realized that Payeras was near death. Gutierrez immediately began administering the Last Rites of the Catholic Church to Payeras, and asking that *Dios Todopoderoso* accept his soul into heaven.

For the past six years, in addition to his duties at *La Purisima*, Payeras had been elected *Padre-Presidente* of the entire Mission chain. He chose to maintain his beloved *Mision La Purisma* as his base, rather than move to San *Carlos Boromeo*, but his new responsibilities required that he periodically travel to all the Missions. Alas, the strain was too much for the aging priest with his long-time coronary ailment.

Upon learning of their very dear friend's death, Morgan and Juan Bautista rode at a fast gallop to *La Purisima*. Anna Maria stated that she was too ill to travel that far, even though she had made the longer trip to Santa Barbara only a few days earlier. By the time that Morgan and Juan arrived at *La Purisima the* entire population of the Mission was assembled in the church, with Payeras' body, draped in liturgical robes, lying in the front of the altar.

During the next three days every resident of *Mision La Purisima Concepcion de Maria Santisma* passed by *Padre-Presidente* Mariano Payeras' body, bidding him *adios* and saying a prayer for the repose of his immortal soul in heaven. Many visitors from *Santa Ines,* as well as from many other missions also came. Vice Governor Ortega, many padres, officials and soldiers, craftsmen and their families all came to view the body of this much-beloved padre. On the morning of the fourth day, with the body beginning to swell and become very odorous, a High Mass of requiem was sung by Padre Gutierrez, de Uria and priests from many other Missions. A fine burial box had been constructed by the craftsmen of *La Purisima* into which Payeras' body was enclosed and lowered into a grave in the Spanish cemetery of the Mission. Thus ended the worldly duties of the man that had supervised La Purisima for more than twenty years and who had been a devoted priest of the Lord for almost forty years.

Morgan was very upset with this sudden passing of his dear friend, for even though Payeras had had trouble with his heart for all of the time that Morgan knew him, this death was still a shock to the man that had been saved from death by insurgent natives many years earlier.

The steady hand of Padre Payeras was sadly missed. With the continuing political difficulties of the new Mexican government, and with the beginning of its open hostility towards the Missions, almost every day presented some kind of difficulty. At most of the Missions the padres were acting as conciliators between the natives and the soldiers. But more and more of the natives began to show resentment, not only for the soldiers, but for the Mission system itself. Many native agitators were very vociferous in their denouncement of the padres and their methods. The religious beliefs that had been brought to the natives by these outsiders was now being questioned more and more. Many of the Spanish soldiers were disturbed when they heard the natives castigate their padres and their religion, the religion embraced by the soldiers and their families since birth and by their ancestors for many generations before.

On February 21, 1824, at *Santa Ines*, one soldier became so enraged at a native that he flogged him severely. Other natives who had witnessed the incident became incensed. From nowhere it seemed, bows and arrows appeared and were now being used against the handful of constabulary soldiers. Then a group of the natives set fire to the Mission's craft shops. The fire spread rapidly, soon beginning to engulf the roof of the church. Upon seeing the church afire, other natives began immediately to extinguish the flames, using all available buckets But before they managed to control the fire it had reached the lower church, burning the sacristy and many of the sacred vessels and vestments.

By the next day, news of this incident brought a contingent of soldiers from the *Presidio* at Santa Barbara. The hostile natives departed quickly to *La Purisima* where they joined forces with the natives there. The natives built barricades on the outskirts of the Mission, expecting that they would prevail against the Spanish. They positioned two old Spanish Army cannons that were used only for ceremonial events, and for a month they held the Spanish army at bay. But eventually the Spanish, by use of their muskets, overcame the ancient weapons of the natives. Several natives were killed, many were taken as prisoners, and others were flogged and ordered to return to their villages. Against the padre's wishes, the Governor ordered strict disciplinary controls over the natives. The Mission system would never again be the peaceful abodes that they had been.

Now Morgan felt that he was stretched beyond his mental limits. He was of course, concerned about his own land and herds, he worried about his father-in-law's rank and land holdings, he was greatly concerned about the Missions, and Anna Maria still remained in a state of indifference to it all. Some relief came when he learned that Iturbide, now Emperor August I, who had known Vice Governor Ortega for many years, sent word of his support for Ortega. Both Morgan and Ortega were greatly relieved that their holdings were safe, and expected that the strife in Mexico City would soon settle down.

But the unrest would not settle, and many *creoles* and *metzigos,* who had expected to gain more opportunities as a result of the new government, migrated northward to *Alta California*, demanding their rights to the Mission lands, and even some of the private estates. They arbitrarily staked out holdings for themselves, stole the cattle on that land, and declared themselves the rightful owners. The Mission padres had no way to prevent this from happening, so the disintegration of the system was taking place before their very eyes.

Iturbide, as Emperor, was also granting land to favored supporters. One of these, *Don* Domingo Carillo, who had been granted land earlier, was given vast additional lands, now encompassing much of the land surrounding Santa Barbara, both the Mission and the *Pueblo*. This encouraged other land owners, such as Morgan's treacherous neighbor Humberto Ruiz, to take advantage of the chaos by usurping land and cattle as well. It was impossible for the Missions or owners of adjacent lands to supervise their vast lands and herds.

To protect his own holdings Morgan had to train his several *vaqueros*, cow-hands, to become sentries and ordered them to shoot anyone that they found rustling his cattle. Because he, and almost he alone, had branded his cattle, his herds were somewhat safer. But gone were the peaceful days of ranching and farming in the foothills of the Sierra Madre mountains.

For a little more than a year it seemed that the new Mexican government might establish peace, at least in Mexico itself. But by 1823 a new power struggle emerged. Another revolt took place, this one led by General Antonio Lopez de Santa Anna, a former supporter of Iturbide. Santa Anna called together a convention, establishing a federal government in 1824, and electing Guadalupe Victoria as Mexico's first president. Victoria was a liberal and was intent on reducing the power, and the holdings, of the Catholic Church. He ordered the secularization of the Mission chain, that is, removing them from the jurisdiction of the Franciscan Order. He authorized the selling the Mission lands, the cattle, and even many of the buildings, to his supporters and various other exploiters. He also ordered the "freeing" of the natives from the Missions.

Morgan wondered, would the chaos never end? It seemed not, for over the next several years nearly every Mission was desecrated, decimated and plundered. Many of the padres left the Missions, returning to their seminaries in Mexico and Spain. The few padres that remained had no way to maintain the buildings, since many of the neophytes returned to their villages, joined in the plundering of the land and cattle, or roamed into the *pueblos* where they hoped to find a means of sustenance.

Through it all, Morgan held on. His son Carlos, now in his mid-teen years, was a great consolation to his father, and it was apparent that he would soon become an apt business man. He was a great help to his father in maintaining the *rancho.* Morgan continued to rely on his old friend Juan Batista also, but Morgan's main concern now was to protect his land and trading business so he might bestow on Carlos an estate of importance, for trade with the Yankees and other nations had continued, even if under extreme difficulties.

Almost daily in the fall of 1824, forty-two year old Morgan, and his sixteen year old son Carlos, would gaze northward along the *El Camino Real,* for Morgan was expecting Hiram Palmer to arrive any day. Palmer had become a close friend of Morgan over the past ten or twelve years. He was the agent for a Boston trading company, and was himself a Bostonian. Hiram had visited Morgan about every eighteen to twenty four months, and would remain on the west coast for two to three months each time, arranging trades and purchases of the hides and other goods that the Missions, Morgan, and other ranchers would offer for sale. They had become close enough friends that Palmer would often stay several weeks at Morgan's *hacienda*, and he had become Morgan's primary courier of letters both to and from his brother George.

"Hellloooo Hiram", Morgan hollered up the trail. Hiram, who was still several hundred meters away, called back his greeting, "Hello Charles, my old friend. How have you been?" As he came closer, seeing the young man with Morgan he said, "And who is that handsome *hombre* with you? Surely that cannot be Carlos. Why Carlos was only a small boy when I visited you last." Palmer dismounted and when they came within reach of each other the two men embraced and shook hands like long lost brothers. "Yes, this is Carlos. He is not only a strong *hombre*, he is also a very fine *vacquero,* and a great help to me in everything here at *Rancho del Sol* ". The two men went into the *hacienda* while Carlos ran to find Juan Bautista to join them. Soon the four were discussing the shipping trade, the political fortunes of the United States, and that of the new nation Mexico. After several glasses of *vino,* Palmer dared ask about Anna Maria, for he knew from his past visits of the

estrangement of Morgan and his wife. Morgan simply
nodded, indicating that the matter was not improved.
Carlos looked away, as if to avoid hearing about his
mother's condition, and Juan dropped his head, also
not wanting to show recognition of the matter being
discussed.

Then Palmer, pulling an envelope from his
pocket said, "Here, Charles, I have a letter from your
brother George. I took the stage to Sturbridge because
I wanted to meet George and his family. I am very glad
that I did so. Sturbridge is such a charming town, and
George and Harriet were so kind to me. And their
children are so lovely. Here, I'm sure that George has
told you all of this, for he read your last letter that you
wrote to him and immediately penned a reply." As
Morgan opened the envelope, Carlos came to his side.
"Here, Carlos, we have another letter from your uncle
and I'm sure some news about your cousins, Abigail
and Charles."

While they sat and read the latest missal, Juan
offered an invitation to Hiram. "Come, *mi amigo*, I
will show you the advances that we have made since
your last visit to *Rancho del Sol*."

As they left, Morgan spoke. "Carlos, let me
read this letter to you, then we will bring your mother
the exciting news." Morgan was trying to sound like
they too, had a normal family, as did George and
Harriet.

March 14, 1829
My dear brother Charles, Anna Maria, and Carlos,
How relieved we are to again receive the
news of your situation. Before receiving your last

letter, we were fearful of you situation. We pray that you are still safe from any harm that may be caused by the turmoil that you described about New Spain. I suppose that it is similar to that turmoil that must have existed at the start of our own new nation. It is surprising to realize that we have already been a nation for almost fifty-three years. And we certainly have seen many changes and advancement over those years, even if at times many matters seemed hopeless.

I will apprise you of our country's progress, but first let me tell you how pleased we are to meet Hiram Palmer. He certainly has been a good friend to the both of us, and how fortunate we are that you made his acquaintance in your business dealings. Imagine, The very cow-hides and goods that you produce come all the way to Boston! Most are used in the manufacture of shoes and boots. The shoe manufacturing industry is having a difficult time to meet the demands of this quickly growing trend, the fine fashions that the ladies are now seeking. But, perhaps you have heard, shoes are now being produced by machinery, not entirely by hand as was done in the past. Not only machinery for shoes, but machines are now devised for the manufacture of cloth, farm implements and many, many other commodities. It would seem that almost everyday another clever person devises a new machine. Such improvements were required by our ever expanding nation.

In our last election, Andrew Jackson was selected by the majority. You may recall that I had related to you how four years ago, our own fine statesman, John Quincy Adams was elected, or rather designated the winner by our Congress. At that time, many believed that Jackson should have been elected. So now we shall see if his "Common Man" platform will really help the less fortunate. Jackson and many in the land, believe that wealthy New Englanders be the enemy of farmers and laborers. To the contrary, I believe that they are largely responsible for the expansion and improvement of our country.

Another matter of urgency is still festering, that of slavery. Jackson favors it, and as you know, most of the northeastern states, our own Massachusetts included, do not. We thought the matter had been settled with the "Missouri compromise", but it seems that with the possibility of additional western territories wishing to become a slave State, I fear that we have not heard the end of the matter. We in Massachusetts thought that by granting our northern portion the right to become a separate state, Maine, that we had offset the Missouri statehood and slavery issue.

In New England many are pleased that Jackson favors heavy tariffs on imported goods but the southern states are very angered by this, as they fear retaliation on the shipments of their cotton and tobacco to Europe. In fact, perhaps your next load of hides coming into Boston will be subject to excessive duty.

Enough of politics! How is your lovely wife? Is she again dutiful? We certainly hope that she has recovered from her delirium as a result of little Maria Consuela's death. And what of Carlos? By now he must be a fine young man, and a great credit to you. We have wondered, Charles, of his education. Has he been able to attend school there in your remoteness? Do schools even exist? We here in Massachusetts have created an educational climate that is a marvel. Nearly every child is now well educated in our public school system, championed by a fine fellow named Horace Mann. Mr. Mann, by the way, is a graduate of Brown College, the same college attended by our dear sister Mary's husband Seth Stebbins.

Speaking of Mary and Seth, they have as yet no children even after these fifteen years of marriage. Mary is now no longer of childbearing age. We dared not ask the reason for their barrenness, but they seem entirely blissful in their union.

From the news that we have read in our periodicals, many folks are moving westward, Charles, across the Appalachian Mountains and across the vast Mississippi river, into areas where large farms and grazing land are available. Many have traveled to a territory called Oregon. Have you heard of this land, north of your Alta California? Many have followed the trail originally traversed by those fellows Lewis and Clarke that I had written to you about. What stout fellows they be! Also, Charles, a new canal has been opened that allowsbarges to travel from the Hudson River, not far from us in eastern New York, all the way to those waterways called the Great Lakes. We understand that many of New England manufacturers are utilizing this means to extend their businesses. Yes! Our great land is indeed expanding quickly and widely.

But it seems that with every improvement for us, we bring distress to others, namely, the native Indians. They are now being forced to leave the land that they had previously moved into when we drove them from our eastern states. I suppose soon, they will be encroaching on your Alta California, seeking lands for their homesteads. Sadly, we read that those who have resisted this forced relocation have been badly treated, even put to death. You recall, Charles, as youngsters, we often encountered native Indians in our village, and never were they offensive. But now we seldom see a native. Those that we knew have died, and their descendants have moved westward, only to be taunted again, due to our country's need to expand.

Charles, I trust that before Mr. Palmer returns to Boston that you will have an opportunity to write me of your situation and of your family's happiness. Until then, may the almighty look down favorably on you all.

With much affection to you and your family, I am,

your loving brother George.

The next day Palmer and Morgan made their business transaction official. Palmer told Morgan to expect the ship of his trading company to arrive off-shore within a few weeks. Palmer continued, "You have done quite well, Charles, to have processed this many hides under the extreme conditions that prevail. Now I want to advise you of another complication, a very serious threat that exists because of your neighbor Ruiz."

Morgan was warned by the agent of a treacherous plot by Ruiz to seize Morgan's land, not by force, but by political chicanery. Palmer related how he had learned that Ruiz had traveled to Mexico City, met with Santa Anna, who was now planning to overthrow the new President Victoria, and again seize control of the Mexican government. Ruiz sought the post of Governor of *Alta California*, in exchange for supporting Santa Anna, and providing financial aid to his cause. Palmer concluded his report by stating, "You know, Charles, over the years, Ruiz' trades have greatly exceeded yours and even some of the Missions. He did this by rustling cattle from the Mission herds. Of course, no one was ever able to prove this was true, so he simply became bolder and bolder. Now he seeks to inveigle his way into becoming the master of *Alta California's* fate." Morgan was disturbed but not shocked at learning of his neighbor's chicanery. Morgan looked pensive. He told Palmer that he would like to have him take a letter back to George. Palmer nodded assent.

By the next morning Morgan had finished writing his letter. In fact, he had it partially written before Palmer had arrived, advising George of the many changes to his land and to his family. Unfortunately, he could not report any improvement in Anna Maria's disposition. As Palmer departed, Morgan gave him the letter, thanked him, and with a smile of hope, said, "I'll see you in another year or two, Hiram. Have a safe voyage, and if you are able to visit my brother again personally, please express my love to him and his family." As Morgan waved goodbye, turning towards his doorway he pondered his next move.

The following morning Morgan and Juan rode to the Santa Barbara *Presidio*, seeking out their old friend *Capitan* Hernandez. Although the *soldatos* at Santa Barbara had not been paid for several years, since they had nowhere else to go for subsistence, many remained there under Hernandez, maintaining order of the *peublo,* whose population of indigents and carousers had grown significantly. The soldiers were dependent on the original settlers for food, and occasional contact with the trading ships for bartering their homemade crafts in exchange for other goods. Like Morgan, they wondered what was to be their final destiny.

When Morgan related Ruiz' plot to Hernandez, the captain assured him that Ruiz would not accomplish his objective, for his men were still loyal to him and were intent on maintaining as much of the old order as was possible. He did say that bloodshed would probably result from any confrontation. Morgan assured the captain that his men were capable of assisting the soldiers if necessary. Morgan then went to advise his father-in-law of the situation, and from there to Mission Santa Barbara to speak with Padre Amistoy. This Padre was one of the few that had remained at his post to try to assure that the Mission buildings would not be sacked by either the natives or the indigents. Up to this point the Padre's stern warnings had kept the indigents and natives from plundering the sacred buildings and grounds.

CHAPTER FIFTEEN
Difficult times...worsening situations

"Alright men, now listen carefully." Morgan was addressing his cowhands, "we must be careful so as to have no trouble with Ruiz or his trickery. I need most of you to start bringing the hides to the top of the bluff so as to toss them to the sailors on the beach, just like we did before. But I can't have all of you doing that, I need two of you to go with Juan and patrol the range." It was now necessary to transfer the hides from Morgan's storage barns to the ship of agent Palmer. The agent said that the ship, the *Pilgrim*, would be arriving off shore about now, after first loading hides, wheat, dried beans and preserved meat at Monterey. Morgan had ridden to the top of the bluff for the past several mornings, scanning the channel waters with his telescope. This morning he had sighted the ship, first under full sail, then as it neared the shore, furling its sails nicely. Morgan reminisced about his days at sea, and thought to himself, 'she carries a fine crew.'

As the ship came into the channel, several Chumash *tamols*, canoes made of lashed-together planks, plied their way across the Santa Barbara Channel waters, the occupants waving merrily to the sailors aboard the *Pilgrim,* who waved back just as gaily. For centuries before, the Chumash channel tribes had traversed this channel in the same manner. Even before the white man arrived, their daily activity consisted of moving pelts and fish from the islands of their habitat. The canoes were highly decorated with pigment colors and beads, not at all like the plain canoes made by their northern neighbors, the Essalen and Salinon natives, who made their canoes of tule reeds.

When the ship neared the land, it dropped anchor a few hundred meters off shore. Then the dinghy boats were lowered and the crews rowed ashore, ready to start loading the hides onto these dinghies. When a dingy was loaded with as many hides as it could safely carry the sailors would row out to the ship for the transfer of the hides to the ship's hold. This method had worked successfully for the last seven or eight trades with the Yankees. This time, however, in this year of 1834, Morgan had to concern himself with the possibility that Ruiz might try to take advantage of the situation, while his men were occupied in this trading operation.

Two of Morgan's men volunteered to join Juan as range guards. "*Bueno!* Now Juan, Martinez, Pedro, I want you to saddle up three of our fastest horses, and take supplies for four or five days out on the range. Better take along some extra horses too. Keep on the move. I know that you can't be everywhere, 'cause it's a big range, but keep moving about. Hopefully, if Ruiz has any idea of rustling, you'll see them and scare his men away. And if need be, shoot to scare 'em away." "Si, si, Senor *Sharlezz*, we understand." was their eager reply. So the men separated. Three to the corral to select their horses, and the rest, with Morgan and Carlos, hiked to the hide-storage barns. Morgan had had the hides prepared over the last twelve months by splitting his men into two groups, each group alternating between preparing the hides and salting the meat, and riding the range.

Morgan was pretty sure that Ruiz was still in Mexico, but he thought that some of his men might believe that Morgan had put his whole crew to work at the shore and they therefore might intrude onto his land.

Morgan was very mindful of the warning that agent Hiram Palmer had passed along about Ruiz' ambitions. He wanted to assign more men to the range patrol, but he had to get the hides loaded or not have any income for the next year. It was a difficult choice he had to make, but in the end he decided, it was his only choice. In the past, in addition to the sale of hides, Morgan had additional income from selling the preserved meat to the military, as well as to some of the visiting trading vessels. He also gave some to nearby Missions, if their own supply was too little to support the large native populations now living at these Missions. And now, since the new government had not paid the military, they were unable to buy their meat supply. They depended on the local ranchers to provide it, issuing notes that the new government would hopefully honor in the future. The Missions, too, had their government stipend discontinued, so that if they needed supplies from a rancher like Morgan, they were unable to pay for the goods. Much bartering transpired.

The loading went well. It took almost three weeks to move all of the hides, Morgan counted 5253 of them, to the crest of the cliff overlooking the beach below. Just as before, the sailors found it amusing to chase the hides as they sailed downward. A few of the sailors had been to this beach before and remembered this unusual loading method. To them, it seemed less laborious than just carrying hides from a barn to their dinghies. The *Pilgrim* had arrived well laden with hides and other commodities from Monterey, and with the addition of this new cargo, was so heavily loaded that its gunwale was near the water. It unfurled its sails one at a time and began to pull out into the channel and then to the ocean waters. Morgan and Carlos watched until it was well away, each wondering when they would again have an opportunity to trade with a Yankee ship, or any other.

The hide-storage barns were some distance from Morgan's house because the stench of the scraped and drying hides was so repugnant that the operation could not be done near the living abode. The men therefore camped at the barn site. When Morgan, Carlos and the men returned to the *hacienda,* they found a note from Juan tacked to the door. Juan and his two hands had returned to the ranch house several times, replenished their supplies and returned to their patrol. It seemed that Morgan's plan was working just fine.

The ranch hands all ambled to their *cabana.,* while Morgan and Carlos went into their *casa.* As they entered, Morgan called out, "Anna Maria, we are home. We have finished loading the hides" He waited for a reply. There was none. Then Carlos called out, "*Madre, padre* and I have returned. We wish to tell you of the events of the past several weeks. We are pleased with ourselves." Still no reply. The two men looked at each other in anguish. Their exhilaration was now gone.

"*Buenas noches Senor Sharlezz, buenas noches Senor Carlos*", Martha addressed them as she entered the room from the *cocina.* "*Senora* has not been feeling well. She has been keeping to her room, with the shades drawn most of the time. I bring her meals but she does not eat much. I am very worried about her." Morgan looked exasperated. He had no idea of what to do. He wondered, is she really ill, or is she feigning her condition to gain sympathy. Either way, he had to find a way to bring her back to the reality of life. She was a wife, but without regard for her husband's needs, and she was a mother, but without apparent love for her son.

Carlos suggested, "Let me try, *padre*, to see if she will respond to me". Morgan nodded his assent. Carlos went to the door of his mother's room and tapped gently. "*Madre*, it is Carlos. May I enter to speak with you? *Padre* and I are greatly concerned about you." A feeble voice replied, "*Si*, Carlos, *entrar*." Carlos opened the door slowly and peered into the darkened room. He entered, closing the door slowly. After about twenty minutes he came out of the room and went to his anxious father. "*Padre, madre* wishes me to accompany her to Santa Barbara. She would like to visit *abuela* and *abuelo*. She is worried about them, the predicament that they may be facing, with all the unrest." Morgan was relieved that Anna Maria was showing some signs of reality by wanting to visit her parents, not apparently hiding the truth from herself. "Oh, *si,* Carlos, *si*. Do accompany her, and stay as long as she likes. And Martha will go along as well."

The following morning Carlos saddled his own horse and two more that he knew to be gentle, for his mother and Martha. As Anna Maria came to the door she glanced at Morgan, then quickly looked outside for

Carlos, and moved to her horse immediately. Martha followed, carrying a pouch of *pan, queso and vino*. Morgan waved after them, but only Carlos and Martha waved back.

That day all fourteen of Morgan's men were able to ride the range to tend the herd. Morgan sent them in several groups and in different directions. In late afternoon one of the riders came hurrying to the *casa* calling, *"Senor Sharlezz, senor Sharlezz"*. Morgan ran outside hurriedly to meet the rider. "What is it, *Pedro?* Is there a problem with Ruiz or his men?" Pedro dropped from his saddle quickly to report. Some of Ruiz' men had been spotted along the southeast corner of Morgan's rangeland, though there were no cattle in the area at the time. Morgan saddled up and the two rode at a fast gallop back to the area. Morgan met several of his men including Juan, at the encounter location. Juan spoke, *"Senor Sharlezz*, we intercepted Ruiz' men, ordered them to leave your property at once. They stated that they were not here to steal any of your cattle, only to claim the land, because *Senor* Ruiz now was the deeded owner. They say that his claim comes from the new *Presidente* of *Mejico,* Guadalupe Victoria. Can this be so?"

"I don't know, Juan, there is so much confusion in the government I suppose anything is possible. I'll ride over to Ruiz' *casa* tomorrow and talk to him. If he got it legally, I'm going to be in trouble. You come with me Juan." The two turned and rode away, leaving four very concerned *vaquero*. Early the next morning, as he had said that he would, Morgan rode to Ruiz' ranch-house. Upon inquiring, he was told that Ruiz had not yet returned from Mexico, but had sent a messenger ahead that he now owned one-third of Morgan's land, and much of the land of Morgan's father-in-law as well. Now Morgan was even more concerned. If there was a confrontation at Santa Barbara, Anna Maria and Carlos might be involved. He returned to his own *hacienda*, ordered Juan to saddle up his own horse, then advised the one man on guard there that they were riding to Santa Barbara. They started out immediately and rode the entire distance at a fast gallop. By the time they reached the Ortega *hacienda* at Santa Barbara they were both exhausted. When entering the *casa*, they looked so disheveled that Carlos and the Ortegas hurried to them. "*Mi Dios, Sharlezz*, what is wrong. Why have you pressed so hard to arrive here?" *Senor* Ortega showed great concern. Anna Maria was present but remained in the background, though she looked very apprehensive also. Upon seeing *Senora* Morgan, Juan left the group, standing unobtrusively near the entry door.

Morgan related what he had learned, then ordered, "Carlos, you should ride to the *Presidio* and tell *Capitan Hernadez* of Ruiz' plot. Ask if he has learned whether the new government has contrived with Ruiz to steal our land." Carlos left immediately, but on his return two hours later, he showed his dejection. Carlos' report was not pleasant. "*Capitan* Hernandez states that has no direct knowledge of any new land deeds being issued to Ruiz, but says that has learned that the new government is indeed issuing deeds to their loyal supporters, not only to men already in *Alta California*, but to others in *Mejico*, of the *mestizos* and many, many of the craftsmen and laborers. And these deeds are for the same lands previously deeded long ago by the Viceroy of *Nueva Espana*."

Vice-Governor Ortega, Morgan and Carlos withdrew to the *oficina*, the Vice-Governor's private office, to discuss the matter beyond the hearing distance of the ladies. Ortega spoke first, "I will send a dispatch rider to the Governor at San Diego to learn if any official news has reached him. Governor Velasquez would surely have been informed of any change in land deeds within his jurisdiction." Morgan looked doubtful, "I'm not so sure *Senor* Ortega. From the rumors that we hear, the new government has become very liberal and shows no respect for the enactments of the previous government. But, *si*, you should seek official direction in the matter." Carlos nodded agreement then added, "Should we not prepare ourselves to defend our land if the so-called new owners try to usurp our rights?" The three looked at each other somberly, nodding agreement at both the plan and the prospects.

The next morning the entire group, less Juan, ate breakfast together. Juan had breakfast with the *vaqueros* in their ranch house, so as not to upset *Senora* Morgan. Even after all these years he knew that Anna Maria had not forgiven him, nor accepted the fact that little Maria Consuela had been killed in an unfortunate accident. He knew that she still blamed him for her dear daughter's death. Just then, Carlos came to the ranch-house. "Juan, my *padre* would like you to join us in the *casa*. We need to discuss our future plans." All four men had just convened in the Vice Governor's office when a servant announced that *Capitan* Hernandez would like to speak with them.

Following the usual greetings, the Captain announced, "*Senor* Governor Ortega, I wish to advise you that I am leaving the army, and will be returning to Spain as soon as I can arrange passage." The four men were stunned. The Governor spoke first in his official capacity. "*Capitan*, I am distressed to learn of this decision, although under the circumstances I understand your consternation. We will dearly miss your command ability, and certainly your friendship. Have you notified your army superior?" Looking disheartened, the Captain explained, "I have sent a letter of resignation to General Montez in *Ciudad de Mejico*, but quite frankly, I don't know if he is my superior. I have received no commands from any superior for nearly one year. Obviously great confusion exists, not only in the political government, but also in the military. I wrote an official resignation, stating my age as my reason, so that I would not possibly be later accused of treason. I had actually expected that when I was eligible for my pension, I would settle here in *Alta California*. After all, I have spent the majority of my military career here. But now I recognize that I cannot expect to have the future life that I had planned. I have relatives remaining in *Espana*. I hope that they will accept my return to their kinship."

Morgan looked hard at the Captain and suddenly realized that Hernandez now looked to be quite an old man. He had not thought about the years since they had first met, and that both are more almost thirty years older now. He thought back to the first time that he saw Anna Maria. She was in the arms of Hernandez, dancing. Morgan always thought that

Hernandez would like to have married Anna Maria, but he was more than twenty years her senior. Her father would never have approved. So Hernandez remained a single man all of his life, married to his army career.

Now Morgan spoke, "Oh, *mi amigo*, you have stunned us with this announcement, though I understand your reasoning. We are all disturbed by the lack of communication and direction of our new government. And in the military, lack of control is inexcusable. *Mi amigo*, we will all miss you, and I know that your *soldatos* will miss you, and your firm but compassionate leadership." Again, all in the room nodded agreement. Each of them embraced the Captain, then shaking his hand vigorously, they wished him good fortune in his future. Governor Ortega was the last to speak, "My son, you know how much I have appreciated your service, and your friendship, these many years. I will personally miss you, as will the people of Santa Barbara. Now let me ask, who will command your troops?" Looking very military, Hernandez, saluted the Vice Governor, then replied, "Your excellency, since there is no other officer assigned here at the *Presidio*, I am designating *Sargento* Montez to become the new commander of the *Presidio* and *soldatos.*" Ortega looked satisfied, "Montez is a very good soldier. A good choice *Capitan.*" With a smart salute to all and a slight bow, the Captain turned and left the office. Ortega, looking very somber, spoke. "*Sharlezz,* Carlos, Juan, whether we like it or not, we have reached the end of an era. Our lives will never be the same again." Each wondered individually how the new era would affect them. From the distraught looks on their faces, none seemed to believe that the future would be as enjoyable as was the past.

They continued their discussion of the matters of defense of their property. "It is now questionable", Morgan offered, "that we can depend on the *soldatos.* We don't know where their loyalty lies." Ortega, looking very pensive, said, "You are right *Sharlezz,* even as Vice Governor, I do not know if I will receive support in matters that I deem necessary on behalf of the government." Morgan inquired of Ortega, "What of your own *vaqueros, can y*ou depend on them to defend your land?" Ortega looked surprised that Morgan would raise such a question. "Why, I believe so, *Sharlezz*, but you give me concern. I have no reason for suspicion of disloyalty, but I suppose I should not assume that my *hombres* are not also affected by the unrest and rumors that abound."

Morgan suggested that Carlos remain at his grandfather's *hacienda* permanently to oversee any defense, but both Carlos and Ortega objected to this proposal. Ortega felt that he and his men would be able to protect against any illegal attempt at seizure, but expressed great concern at the possibility of a legal usurpation of his land. He did not know if, or how much longer, his superior Governor Velasquez, would be the presiding officer of *Alta California*. It was Velasquez that had assured Ortega that there would be no seizure of the lands granted by the former Viceroy, appointee of the King of their country, *Nueva Espana.*

Now Carlos spoke, "No *padre*, I will remain here as long as *madre* remains, but I will return to *Rancho del Sol* when *madre* does. It is my land as well as yours you know." Morgan replied, "You are right

Carlos. *Si,* remain with your *madre* and bring her home safely. Come, Juan, we better start back ourselves." Soon, both Morgan and Juan were mounted and with a wave to the others, began their gallop north, along *El Camino Real.* After riding several hours they stopped to let the horses rest and take water from a small nearby stream. "Do you realize where we are, Juan", Morgan asked. At first Juan did not seem to understand the question, but suddenly realized the point of Morgan's inquiry. "*Si, Senor Sharlezz.* We are only a short distance from the painted caves of my ancestors. The caves which we visited together those many moons ago." Morgan reminisced, recalling the joy of those early years. He and Juan had come far together, each with a dream of the future. "And you, Juan, do you recall our youthful dreams. Me to marry Anna Maria and to own a rancho. And you?" Juan just smiled, "I had no dreams, *Sharlezz.* I was content to be a friend to you." Morgan thought of Juan's answer and once again realized that after the death of his beloved Angelica and her infant, his dreams were shattered. After that he must not have expected much joy in life.

"Well Juan, we had better get going again." The two began to ride at a slow pace now, as if not wanting to return to the troubles of life, but to laze in the enjoyment of yesteryear. As they rode along Morgan conversed with Juan, "I wonder why Ruiz rode all the way to *Ciudad de Mejico.* Why did he feel it necessary to do that?" Continuing his own thoughts he added, "Why does he think that he has a right to the land that was deeded to Vice Governor Ortega, and then to me? After all, it was the government's land to assign to anybody they wished. We didn't steal it." At that, Juan first smiled then broke into a laugh. "What is it?, why do you laugh?", Morgan asked. "Oh *Senor Sharlezz*, I mean no disrespect. I know that King of *Espana* felt that this was his land to dispose of as he wished. But did he not steal it from my ancestors? My people did not believe that a piece of parchment or paper entitled anyone to certain parts of the land. My ancestors believed that the land belonged to all, to be protected, and that its use was granted us by *Madre* Earth and *Padre* Sun. Is it not true that the white man has stolen the land from us."

Morgan had never heard Juan speak so sternly before. *"Si,* you are correct Juan. The white man has stolen the earth, from the ocean to the east, and all the way to this ocean. But, Juan, each changing of the moon brings more changes in our lives, and we must accept them." Morgan was trying to express to Juan his own regret, but he felt that he was doing a poor job of it. They rode the rest of the way in silence, each hoping that their friendship would continue in spite of their recently revealed differences.

They reached *Rancho del Sol* at sunset. They unsaddled the horses, wiped them down, and placed them in the coral. Then each went to their awaiting bed, Morgan in his *casa* and Juan in the *cabana* of the *vaqueros*. Early the next morning Juan came bursting into Morgan's bedroom. It was only one hour after dawn. *"Senor Sharlezz*, arise *pronto*. Ruiz and two of his *hombres* are riding towards us. They are riding very slowly, I believe to show that they mean no harm." Morgan leaped from his bed, tore off his nightshirt and began to dress. "Well Juan, I guess we'll soon know what Ruiz and the new government have in mind for us."

They met Ruiz and his men in front of the *casa*. "What can I do for you?", Morgan asked, trying to sound casual and without emotion, though inside he was quivering slightly. Ruiz replied, also trying to sound non-combative, "I've come to deliver to you your new deed, signed by *Presidente* Victoria himself. When you read it, you will realize that you are losing two-thirds of the land that you originally stole from the former country of *Nueva Espana.*, one third to me and one third to several natives that have helped our new government, by helping to dismantle the Missions." Morgan was very concerned about the 'dismantling of the Missions', but his immediate thought was, 'How important is Ruiz, that the President himself would be involved in land deeds?' Before he could offer a reply, Ruiz spoke, almost as if reading Morgan's mind. "After all these years of injustice, when I learned that my former army comrade General Augustin de Iturbide was to head the government, I left immediately to visit him. But he has instead allied himself with *Presidente* Victoria, and as a personal favor to Iturbide, Victoria signed several deeds, among them the ones affecting yours and your father-in-law's ranchos. You see, before I came to Alta California I was a *Capitan* in the Army of *Espana,* serving under *General* Itubide*"* But I left at the end of my service term, wishing to establish myself as a rancher in this new land."

Morgan realized that if what Ruiz said was true, there was little chance of reversing the new government's decision. Still he protested, "The new *Presidente* has no right to nullify the edicts of the previous government. These lands were legally deeded to the present land owners."

But Ruiz rebutted, "No, no *Senor* Morgan. The land always belonged to the government. When it is deeded to us, we are but caretakers. All of the land formerly belonged to King Ferdinand, but now it belongs to our new country of *Mejico*. The new officials can assign the care taking to anyone it wishes."

Morgan was very upset with Ruiz' explanation. It sounded all too true. He was losing a third of his land to the man that he loathed, the man he never trusted, and another third to rebellious natives. Morgan began again to protest. Ruiz interrupted, "It is of no purpose to protest. The deed is signed by the highest ranking officer of our new country of *Mejico.* In fact, *Presidente* Victoria was kind to you. Many previous deed holders have had all of their land reassigned to the citizens of *Mejico.* "

Ruiz and his men turned and rode away from Morgan's home. Morgan and Juan very dejected. 'What was he to do now Morgan wondered. Juan stood in silence knowing that his *amigo* and *patron* was feeling great despair. From the first time that Juan had met Morgan, he always had a plan for the future and was always optimistic. But Juan understood the gravity of this situation and realized that Morgan's whole future, and that of his son Carlos, was now in doubt.

Morgan summoned the few men who were at the *cabana* to come to his house. Sitting on the front *portico* Morgan explained to the men what was happening. All the men let out sounds of surprise and disgust. Now they, too, wondered about their future.

303

All were unmarried men with no family or ties except to their employment at the *Rancho del Sol.* That was their home and Morgan was like a father to them, even though some were as old, or older, than Morgan. Juan then spoke to them, asking that they ride out to the other men, relieving them so that they could return to hear the bad news from Morgan himself.

For the next several days the ranch was a sad place. Everyone was in a dejected mood. All waited, and hoped, that Morgan would offer a plan to overcome this disaster. Should *Senor* Morgan not ride to San Diego, or even *Ciudad de Mejico,* if necessary, to correct this error, the men grumbled. Morgan himself had thought of this possibility, but felt it would be futile. The new government certainly would feel no loyalty to him, or other ranchers like him, that were granted the privilege of land ownership by the former rulers. Although he did not like losing any of his land, he was less resentful of the portion being reassigned to the natives or the *mestisos,* for he recognized that their lives would be much improved from the poverty that many endured. But why Ruiz? Why should he be rewarded? He has shown no great effort on behalf of the new government. And he was always willing to disobey the laws of the former government. This part of the transaction was greatly disturbing to Morgan.

Although Morgan had not been attending Sunday mass regularly at *Santa Ines* or *La Purisimo,* he felt the need to go to church and pray, not just for guidance, but for a miracle. He summoned Juan. The two saddled their horses and began the half-day journey to *Santa Ines.* As they approached the Mission, it was obvious that things were not normal. The native women were not at the *lavenderia* in front of the Mission, singing as they washed their clothes. This ritual occurred on almost every day of the week. And no men were in the gardens or vineyards, doing their usual tasks. Morgan and Juan tied their horses to the hitching rail in front of the Mission and went inside to the *padre's oficio*. Padre de Uria was seated at his table with his head resting between his hands. Upon hearing the footsteps he looked up with a painful expression. "Oh, *Sharlezz, mi amigo*. Juan, *mi amigo*. It is so good that you have come." Morgan and Juan looked at each other with puzzled expressions. "What's happened, Padre, things don't seem to be normal here today", Morgan commented. "Oh, *ninguno, Sharlezz*, nothing is normal.", was de Uria's anguished reply. "I no longer have a Mission. It has been rented by the new government. Leased to a *diablo* named Jose Covarrubias. He is a friend of the new Governor of *Alta California*, Felixo Chico, who granted the mission to Covarrubias for a paltry sum. Oh, *mi Dios!* What is to become of our beautiful Mission? What is to become of the native neophytes? With no church, where are we to honor *Jesucristo*? Oh *mi Dios!"* Plainly Padre de Uria was in agony and in seeming disbelief at the decisions of the new government. 'So it is not only me that is victimized", Morgan thought. He spoke to the priest, "Padre, how do you know this? Who has informed you of this?" The padre extended a piece of paper to Morgan. It was certainly an official looking document. And it was indeed signed by the man who was apparently proclaimed the new Governor, the one replacing Velasquez, *Senor* Ortega's old friend. As Morgan read it, he too became infuriated. He held the paper toward Juan, who declined to read it. Morgan continued to study the document. "*Padre*, you are correct. The Mission has indeed been rented to *Senor* Covarrubias, and for a few hundred *pesos*. All of these beautiful buildings, rented for a few hundred *pesos*." Morgan glanced again at the document. "Wait, Padre, all is not gone. In this new deed the church is granted the right to retain the padre's quarters, and, you are allowed control of the church. These portions are excluded from the grant to Covarrubias." The three men seemed a little more relieved. But it was difficult to feel any elation, knowing that this large Mission compound was being turned over to a stranger, and one who was apparently not religious, for if he were, he would not have accepted this lease from Governor Chico.

As Morgan returned the document he spoke to de Uria, "Padre, there is much to do. Can we sound the bell to call the neophytes together. We need them to clean out the store rooms and move the furniture and supplies, before Covarrubias arrives." *"Mi caro amigo"*, the Padre replied, "it is too late for that. *Senor* Covarrubias is already at hand. It was he who delivered this document only a few hours ago." Morgan started to reply, "But let us..." he was interrupted by a stranger entering the *oficio*. "*Me llamo* Covarrubias. I am the new owner of this property. And who are you two to trespass here?" Morgan showed his irritation, "We are not trespassing, *Senor*, we are here as guests of Padre de Uria, who has the right to use this portion of the Mission compound, as stated in the document that you delivered to him." The man's reply was intended to taunt Morgan, "No, *senor*, this *oficio* is not part of the padre's quarters, nor of the church. You are all trespassing on my property. I order all of you to leave." Padre de Uria now spoke, "*Senor* Covorrubias, surely you will allow me this small room in which to conduct my duties. I have temporal matters to administer, as well as priestly duties to perform."

Now Covarrubias laughed heartily, "Oh!, so you have temporal matters to attend. What are they, *senor*, to sell the wheat that I now own; to sell the tallow that I now own; to sell the carpenter's tools, the saddle maker's tools, the blacksmith's tools. No, *senor*, you may not allow any of these materials to be removed from the mission buildings. I own all that is within these buildings. So you see, you will have no need of an *oficio*. Now remove your holy books, your holy statues and your holy pictures, before I throw them to the *viento.*" The padre was astounded. Morgan was furious. Juan was bewildered. Morgan spoke, "So you are an *hombre* who does not believe in *Dios*. You have not recognized all that the Almighty has given you." Covarrubias derided Morgan's comments. "No, what I have, I have earned, or have taken. I am a man that believes only in the strength of force, and in himself. So now, *hombres*, remove yourselves *pronto.*" He placed his hand on the handle of the pistol that he wore, awaiting Morgan's and the others next action. Morgan spoke to his friends, "Come, it appears that for now, this *diablo* has the upper hand. We must move all that is sacred to the church building." The three began to gather all that they could carry in their arms. The church building was connected to the end of the portico, only a few steps away from the *oficio*. Two trips by each accomplished the move. As a temporary resting place, they placed all on the rear pews of the church, then began to confer on their next move. "Well, Padre, it seems that you have a quandary here". Morgan spoke, "You had better observe the rules of this *diablo* Covarrubias, or he might try to injure you. What in the world causes a man become such a devil?" Padre de Uria spoke philosophically, "There have been many men like him in the world since the beginning of time. They may prevail for a while but not forever. I think that we should now all pray for the conversion of such men, that they be brought to see the will of *Dios*." The three men walked to the altar rail of the church and knelt. De Uria, placing his hand to his forehead, began, "*En el nombre del Padre...*" Morgan and Juan joined him, "*...y del Hijo, y del Espiritu Santo.*" The three recited the Lord's prayer then several Hail Marys.

Morgan and Juan departed the padre's company, wishing him good fortune in his dealings with Covarrubias and offering to help in any way they could. They promised to be in contact with de Uria often. As they rode back to their ranch they discussed the contemptible actions of the new government. They spoke of the situation at *Rancho del Sol.* and the adjustments that would need to be made due to the loss of so much land. Then they spoke again of the man Covarrubias and poor Padre de Uria's plight. They decided that they had better attend Sunday mass every week, not just for their souls, but to keep aware of the distressing situation at *Santa Ines*.

As they reached their ranch a rider approached. They recognized him as one of *Senor* Ortega's *vaquero*. Morgan called to him, "What message do you bring. Is there a problem at the Vice Governor's *rancho*?" *Si, si, Senor Sharlezz,"* he called back to Morgan. He was now near Morgan and Juan, but remained in his saddle as if to quickly depart again. "The dispatch rider that was sent to San Diego by *Senor* Ortega has returned. He has notified the Vice Governor that Governor Velasquez has been removed from office and a new man, Felixo Chico has been appointed Governor of *Alta California. Senor* Ortega wishes you to know that he has now received the notice that his former deed is without sanction, and that much of his land has been deeded to a man named Carillo, a supporter of the new government, and a portion to *Senor* Ruiz. Also, *Senor* Ortega wishes you to know that your deed is also in jeopardy." Morgan ordered the rider to return with the message for the Vice Governor that he is aware of the new Governor's appointment and that he has been notified that he will lose much of his land, but not all. The rider quickly departed.

On arising the next morning, Morgan decided that he must meet with his *vaqueros* to tell them of his need to reduce their numbers, and yet contain his herd within the bounds of his new land limit. It would be difficult to round up all the cattle and keep them more restricted, but if he allowed them to wander, many would be rustled by the new arrivals and claimed as their own, even though branded with the mark of *Rancho del Sol.* He had just finished instructing his men about the new conditions when another of Ortega's cowhands came riding in at a very fast gallop. "*Senor Sharlezz*!", he called. "*Senor* Ortega has become very ill. *Senora* Morgan urges you to return to Santa Barbara as quickly as possible."

Morgan saddled his horse and departed at a fast gallop alone, leaving Juan in charge of the new ranch plans. Upon arrival at *Senor* Ortega's *casa*, he was met at the front door by Anna Maria and Carlos. "Oh! *Sharlezz*", Anna Maria spoke with tears, "I'm am so happy that you came. My poor *padre* has taken very ill. His heart is painful. First he received the sad news of losing his land. He was already expecting that tragic information. Then he was told of the removal of his dear friend Velasquez from office, followed by the news that many *soldatos* are refusing to take orders from *Sargento* Montez, and are stealing land and cattle from the mission herds. *Padre* uttered "anarchy", then collapsed." Carlos too, spoke to his father, "Oh, *padre*, thank *Dios* you are here. We are all very distressed. We know not what to do. We quickly summoned Doctor Gonzalez, but he offers little hope for *Abucio's* recovery. We are praying, and Padre Amistoy is with *Abucio,* but he does not respond." They led Morgan to the bedroom of *Senor* Ortega. There they found *Senora* Ortega praying outside the door. Padre Amistoy then came from the bedroom. "I have given the *Senor* Extreme Unction, the last rites. Please continue to pray for his peaceful passing." With those words, *Senora* Ortega began to utter loud sobs. "Oh, *mia Dios*, please let my dear *esposo* live." The bedroom door again opened. The doctor came out, looked at the five standing expectantly, and shook his head. "*Senora*, I am sorry, but your *amado esposo* has passed away. His heart could no longer withstand the pain."

The *Senora* slumped into a chair while Anna Maria quickly knelt, laying her head on her mother's lap. As the mother stroked the hair of the daughter, the two women cried loud sobs. Morgan placed his arm around Carlos shoulder, and with a strong embrace said, "I am so sorry Carlos. Your grandfather was a wonderful man. He is the victim of these trying times in which we continue to live."

CHAPTER SIXTEEN
Pleasant recollections…
sad happenings…wild ideas!

It was an especially beautiful springtime in 1840. The trees were budding and many flowering bushes were already in bloom. The winter rains had been mild, just enough to fertilize the new plants and invigorate the old. The nights were still cool but the midday temperatures were very pleasant. Morgan was pleased with the way things had turned out. Not at all as dire as he had thought might be the case several years before. Now he often rode his favorite horse, *Pacifico,* to the top of the bluff overlooking the ocean, and surveyed the view of the coastline. He could not help but reminisce about how he came ashore that night almost forty years before. 'My, was it that long ago?', he thought.

He recalled the year or so that he had spent as a pirate on Hippolyte Bouchard's corsair. He wondered if Bouchard had ever been caught, as so many of the pirate captains had been. For with the growth of commercial shipping by the Spanish, Portuguese, British, and even the United States, these countries had become much more aggressive in their pursuit of pirates and buccaneers. The practice of piracy on the high seas and the land assaults such as Bouchard had made on Monterey were now almost non-existent. Since the pursuit of pirates by these nations was generally successful, Morgan believed that Bouchard surely must have been taken by one nation or the other.

He was certainly glad that he had not remained with that lawless band of freebooters. As Morgan reminisced about those years he shuttered to think about why he had been so foolish as to have believed the sailors that enticed him. 'My, how life would have been different if I had not escaped over the side of that ship', he reflected.

As he spied a ship passing well out to sea, he raised a telescope to his eye to determine its nationality. This one was flying the Union Jack of Britain. The ship was traveling with its gunwale riding close to the water. No doubt she had a full cargo taken on at San Francisco or Monterey. Then he realized that he had not seen a Russian ship for several years now. The Russians had discontinued their pursuit of seals, otters and whales off the California coast, now remaining to the north, where they could catch large herds of these mammals without interference.

Turning his gaze inland to the north, he remembered again his coming ashore long ago He recalled how he had met his good friends Padre Payeras, Cimkonah, Juan Bautista, Angelica, Padre Castellanos, *Capitan* Hernandez, and so many more. At the memory of Payeras, Cimkonah and Angelica, he would say a silent prayer for them. His beautiful little girl, Maria Consuela came to mind, and his father and mother-in-law *Senor* and *Senora* Ortega. He prayed silently for them as well. He wondered if his friend Castellanos was still in San Francisco, or did he too abandon his post when the new government had disbanded the Mission holdings. If he had, who could blame him. As if overnight, the padres had become the enemies to the many who had championed their efforts before. 'My how quickly life changes!', he thought. But here on the pleasant *Rancho del Sol,* life had been extremely enjoyable for many years now.

After the death of his father-in-law, Vice Governor Ortega, Morgan had begun keeping a journal. At first he felt it to be a protective document in the event that some government quasi-official tried to cheat him further of his land and holdings. But actually, after the initial turmoil of the new government's edicts, most matters settled down pretty well. Now, in addition to the events of the day, Morgan had been noting the many changes that were occurring, to the native peoples, the influx of new settlers from *Mejico,* and even of more Americans and Englishmen into the *pueblos.* It seemed that with every ship arriving in port at either Monterey, San Francisco or Santa Barbara, which he visited often, he noted or heard of some of the crewmen remaining in California. These were industrious individuals, more inclined to open shops or establish fisheries or ranches, taking advantage of the opportunities that some of the Mexicans seemed not to recognize. Of course with their encroachment, differences between them and the natives or Mexicans occurred often. The local *alcalde,* the justice of the peace, would find it necessary to arbitrate matters, for although the law of the land was *Mejicano,* these new Americans and Englishmen believed the laws with which they were familiar were more sensible.

The greatest difficulty that these new pioneers found was with the *administradores,* the government appointed administrators of the rules and regulations that were being implemented in *Ciudad de Mejico,* the seat of the new country. Most of these administrators were petty politicians that had been rewarded with a post in the expanded government. Most were as much concerned with developing their own fortunes as they were at enforcing compliance with the new government's laws. The payment of a few *pesos* would most often eliminate the so-called infractions.

Over the past few years many unexpected developments had occurred in Morgan's favor. Not only did he not have to lay-off some of his workers, he did in fact have to hire many additional ranch-hands as well as craftsmen to help run *Rancho del Sol.* Thankfully, his son Carlos was a very capable manager. Due to Morgan's tutelage over the years, was intimately familiar with every aspect of ranching. The *rancho's* staff now numbered more than four dozen people, plus the wives of some of his cowhands and craftsmen. With these families there were many children about, so several of the wives became teachers, cooks and bakers for what was now almost a *pueblo* in itself.

Morgan turned back the pages of his journal to see when last he had received a letter from his brother George. It had been several years. He had written George last in 1832, ('my, could it have been so long ago?'), informing his brother of his good fortunes, and of the growth of his fine son, Carlos. He avoided telling much of Anna Maria's condition. He noted from his journal that he had received a return letter in April 1835 from his sister-in-law Harriett, containing the sad news of his brother's and sister's deaths. He extracted the letter from the back leaf of his journal and read it for the fourth or fifth time.

23 November 1834

My dearest brother-in-law Charles,

It is with great sorrow that I inform you of the death of your beloved brother George. I also regret not having written you much sooner, but the disease from which dearest George suffered was so debilitating and painful that I spent almost my entire day trying to provide some little comfort to him. Unfortunately, there is not much treatment for this terrible disease, arthritis. George first showed symptoms many years ago, but of recent times the pain was so severe that we were unable to maintain our farm, nor take care of himself very well. We were forced to sell the farm and land two years ago and to move into town. George was a loving husband to me and devoted father to our children. We shall miss him greatly.

I also sad to inform you that your sister Mary has passed away She found her heavenly bliss at about the time that we moved into town. For the last few years of her life she suffered many pains in the heart, until finally she succumbed. Poor Seth is devastated. He had sold his hardware store so that he could attend Mary in her distress. He remains a sad figure here in town.

Our dear daughter Abigail, now nearing 25 years of age, has been married for nearly seven years and has three lovely children. Her husband is a bank administrator. They reside in Worcester.

Our son Charles, your namesake, has completed his studies at Harvard and is pursuing additional studies to become a lawyer. He is very handsome and intelligent. This trait seems to run in your family.

While visiting Harriett and her family in Worcester I noted a new Catholic Church and one of those priest fellows. I presume that he is like those that you are so friendly with there in California. This church, and the priest, are the result of a strong influx of immigrants from Ireland. They, and the immigrants from Canada, constitute the primary work force for the many mills that are prospering in the area.

Charles, I am again apologetic for not having informed you sooner of this tragic news. I do hope that you understand the circumstances.

Be assured that you and your family will continue to be in our thoughts.

Your loving sister-in-law,
Harriett.

P.S. We were most pleased to learn of the successful ranching enterprise that you have developed. We hope that your good fortune continues. George was most pleased to know that you prosper well in your far away California. We send our best regards to your dear wife and your son Carlos. Dare we hope that someday we will meet you and your loved ones?

When he received that letter, Morgan had given serious thought about returning east for a visit. After all, it was possible now to take a stagecoach all the way to St. Louis, and from there board the new steam locomotive that traveled to New York City. And

317

another short coach ride would bring him to Sturbridge. Following just this brief consideration, he quickly decided that such a trip was not practical.

When he commented to Carlos about his fleeting thoughts Carlos was more excited about such a trip, not for him, but for his father. He stated that he would remain to oversee the ranch operations and that his padre should return to his home village. Further, Carlos suggested, his padre should visit Washington, to meet with his long-ago friends Nathaniel Aldrich and his wife Becky. Aldrich was now the United States Senator from Massachusetts and was the chairman of The Committee on Territorial Matters. Perhaps he could help by interceding with the President regarding matters of the Missions' difficulties. No, Charles retorted, that was of no importance to the President of the United States. Carlos, not wishing to oppose his father, relented with the jovial comment that his father must be getting old. But during the next few days Carlos secretly penned a letter to his father's friend Senator Aldrich and had it dispatched by a rider to the port of Monterey.

Morgan had told his son that here on his ranch, with the increase of cattle, horses and swine, and yield of crops, barrel makers, dairymen, blacksmiths and a number of other craftsmen that were employed, all needed his attention. He stated that both he and Carlos' attention was necessary to run his now vast *rancho*. And he felt that his personal direction was necessary, even though Carlos was a fine assistant.

Indeed, Morgan's holdings had not been reduced as he had earlier expected, but following the initial loss of some of his land, he gained a substantial portion of it back through a completely unforeseen circumstance, an event which created the basis for many new opportunities.

About six years after the confrontation with Humberto Ruiz regarding the land deeds, Morgan was summoned to Ruiz's *hacienda* by one of his men. Morgan rode there with some trepidation about his personal safety and with much curiosity as to why Ruiz summoned him. Following an unusually courteous greeting, Ruiz related an amazing tale to Morgan. First he explained why he was enraged that Morgan had received a land grant from Vice-Governor Ortega. "You see", he explained, "I expected to be named the Vice-Governor, not your father-in-law." Morgan could not hide his surprise at this incredible statement. Ruiz continued, "so I was naturally jealous. I had been promised the position by my former superior, General Augustin de Iturbide" Another surprise look on Morgan's face caused Ruiz to smile very slightly. "Of course at the time that I served under him, many years ago, he was a mere *Capitan*. But when he gained higher rank and became quite powerful, he tried to get me appointed. But because I was not friendly with *Alta California's* new Governor Joaquin de Arrillaga, and because I was not of the *peninsular* class, I was born in *Nueva Espana* you see, I was not regarded by those in political authority to be worthy of the appointment, even though I had served the King in his military service for more than three decades."

So far, Morgan was very bewildered. Why was Ruiz now relating his life story to him? Ruiz sat calmly, while both men sipped on glasses of *tequila*.

Continuing his story, Ruiz added, "So as an appeasement to Santa Anna, the governing officials begrudgingly agreed to grant me this land. Of course, I felt that I had earned it, having served King Carlos for so many years. And then you, a *novicio Americano*, you were given the land just because you married Ortega's *hermoso hija,* his beautiful daughter. Of course I was jealous of you!" He sipped more tequila. He was now more relaxed but at the same time intense, as he unfolded more of the story. "So you are wondering, why did I ask you to meet me here, eh?", he looked inquisitively at Morgan, who did indeed show a puzzled expression. "Well, *mi amigo*", Ruiz continued. With that '*mi amigo*', Morgan smiled very broadly. Ruiz smiled too. "Oh, *si Senor*, over these several years I have mellowed towards you, for I have observed your calm demeanor, even when we might have been more aggressive towards each other. I have come to respect your ability as a *ganadero,* a rancher, you know. But more than that, I have learned of your kindness to others who are less fortunate than you. And, though you may not believe it to be so, I am a kind person also, as you will understand soon enough." Now Morgan was really wondering, 'what in the world is this fellow leading up to?'

Ruiz continued to explain further. "I have been a *soltero,* what you call a bachelor, all of my life, so naturally I have no heirs. I have arranged that upon my death, half of my very extensive land holdings, and all of my cattle, will be apportioned and deeded to each of my long-time *vaqueros*. They deserve this compensation for their loyalty. They have worked diligently on my behalf. I am also providing them with some monetary rewards, of which I have accumulated a small amount." Again, Morgan was confused by this explanation of Ruiz's personal decision regarding his estate. "Now, *mi amigo senor* Morgan," Ruiz continued, "I want to explain what will become of the other portion of my land, the portion that was once yours." Now Morgan began listening very intently, anxious to hear of Ruiz's decision regarding the land taken from him by the changed governmental deeds. "That land I offer for sale to you, now, at a very reasonable price," Ruiz declared, "the proceeds to be added to my estate, and subsequently divided among my faithful *vaqueros*, so that they will have some *pesos* with which to expand their *ranchos*." Morgan was indeed interested in obtaining that land again. At first he was going to express his opinion that the land was really still his, but then he decided not to treat the matter as a litigation. Morgan accepted Ruiz' proposal and they quickly settled on a price and an arrangement for payment.

Now ready to depart, Morgan bowed to Ruiz, shook his hand and stated, "We have made a bargain. I appreciate that you have included me in your ultimate plans." As Morgan walked to his awaiting horse, he was accompanied by Ruiz's closest *vaquero*. "It is too bad," the man stated, "that such a fine man as *Senor* Ruiz will die at an age when many men continue to enjoy a robust life." Morgan stopped quickly, "Why do you say *Senor* Ruiz will die?" The man seemed surprised that Morgan did not know. "Oh, I thought that *Senor* Ruiz explained about his health." Morgan thought back to this just concluded meeting and realized that Ruiz' skin looked yellowish, but he had not thought about the fact earlier. "What of *Senor* Ruiz' health?", Morgan asked. The man replied, "Oh, when *Senor* was a young soldier in the area of *Chiapas* in the south of *Mejico*, he contacted a disease from an *insecto*, how you say, a mosquito, that affects many parts of the body. After these many years, he has become much more worse. He expects to die within a few months. Many former soldiers who served with him have already died of this yellowing disease."

Now Morgan wondered, should he go back to see Ruiz and express his sympathy? No, he decided. If Ruiz had wanted him to know of the disease and its consequences, he would have told Morgan. 'Thank the Good Lord, I have my health', Morgan reflected. Thus Morgan's *ranchero* had become enlarged, more productive and more prosperous.

Nowadays in these late afternoons, as Morgan sat on his *portico* facing west, and when the tide rolled in, he could hear the pounding surf, even though it was several hundred meters from his home. It was pleasant to sit in the sun and make his daily journal entry. Often, he would glance back at earlier pages and remember the events of a particular day, some pleasant, some unpleasant, some even frightening.

After *Senor* Ortega's death, almost six years ago now, Anna Maria had brought her mother to live at the Morgan *casa*. This often required some indulgence on Morgan's part. He was always pleasant to *Senora* Ortega, but often her interference with his wishes required him to control his normally even temperament. To improve life for all, he had the *casa* expanded so that the *Senora* had her own "domain". She had brought her own favorite servant, Magdalena, with her when joining the Morgan household. The new maid in the kitchen required patience by Martha, but soon Martha's and Magdalena's compatibility formed a mutual understanding for the use of the *cocina*. In fact, in a reasonable amount of time they became good friends. Magdalena was the older of the two, about the age of Morgan and Juan Bautista. Juan had not overlooked that fact. It soon became noticeable that he came to the kitchen more often than he had before. Morgan surmised that there might be some romantic interest by Juan, and Magdalena did not show any objection to his visitations.

The additional rooms to the *casa* had been built by Ignacio Remirez, who had moved to Morgan's ranch after the closing of the *La Purisima* Mission. Ignacio and his wife Rosa, and their six children, had all moved into a small *cabana* that Ignacio built on land that Morgan granted to him. In addition to his carpenter craft, Ignacio had also become a fine wagon-maker. With the expansion of Morgan's ranching and farming, many wagons were now being used to haul produce, tallow, and sometimes even the many hides, to Monterey where the continuing trade with the foreign vessels was flourishing better than ever. Roberto and Margarita Mendez and their four children had also become a part of the *Rancho del Sol's* work force, Roberto as a fine saddle maker and Margarita as a seamstress. Though the clothing made by Margarita was mainly for the residents of *Rancho del Sol*, Roberto's saddles were of such fine quality that they were in demand as a commercial product, sought by both Californians and the agents of the many trading ships.

Together Ignacio and Roberto had built a fine surrey, beautifully finished with lacquers that Morgan obtained from a French ship. Now that the lanes to Santa Barbara were widened and improved by the many wagons that traversed them, the surrey was used often by Anna Maria and her mother to travel to Santa Barbara where they visited the graves of *Senor* Ortega and little Maria Consuela. They also visited many friends still remaining in the *pueblo* of Santa Barbara. Surprisingly, after the governmental confusion settled down, social life again became a nicety enjoyed by the residents. In fact, some of the former craftsmen at the Mission compounds had established their own craft shops or began ranching or farming on small plots and many had become minimally successful. They were now also a part of the social circle. The immigrant Americans and Englishmen were also welcomed.

Another event had greatly affected the Morgan's family life. About six or seven months after the departure of *Capitan* Hernandez, a new officer was appointed to command the *Presidio.* He was *Capitan* Diego Cordova. The good Captain was a widower who had a beautiful daughter, and although she was just a few years younger than Carlos, who was now twenty-seven years of age, she was still unmarried. Soon, a courtship between Carlos and the lovely lady, *Senorita* Carmencita Cordova, had begun. After about one year of courtship, in June of 1836 Carlos and Carmencita became man and wife in a grand wedding at Mission Santa Barbara. The nuptial mass was celebrated by Padre Jose' Rodriguez, who had succeeded *Padre* Amistoy a few years earlier. Amistoy had retired to the Franciscan's seminary in Mexico City. Carlos and

Carmencita now resided in their own *casa* on the *Rancho del Sol*, on a beautiful knoll, also overlooking the Pacific ocean. To add to the joy of life, Morgan and Anna Maria were now the grandparents of two lovely girls, Maria Elena, now almost three years of age, and Maria Terese, just a little more that one year old.

With the return of Anna Maria's mother into her daily life, Anna Maria became more pleasant, even mellow at times. She still forbade Morgan conjugal pleasures, and still insisted on separate bed chambers, but at least she was congenial and conversational. This eased the abrasion between the two so that all could enjoy their meals together. Besides, at age fifty-eight, Morgan's desires for affection had waned somewhat. He had long ago adjusted to the life of a bachelor.

The two Morgan families were now in the custom of attending Sunday mass together at *Mision Santa Ines*. But it seemed that each Sunday the Mission was becoming more and more forsaken. Without craftsmen or neophytes to tend to its corporeal needs, the church and the small padre's quarters were becoming dilapidated. Then one Sunday morning, after completing the celebration of the mass, Padre de Uria announced to his small congregation that he was returning to the Franciscan's seminary in *Mejico*. It was a tearful goodbye in which everyone expressed their gratitude to the Padre for his service to them for so many years, and it seemed that each person wished to reminisce with the Padre about some important incident or event in their lives.

Morgan himself recalled an incident that had occurred just a few years before. On that particular day, a neophyte came running to Morgan's *casa*, panting so hard that he could hardly narrate his story to Morgan. The young man related how the leaser of the Mission buildings, one *Senor* Jose' Covarrubias, and Padre de Uria were engaged in a fierce argument. Morgan immediately saddled his horse, pulled the young native onto the rump of the steed and rode at top speed to *Santa Ines*. On arrival he found the two men still involved in their dispute. Contrary to a previous understanding by the two, Covarrubias was now insisting that the Padre had no right to use the Mission courtyard for his daily walk. As in most Missions, it was the custom of the padre to walk the courtyard perimeter while reading his *officio* prayers, the daily requirement of every priest.

As soon as he realized the cause of the disagreement, Morgan arbitrated between the two angry men, proposing that a new wall be built to create a private portion for the priest, and the remainder of the courtyard for *Senor* Covarrubias to use as he saw fit. The two men agreed and for the next several weeks Morgan rode to the Mission daily to construct the wall with the help of Juan, a few neophytes and several of his own *vaqueros.* Some of Morgan's men had not been to the Mission for many years, ignoring their Catholic religion's tenet to attend mass every Sunday, and they were astounded at the poor condition of the buildings. Most had been converted to use as cattle stalls and swine pens, wheat and oats storage, or other shameful uses. One portion was even being used as a *cantina* and brothel.

Morgan himself had been witness to the gradual degradation, but the men had not realized the degree to which the facilities had been allowed to erode. They were dismayed at the conditions. Where roof tiles had been removed for resale, the beams and the adobe were now exposed to the elements and were showing their decay. There was no way to prevent this erosion without the help of the neophytes, who had now departed the Mission, returning to their own destitute villages, or were trying to eke out a subsistence on a piece of the former Mission *rancho,* with a few cattle or swine that they had purloined.

After building "the Padre's wall", Morgan could do no more for the Mission. His vital role in its development was now ended, just as was the Mission's own role of converting and "civilizing" the natives. The new government in *Mejico* cared nothing for the mission properties once they were rented to exploiters like Covarrubias and later sold to the exploiters, like Jose' Carillo.

For the next several years the Morgan families, that of Charles and that of Carlos, occasionally attended mass at the Mission Santa Barbara, which had avoided decay because of a few faithful neophytes and many of the nearby soldiers who had helped with maintaining the beautiful church and padre's quarters. But life had certainly changed for the Morgans, and more changes in their lives were inevitable.

While returning from one of their Sunday visits to *Mision Santa Barbara*, *Senora* Ortega suddenly began to gasp and hold her hand to her breast. "What is it, *Madre?",* Anna Maria had both fear and anxiety in her voice. The *Senora* was unable to reply, just motioned that she had pains in the chest and it was obvious that she was having great trouble breathing. It was late afternoon. Morgan turned the surrey around immediately and urging the horse to a gallop, headed back to Santa Barbara. It took almost two hours to return to the *pueblo*. Morgan drove immediately to the home of Doctor Gonzalez.

Morgan and Carlos gently carried the *Senora* into the doctor's house, but as soon as he realized her condition, he turned to Anna Maria, Morgan, Carlos and Camencita, and shaking his head to and fro, indicated that it was of no hope. With this, Carlos hurried out and galloped the horse up the hill to the Mission. Within a few minutes he returned with Padre Rodriguez in his company. The Padre immediately began to administer Extreme Unction, the final sacrament of the Catholic Church. At the sound of the Padre's voice, *Senora* Ortega opened her eyes, smiled slightly, closed her eyes and gasped. It was her last breath.

With many prayers, the group then took *Senora* to the Mission church where her body could repose for the night. The group found quarters for the night with several different friends in the *pueblo,* and the next morning, following a Mass for the Dead, *Senora* Ortega was committed to her newly dug grave, beside her husband and granddaughter Maria Consuela. Everyone in attendance at this hastily arranged funeral agreed that all three of these fine persons were now angels in heaven.

The drive home by the daughter of the deceased, her spouse and their son and his family was a very sad ride, taking from late morning and well into the night. Almost no words were spoken during this entire time. Upon reaching their *casa,* Anna Maria went immediately to her bed chamber, remaining there in mourning for several days Morgan was distressed, believing that Anna Maria was reverting to her previous state of depression. He surmised correctly. The only time that Anna Maria came out of her room was when Carlos and her grandchildren came to visit. Morgan thanked God for those children, for he believed that they were the only reason that Anna Maria did not lose her sanity. Morgan and Carlos spent more time together now, overseeing the activities of *Rancho del Sol*, and generally consoling each other. Again, one had effectively lost a wife, and the other a mother. Their renewed closeness brought back memories to Morgan, of how when Carlos was a young man, the two would sit on the *portico* in the evening, usually discussing matters of the *rancho* and listening to the cowhands strumming guitars and singing their songs of *Mejico*. Often, some of the wives would join them, breaking into dance, with everyone shouting to show their merriment. Now Morgan shook his head, wondering where all the years had flown. Carlos was now a married man, a father, and a *hacendado*, a land owner, and a son of which Morgan could be proud.

About a year later, Morgan learned that a young sailor from Boston was spending some time in the *pueblo* of Santa Barbara. Naturally he was anxious to meet this young man so that he could learn of the latest news from his native New England. Morgan, along with Juan, had ridden to Santa Barbara to find this man. After several inquiries they was directed to a handsome *yanqui* who was sitting on the pier with notepad at hand. Morgan recognized him as one of the sailors that had chased after the hides that went sailing down from Morgan's cliff in years past. Morgan introduced himself and Juan, asking if the young man was really from Boston. The man replied, "Oh, yes indeed. I am from Boston. My name is Richard Dana. I am a seaman on the ship *Pilgrim,* but I have been ordered to remain here to assist our company's agent. He has not yet arrived, but I expect him on the next ship from Boston." Morgan smiled broadly, "So, you are of the crew of the *Pilgrim.* I have dealt with her in the past. Is Simon Hayden still her Captain and is Hiram Palmer still your agent?" Dana assured Morgan that the Captain was still in command, but Palmer had married and chosen to remain in Boston rather than leave his bride for long periods of time. Dana then explained his own background. He had not run away from home to become a sailor as had Morgan. He had signed on as an adventurer, and to obtain first hand experience for a book that he planned to write. "Oh, so that is the reason for the notepad, eh?", Morgan asked. "Well I have been keeping a journal myself for several years. Perhaps you would like to read some of it." "Yes, indeed" was the young sailor's enthusiastic reply.

The trio withdrew to a nearby *cantina* so that they could be more comfortable. Morgan explained that he was hopeful of receiving another letter from his brother in Sturbridge, the one that never came. He had expected Palmer to bring it, but now knew that he would never receive it. He asked Dana for the news from Boston and the United States. Dana told of the election of Martin Van Buren, Vice president under Andrew Jackson, to the Presidency. The Whigs had nominated William Henry Harrison, but although he was a war hero, having defeated the Shawnee Indians at Tippecanoe, and an officer in the War of 1812, he could not overcome the popularity of Jackson's Democrat party.

Dana spoke of the tariffs enacted by Andrew Jackson and their effect on New England and the port of Boston itself. The southern Senators called it the "Tariff of Abomination", and said that it was the cause of the great depression that was then occurring in the United States. Morgan now wondered of the effect of this depression on his family back in Sturbridge. Perhaps that was why he had not heard from George.

Dana related the startling news of Americans that had settled in the Texas Territory, of their revolt against the Mexican troops, of Mexican General Santa Anna leading his troops into battle, defeating the Americans at the battle of the Alamo. Then, he continued, the Americans, under command of Sam Houston, again attacked Santa Anna's army, defeating it, taking Santa Anna captive. To secure his own release, Santa Anna signed a treaty granting the Texas Territory independence from Mexico. Dana said that Santa Anna was removed from office by the powers in Mexico City, since they did not agree with this treaty. "But", Dana continued, "many of the American settlers in the Texas Territory want it to become a part of the United States."

Morgan and Juan were astounded at this news. Why had they not learned of this before? "I suppose that the Mexican government did not wish us to learn of this", Morgan surmised, "due to their own embarrassment that Santa Anna and his army could not withstand the rag-tag American fighters." Looking anxiously to Dana, Morgan asked, "So what do you think of the possibility that Texas will become a part of the United States?" Enthusiastically, Dana replied, "Why I think they will indeed someday become part of our country. President Van Buren has appointed General Zachary Taylor to command American cavalry troops in the Texas Territory, to protect the settlers there. He is a noble soldier. The Mexicans had better not try his patience."

The afternoon had flown swiftly. Morgan and Dana made an agreement to meet again so that Dana might view Morgan's journal, but as a matter of fact, within a few days Dana was called aboard his vessel before he could make the visit. Morgan and Juan had returned to *Rancho del Sol,* discussing all the way, the events of the Texas revolt and wondering what effect it might have on *Alta California.*

Arriving home Morgan was surprised at the vitality of his wife, who had obviously dispelled her depression. In fact, she was exuberant when she informed him of her new intention. Somewhat gustily she announced "I am leaving for Santa Barbara in three days." Well, Morgan thought, there was nothing terribly surprising about that, except the sudden change of mental alertness. Anna Maria continued, "From there I shall take a coach to Los Angeles where I hope to speak with Governor Manuel Michaltorena and newly appointed Bishop Francisco Garcia Diego y Moreno." Morgan's mouth was agape. "You hope to do what?", was Morgan's doubtful reply to Anna Maria's astonishing announcement. "*Si* ", she replied. "*Madre* and I had been thinking about the matter for some time and now I have decided to do something about the need for additional *sacerdotes*, you know, priests." Morgan showed even greater puzzlement and more exasperation. "What in the world can you do about getting more priests? That is the job of that new Bishop in Los Angeles or even the Archbishop in *Ciudad de Mejico*, not of a *senora* in remote *Alta California*."

Anna Maria was again ready with her rejoinder, "That has been correct, up until now." She had emphasized the 'has been'. She continued, "Since more priests are leaving *Alta California* than the Archbishop can seem to assign here, I will ask him to establish a seminary here. I believe that many young men, both *Mejicano* and neophyte, would like to serve *Todoposeroso Dios*, but cannot travel to *Ciudad de Mejico* to enter the seminary there. Earlier today I have ridden to visit *Senor* Carillo, the new owner of the *Santa Ines* mission buildings. I have explained my plan to him. He has generously offered to allow the use of one of the buildings for an advanced *instituto*, a *colegio*. It can later be developed into a *seminario.*"

"Why that's foolish, Anna Maria", Morgan replied sarcastically. "The mission buildings are in very poor condition, and with that brothel nearby you would not want devout young men in the area." Anna Maria was ready with her answer, "Well *mia amado*" she taunted, "*Senor* Carillo has already evicted the ladies of the brothel and has agreed to help me repair one of the buildings, the former *convento*. So you see, all things are possible with the help of *Todopoderoso Dios*. Hopefully He will inspire you to understand and offer no difficulty for me about my plan."

Morgan was not sure how to react. He decided not to argue with Anna Maria, but he felt it necessary to point out potential difficulties. "You realize Anna Maria, that to gain an audience with the very busy Governor and Bishop may not be possible. And further, are you prepared for such a long journey? During the weeks of time that will be needed for this trip many adverse conditions can be expected to be encountered. The weather, insurgent natives, drunken *soldatos!*. The public coaches are not safe for women. Have you thought about these matters?" Anna Maria's reply was simply, "*Todopoderoso Dios* expects me to do this and He will provide all that I need. And further, I believe that this *seminario* will be a fine tribute to *madre*, who believed strongly that we need more priests. Martha and I will leave in three days, on *primero de Mayo,* and we shall be traveling in the month of *Santa Maria, Madre de Dios* so how can we encounter any difficulties." Shrugging his shoulders and shaking his head side to side, Morgan left the room, uttering, "*Vaya con Dios. Hasta luego!*" as his last retort.

The next two days were very busy. Morgan had conceded to himself that Anna Maria was determined to go through with her plan. He felt that he had no choice but to see that every aspect of her needs would be provided. Her personal safety was his primary concern. He said that he would not allow her to ride a public coach alone, so he ordered Carlos to convince his mother that he should accompany her. At first Anna Maria disagreed, stating that it was not necessary, but she then reluctantly agreed with this demand of Morgan. Also, it was agreed that Martha should accompany Anna Maria to serve her and to act as her *duena*. Then Morgan conceived a new plan. He arranged for the oldest son of Ignacio Remirez, who was now one of Morgan's cowboys, to drive Anna Maria and Martha in the surrey. Remirez would be a good helper to Carlos and he would be available in the event that any repairs to the surrey might become necessary, for he too was a fine wagon maker and blacksmith. In addition, *vaquero* Martinez would follow the party in a buckboard wagon. He was a burly man so he could thwart any would-be attackers. Morgan had already instructed him to hide a musket under the seat of the buckboard. Carlos would ride with Martinez in the buckboard, with two spare horses in trail. The buckboard was loaded with enough supplies for both humans and horses, and Carlos was secretly carrying a goodly amount of *pesos* that his father had provided, to buy more supplies along the way, and to pay for board for several days in Los Angeles. Morgan now felt that all contingencies had been considered.

As the group was ready to depart on the appointed morning, many people were on hand to offer their best wishes for a safe journey. Anna Maria suggested that they all join her in the recitation of *El Padro Nuestro* and *El Avemaria*. Each prayed fervently for the person that they cherished. Ignacio and Rosa Remirez and their children were all present to offer *"Vaya Con Dios"* to the party, especially to their son who had never before been away from home. Juan, too, was present to offer *"Hasta luego"* to all. Then Morgan suddenly offered, "Anna Maria, Carlos, I think that Juan Bautista should also accompany you.

He will be of great assistance in all possible matters, good or bad."

With that Anna Maria jumped up from her seat, "Oh no!, *ninguano!,* I will not permit it!" Morgan could not believe that after all these years Anna Maria had not forgiven Juan for what she believed to be his grave error in their daughter's death. "Oh alright", Morgan conceded, knowing that there would be no point in opposing Anna Maria's determined attitude. Carlos had shown pleasure at his father's suggestion, but now he also accepted the inevitable. He would have enjoyed the companionship and conversation of Juan. He was obviously not pleased to have to depart from his lovely wife and his dear children. They too, were on hand to wish the party *"Vaya con Dios."* Carlos assured his father that he would send word of their whereabouts and safety. He would do this by sending letters via any northbound rider, asking that they forward the letter to *Rancho del Sol*. Both had faith that strangers would help other *compatriata* and fulfill the request.

So, on the beautiful morning of *primero de Mayo*, the little party of travelers left *Rancho del Sol* on a quest that Morgan believed to be an impossible objective. Magdalena too, had been among the well-wishers and as the crowd dispersed Morgan called her. When she neared he said, "Magdalena, please plan to stay with *Senora* Carmencita and the children until *Senor* Carlos returns. She will need your assistance. I will manage *bueno suficiemente*. Do not worry about my welfare. Go now with the *Senora*. Magdalena nodded her understanding of the situation, bowed to Morgan, and left to gather some of her belongings, so that she might stay at Carlos' *casa* for a while. Camencita heard her father-in-laws directive and thanked him for his concern. She invited him to join them for *desayuno y cena* at any time.

When the wives of Ignacio, Roberto and the others overheard Morgan directing Magdalena to leave his service, they also immediately invited him to their *cena mesa*. None were going to allow *Senor Sharlezz* to go hungry. Morgan smiled and bowed, nodding acceptance to all. He had estimated that the trip of the party to Los Angeles, a distance of about 200 kilometers, with stops along the way, meetings with the officials, and the return home, would require three to four weeks. He knew that that would be long time to cook his own meals, so he graciously accepted their sincere invitations. He knew also that he would be welcomed to join Juan and the *vaqueros* on their *patio* at any time, to partake of their delicious open-fire cooking. So he worried little about his stomach, but was very worried about the safety of his journeying family.

CHAPTER SEVENTEEN
Bien Venido Americanos

Almost three weeks after Anna Maria and her party had left for Los Angeles, one of Morgan's men came running to the *casa*, calling to Morgan that a rider was approaching. Morgan came outside immediately to greet the rider. "This man has a message for you *senor*", Morgan's cowhand addressed him, "he says that he received it from a rider that arrived in Santa Barbara yesterday. He says he was asked to deliver it here on his way to San Francisco." Morgan reached up to shake the hand of the rider, then accepted the folded but unsealed letter. "*Gracias senor*." Morgan addressed the rider. "*Mucho gracias*. I had been hoping for this communication from my son. I greatly appreciate that you have helped me, even though I am a stranger." The man simply replied, "*De nada*. I am pleased to be of service. We must all help each other. That is the *precepto dorado*, is it not?" As he started to gallop away he said, "I hope that your *esposa* can convince the Bishop of her wishes." Morgan looked after him, realizing that he had read the unsealed letter, just as everyone who handled it must have done. Morgan thanked his own cowboy for his help, and as the man turned away. Morgan retired to his *portico*. Sitting in a rocking chair, he read the letter.

Cuarto de Mayo, 1841
My dear Padre, This is my first opportunity to write you. I know that you must be very concerned about our welfare. We are all of good

health. Madre is very well and full of vitality. Her resolve to have this colegio established has given her new vigor. Martha, young Ignacio, Martinez and I are all of good fortune.

We arrived in Los Angeles two days ago after an uneventful journey. For each night of our travel Madre and Martha were welcomed into the homes of very gracious families, while we men slept on their portico or in their cabana. Here in Los Angeles we are residing at a dwelling for travelers, la Posada de San Cristobal. Upon arrival, however, Madre desired that we first visit Mision San Gabriel Arcangel. But we learned that the wonderful Padre Estenaga has recently left this Mision after many years of faithful service. We also learned that this once beautiful Mision, like the others, is in a most derelict condition. *The* rancho has been apportioned away to many Mejicano and natives, and the neophytes have all scattered.

We went instead to The Church of Our Lady of the Angels, a recently built church in the pueblo. We went there to pray for the success of our venture. We thanked Dios for a journey without incident and asked Him to grant us future success. Our prayers may have helped.

Madre was able to obtain an audience with the Governor Manuel Micheltorena the very next day. His reputation of being a pleasant fellow certainly proved to be true. He is in agreement to allow the establishment of the colegio, if the present owner of the property has no objection, (we know that *Senor* Carrillo does not) and if newly appointed Bishop Francisco Garcia Diego y Moreno does not object. **Madre expects that when she is able to gain an audience with the Bishop, he will question the Church's ability to finance the colegio and to provide an instructor. Madre will reply that <u>we</u> will provide the financial needs, and that <u>she</u> shall obtain the services of at least one padre as the first step, a promise that I hope she can fulfill.**

Padre, this pueblo of Los Angeles has grown significantly. It now has more than one thousand residents, consisting of many wonderful and industrious Mejicano, Creol and native peoples. Of course, just as in San Francisco, there is the undesirable element as well. Unfortunately, the soldatos, who are assignedto maintain good order, are often the cause of disturbances. They very often antagonize the local natives, mostly of the Gabrielino culture.

And so, Padre, pray as we have, that this wonderful inspiration of Dios will be granted through the intercession of el Espiritu Santo. And thank Him for providing Madre with this nuevo animation.

As soon as I am able, I will forward another communication, hopefully to inform you of the Bishop's approval.

Mucho afecto, Carlos.

Morgan was surprised that Anna Maria had already met with the Governor and was pleased that Carlos too, was as enthused about the formation of a college as his mother. He was pleased also at Carlos' happiness because of his mother's new found vitality. Morgan felt some elation himself, mostly at his wife's apparent return to her previous vivacious self. Wouldn't it be wonderful, he thought, if we could live as husband and wife once more. Or was that too much to hope for?

The next week seemed to pass very slowly. He knew it was because he was hoping for another letter from Carlos. He calculated in his mind the number of days that they had been gone. It was now more than three weeks. He wondered if Anna Maria had yet met with Bishop Moreno, and he wondered what the Bishop's reaction would be. Then a chilling thought came to him. What if the Bishop refuses to grant permission for the establishment of this proposed college? What would that do to Anna Maria's self-esteem, to her new spirited attitude? Oh, God, do not let that happen, he thought.

Without Carlos at hand Morgan felt that there were many details in which he should involve himself. Or was he just looking for some kind of activity to pass away the time? After all, his men had been doing their jobs well for many years, so why should he interfere. But when he did do so, the men understood, and made Morgan feel that his involvement was helpful.

But Morgan still had an itch to do something, something important. Maybe he should ride to Santa Barbara to consult with *Capitan* Cordova about new developments in *Ciudad de Mejico*, any concerns for the safety of the area, any news of the Texas matter. Then he realized that he was only feeling anxiety. But he wanted to do something! He had an inner feeling that something was imminent.

Late the next day the same rider that had delivered the message from Carlos was returning to the south. He stopped at *Rancho del Sol* to rest and asked for a meal and a bed for the night. Morgan gladly provided both. He told the man to go to the corral, that the men would feed him well and give him a cot in their *cabana.*

The next morning, as the men were all at breakfast, Morgan strolled out. He heard the men in great commotion. He hurried to find what was the cause. As he approached, Juan hurried towards him. "*Sharlezz*, this rider has given us truly amazing news." Morgan asked anxiously, 'What is? What is it that he told you Juan?" Juan spoke excitedly as all the other men crowded around, "*Americanos* are arriving in the north in large numbers. They have used many wagons. Whole families are among them. They have driven their wagons all the way from your part of the world, *los Estados Unidas.* They have crossed the *plano tierra* and climbed over the *grande montana,* descending on our side of the great mountains. They have used very large wagons with many horses and oxen pulling. He says that they have been traveling for almost one year. And more are coming!"

Morgan was astounded. Was this man correct, or did he have too much *tequila*? He found the rider calmly sipping his coffee from a tin cup. "Is this true *mi amigo*?", he asked, "are there *Americanos* to the north that arrived by wagons across the flat-land and the mountains? Did they not arrive by sea?"

The man calmly restated to Morgan that the *Americanos* did indeed arrive by *grande barkos d'tierra.* "There are many, and still they come. They use wagons as large as boats, but these boats have wheels. And in their long trains there are more than *curarenta carto,* how you say, forty wagons ", he insisted. Morgan was amazed. Should he ride north to see for himself if this man was truthful. Why would he lie? How would he know of the wagons unless he saw them. He asked, "Did you see these *Americanos* yourself?" "*Si, si, senor.* I saw a few of them. They are now making *cultivar,* what you call growing the food. Some are along the trail. They wave at me as I pass. They have made *casa,* or *cabana.* Some have many children. They all work in the field."

This is remarkable, Morgan thought. He looked to the east at the mountains, then northward where the mountain tops were even higher. He showed his astonishment when he asked his own men, "Do you think it possible that wagons could be driven over those peaks?" One of the men replied, "We have never heard of such an event, *Senor Sharlezz.* We know that there are *pasa* where tribes from the flatlands have crossed the mountains, but they journey by foot. And the *Mojave* tribes have occasionally traveled here from their desert regions. But always by foot, or sometimes by horse, but it does not seem possible that wagons could be driven over these *alta Montana,* as he says." Morgan was now even more anxious to see for himself. But he dared not leave. A letter from Carlos might arrive. Or possibly Anna Maria, Carlos and the others might return any day. He had best not leave now. 'But imagine', he thought, 'Americans coming across the land, all the way from the eastern coast.' Now he wondered what would happen in the *pueblos* of San Francisco and Monterey. Although there were now a few Americans, mostly former sailors, would these *pueblos* welcome many Americans, farmers who would want land to settle, raise cattle and crops, become citizens of *Mejico*.

The rider finished *desayuno,* waved *adios,* and continued his ride on the trail southward. Morgan's men all continued to discuss the surprising news until Juan finally told them to return to their duties. Everyone, Morgan, Juan and the *vaqueros*, all wondered what effect these new settlers might have on their lives. As they ambled off to the corral or the barn or the *cabana*, each could be seen shaking his head or could be heard mumbling to each other or to themselves.

For two more days the men spoke of almost nothing except the *Americanos.* Anytime that Morgan approached one of them, he would ask, "Do you think it is true, *Senor Sharlezz?*" Even with some doubt in his voice, Morgan would reply, "It is possible. *Americanos* are very venturesome people."

Late on the second day some of the men came hustling to the *casa.* "The *Senora* and *Senor* Carlos, they are returning." Morgan sprang to his feet and hastened out the door, looking to the south for a sign of the wagons. Sure enough, they came into view from a wooded area, all occupants waving as they saw their reception committee. Shouts of *"Bien venido"* were exchanged by everyone. When the surrey stopped, Anna Maria stepped down quickly. Morgan was there to help her by holding his hands around her waist. She did not resist his hold. In her excitement she placed her arms around his neck and offered a slight kiss on the cheek. Morgan was surprised and delighted. He had anticipated that Anna Maria might be in a good mood, but he never expected such a welcoming gesture.

Carlos disembarked from the buckboard, hurrying to his father. He also embraced his father, kissing his cheek. *"Padre!* We have had a most successful journey. *Madre's* hopes are fulfilled. Bishop Moreno has agreed to allow the establishment of the *collegio!* Is that not *marvilloso?"*

Morgan exclaimed his agreement, *"Si,* that is wonderful!" Then welcomed the other members of the party. "Come, come everyone to the *casa*. We will take wine and celebrate this great occasion!" Everyone came to the *portico*. As word spread, the craftsmen and their wives and families all gathered around also. Morgan announced, "We have wonderful news. *Senora* Anna Maria, with the help of *Senor* Carlos and the others, has received permission to establish a *colegio* at *Mision Santa Ines*." Although all did not understand the implication of what Morgan meant, they all cheered, *"Ole! Ole!"* as they raised their cups and drank *vino*. Anna Maria thanked all for their salutations then suggested that they all retire as it was evening already, and a big day awaited them tomorrow.

As Carlos and his lovely wife Camencita left the group they had their arms about each other's waists. Magdalena noticed, and saying nothing, gathered their two little girls and started carrying them to their home. Juan also had noticed. When he saw Magdalena struggling to carry both children, he hurried to her side and took the older girl from her. Juan and Magdalena looked ardently at each other. Morgan had noticed the sexual excitement shown by both couples. 'It has been a long separation for them, hasn't it' he thought.

Morgan was now anxious to see what his own bedding arrangements would be this night. Anna Maria, retiring to her bed chamber, expressed to Morgan that she was very tired. He had to admit to himself that that would, no doubt, be a true statement. But he had hoped that in her exhilaration she might welcome him to her bed. He went to his own room feeling very dejected. The excitement exhibited by Anna Maria, and the brief touch of her body against his as she dismounted the surrey, had caused stirrings within him that he had not had for a long time, feelings which he did not believe he could have any longer.

For a few minutes he stood in the dark of his room. He removed his boots quietly, then went barefoot through the *cocina* to Martha's bedroom. He tapped very gently on the door and pushed it ajar slightly. Martha's voice from the dark within whispered, *"Entrar, Senor Sharlezz.* Come in. I expected you. I am glad that you have come. I can help you." Morgan entered and within a few seconds was beside her. Martha whispered, "I saw your great disappointment when *senora* left you. I know that you are in need of an *enamorado* tonight." They embraced passionately. An hour later Morgan whispered, "We must never speak of this." Martha held him tighter, "Oh, no *senor*, we must never!" Then Morgan slipped back to his own room.

The next morning at breakfast Martha was very cheery. Sensing this, Anna Maria asked, 'Did you sleep well last evening Martha." Martha's reply was nonchalant, "Oh, *si, senora*. I was very tired, so I slept very well." She glanced at Morgan who had his head down, digging his spoon into *pomelo*. "Is that

346

grapefruit tasty *senor?* ", she teased Morgan. "And how did you sleep *senor?"* Morgan tried not to blush, but he did. Hoping that Anna Maria would not notice, he replied casually, "Oh yes, I too slept well". In fact, Anna Maria did not notice Morgan's redness, for she seemed not to be listening to the banter. She was in a contemplative mood. But bringing herself back to the conversation she said, "Very good. We have all had a restful night." Morgan waited to see if she would indicate any suspicion. Martha, too, stood motionless for a few moments. Anna Maria continued, "Now *Sharlezz*, I would like you to join me." Morgan looked up in surprise. "Join you?, join you where?", he asked. "To *Mision Santa Ines.* We shall speak with *Senor* Carillo." Wasting no time, Anna Maria went to her bedroom to change into riding clothes. Morgan went to the corral to order that two horses be saddled.

As they rode together Anna Maria was very pleasant, and very excited as she spoke again about the *colegio.* When Morgan felt that she had exhausted her thoughts and conversation about the college he began to speak with some excitement himself. He told Anna Maria of the new American settlers in the Sacramento Valley. She showed surprise, especially when he told that they had arrived overland, all the way from the east. He pointed out that with the Texas settlers wanting to join America, and with so many Americans arriving in California, he speculated as to whether it might become a State of the Union. Anna Maria was amazed to learn of the new settlers. She too, showed much excitement at the news.

They were passing a pleasant grassy clearing. Anna Maria suggested that they let the horses rest.

They tied the horses to nearby bushes, then walked together a few steps. Anna Maria stopped, then sat. *"Sharlezz*, it has been a long time since I have worn riding boots. Could you help me to remove them for a few minutes?" Both started to speak at once, but Anna Maria let Morgan begin. "Anna Maria, I missed you very much while you were away. I'm very happy that you have taken on this new challenge. I know that you will fulfill your plans for the Church, to create a seminary for new priests. I can sense how excited you are about this plan." Then, looking over her still slim body, Morgan changed the subject. "Anna Maria, it has been many years since I saw you in riding breeches. You still look very ravishing in them. No petticoats now hide your beautiful body."

Anna Maria looked into his eyes and said, "Oh *Sharlezz*. I am excited, and while traveling I came to realize that I have been very selfish. I have shown much disregard for your affection. I hope that you will forgive me." Morgan was stimulated. 'After all these years', he thought, 'Anna Maria will once more be my wife.' "Oh yes, Anna Maria, I do forgive you. I know that many sad events have occurred in our lives, but we have much to be thankful for, much to appreciate." They embraced passionately. Soon they were laying on the grass fondling each other with great urgency. "Oh, it has been so long, hasn't it *Sharlezz*?" Anna Maria exclaimed. Morgan tried not to think of last evening. "Oh yes, my love, it has been far too long. I need your passionate love. I need it now." The two performed almost as they had on their wedding night. Morgan was surprised that he had as much vigor as when he was a young man.

Several hours later, when they reached the Mission, they went to find *Senor* Carillo. They found him sitting in the former *oficio* of the padre. Anna Maria quickly advised him of Bishop Moreno's approval of the *colegio*. She outlined the three conditions, *Senor* Carillo allowance to use the property, the financial support of the Morgans, and the agreement to obtain a priest to administer the seminary. Carillo was obviously surprised. Maria then reminded him of his agreement to allow the use of a portion of the Mission for this purpose. "Oh, my dear *senora.* I had not the least expectation that the Bishop would permit this *collegio.* I spoke hastily when I had told you that I would allow the use of my property." Looking very upset, Morgan moved a step forward, "Now Carillo, you had assured my wife that if the Bishop approved her plan, you would grant her the use of part of your property. Now you must hold to your part of the bargain. You're not a man who is not trustworthy, are you?" Carillo appeared a bit fearful, but Morgan backed away a step so as not to intimidate him. After a moment of thought Carillo said, "Very well, *senor y senora*, since you are to suffer the financial burden, I will agree to allow the use of the former *convento.* Parts of it need to be rebuilt, but it is repairable. You may begin the repairs whenever you wish." Morgan remembered that the former priests' quarters were quite large, made up of several rooms as well as a large study room. "Oh, that will be most suitable", he replied. He looked to Anna Maria for her agreement. "Oh, *si, Senor* Carillo, that will be very suitable!", she responded with her excitement showing. Morgan could not help but recall, 'She looks as alluring as that first day I saw her'. Then Anna Maria added, "We will set in writing the terms of the occupation of the property. It must include an area in the courtyard for the young men to pray, to contemplate and to take physical exercise. Do you not agree? We shall each sign this agreement." Carillo realized that he was dealing with a very determined woman and Morgan realized for the first time that his wife was very astute. Both Carillo and Morgan nodded that they agreed with Anna Maria's suggestion.

"Oh, *Sharlezz*, I am so happy! We will have Ignacio, Roberto and some of your *vaqueros* start the rebuilding *manana! Si?"*, Anna Maria exclaimed. *"Si, mi amor!, manana!"*, Morgan happily agreed. Changing her thoughts quickly, Anna Maria added, "And now we must find *Padre* Castellanos". "Castellanos?" Morgan repeated in amazement, "why must we locate Manuel? We haven't heard from him in many years. Why, we don't even know if he remained in *Alta California!"*

It was now mid-afternoon. Maria commented on the hour and stated that they had better leave for *Rancho del Sol*. Morgan agreed. They departed and a few hours later were at the same spot where they had made love in the morning. Morgan looked anxiously at Anna Mara. She understood his look, and answering his non-verbal question, she stated, "Not now Sharlezz. We will best keep riding for home, for it will be evening when we reach there." Morgan agreed, "*Si*, Anna Maria, we'll keep riding. But perhaps we will skip the *cena* meal and go early to bed." Anna Maria disagreed with him. "No, we shall take a light supper," then with abroad smile added, "then we shall go to bed."

They reached their home a short time before dusk. Martha met them, inquiring if they would like to dine. "*Si*, Martha", Anna Maria replied. "A very light *cena*, then we shall retire. We are both tired from this days journey." From the looks on their faces and the glances exchanged between them, Martha suspected that they would enjoy one bed tonight. She served the meal quickly then went out the rear door of the *casa*. She waved several times towards the corral, finally catching Juan's eye. He sensed urgency in her motions. He ran to her. "Juan! The *senor* and *senora* are to sleep together tonight. I am sure of it. I could detect it in their eyes and smiles to each other. All is well, finally." Juan showed great surprise but more happiness. *"!Caramba!"* he exclaimed, "Oh thank *Dios*. Finally they are together again. I wonder what has brought about this wonderful reunion." Martha thought about her tryst with Morgan the previous night. "Oh, I am sure that after all this time, *Senor Sharlezz* was most anxious for *Senora's* love. And he must have found the words of love that the *Senora* was waiting for." Juan repeated *"!Caramba!* This is wonderful. We are now a family again!" "Go! tell *Senor* Carlos the good news", Martha directed, "I'm sure that he will be most pleased."

Early the next morning Morgan went to the corral to find Juan. "Juan, we are starting a ride to San Francisco today. Saddle two horses and select two others to take with us. We will be riding at an urgent pace." "*Si, si*, Sharlezz. But may I ask why this ride and why the urgency?", Juan asked. Juan was astonished at Morgan's answer. "We go to seek Manuel Castellanos, Juan. If we can find Him. If we do, we will try to convince him to come here to be the instructor to the young seminarians at the new *colegio.*" Again Juan showed his astonishment. "But *Sharlezz*, we have not known of *Padre* Castellanos' whereabouts for many, many years. Do you really believe that we can find him?" Morgan replied with much emphasis, "Well, we're sure going to make a good try. Get some hardtack and water. Also, some *vino*. Fill several saddle bags. We may be gone quite awhile. Can you be ready in one hour?" Juan's reply was positive, "Of course, *Sharlezz*."

As Morgan returned to the *casa* Carlos was there awaiting him. "*Padre!*, *Madre* tells me that you are riding to San Francisco to seek out *Padre* Castellanos. Do you believe that you can find him?" Morgan smiled as he thought 'everyone seems to doubt that this is a wise trip'. "Well, Carlos, *Madre* has the premonition that we can find Manuel. And further, that we can convince him to come to *Santa Ines*. So we must try." "Of course, *Padre*, you must try", Carlos replied. Then with a pleased look and sound he said, "I understand that you and *Madre* are sharing the same bed now." Morgan smiled broadly, "Yes, Carlos, after all these years, *Madre* and I have once again become *amoroso*. Are you pleased? Does everyone know?" Carlos spoke joyously, "Why of course, *Padre*, Carmencita and I are most pleased. It is the most wonderful news. It is certainly the will of *Dios Todopoderoso!*" Reddening some and continuing to smile broadly, Morgan nodded his assent.

Quickly changing the subject Carlos stated vigorously, "And *Padre*, we have heard the news of the *Americanos* coming over the mountains in many large wagons. That is amazing. Do you think that you will find any of these *Americanos* when you ride north?" Calmly Morgan replied, "Likely so, Carlos, likely so. It will be very interesting to confront them. I doubt that they expect to meet a fellow yankee here in California". Carlos nodded, "Oh I believe that you are correct *Padre*. And I did not have an opportunity to tell you that when we were in Los Angeles we saw a few *gringos*, oh excuse me *Padre*, we saw a few *Americanos* there. We were told that they had walked into the *pueblo* all the way from Arizona, across the sand hills and mountains. It seems unbelievable. They had no wagons, only some burros to carry their goods. It took them nearly a year they said. There were several of them. A man called Hedediahaa Smeeth was the first a few years ago, but others quickly followed." Morgan interrupted, "In *ingles*, we call that name Jedediah, a pretty common name. And the other name is called Smith. That's also a very common name among the English and the Americans." Carlos continued somewhat excitedly, "Oh, *si,* I understand. And *Padre*, they have already obtained land grants and are raising cattle and growing wheat and have plentiful grape arbors."

"My word", Morgan replied. "All the way from Arizona Territory! Why next I suppose some of those adventurers from Texas Territory will also move in." Morgan now hoped that he would indeed meet some of those Yankees that were in the north. No doubt they could tell him what was happening. Why, when he left

Massachusetts forty years ago, many folks were already migrating westward. But they went to Indiana and Ohio Territories. That was pretty far west, but not nearly as far as these folks up north had come.

"Are you ready, Juan?", Morgan called. Juan replied emphatically, "*Si, Sharlezz,* I am *prepardo.* The horses and the provisions are ready for this long journey also." Morgan looked toward Carlos and advised, "Well Carlos, we are ready. I don't know how long this journey might take. Look after your *Madre* well, and ask *Dios* to be with us as we travel." "*Si, si, Padre. Vaya con Dios*", was Carlos' concerned reply. Then as Morgan and Juan rode off, Carlos thought, '*Padre*, you are *un marveloso hombre.*'

By mid-day they had reached the area of *Mision La Purisima.* "Do you wish to stop *Sharlezz?*" Juan asked. Morgan thought a moment. He quickly reminisced about the years past, of his good friend Mariano Payeras, of Cimkonah, of Angelica. But knowing that the Mission was now largely impoverished he replied, "No Juan. There is nothing here to stop for. Gone are the days of the Mission's glory. Gone are the days that we cherished, and the friends that we loved." Immediately he realized that he must have stirred up a sad memory for Juan. "Juan, if you want to stop, maybe to visit the cemetery, we can certainly do that. We are not in such a hurry that we must pass by." Juan looked sad. He replied, "*Si, Sharlezz.* If you do not mind, I would like to visit *mi amado.*" Morgan perked up. Wanting to sound supportive, he replied, "We sure can do that Juan. And we can say a prayer there for Angelica, her *bebe*, and for *Padre* Payeras and Cimkonah too."

So the two men rode off the trail a little and proceeded to the cemetery of the now abandoned Mission. They offered brief prayers over the graves and moved along. After riding up *El Camino Real* a few more kilometers, they stopped for food and drink. Morgan could see that Juan was still sad. Even after all these years, the thought of his beloved Angelica brought sorrow to his heart. Morgan tried to be philosophical. 'Come on, Juan. We can't let the sorrow of the past affect our future. We have an important objective ahead. It won't be easy to find Manuel, if he's still in California, and if he's still alive." Wanting to change the subject, Morgan was about to ask Juan how his relationship with Magdalena was going. Then he suddenly realized that this would not be an appropriate time to bring up that matter. Instead, he said, "Alright Juan. Let's mount up and continue on. We need to reach *San Luis Obispo* by nightfall." Juan, also appearing to want to change the subject, agreed, "*Si. Si!* We must move ahead. There are many kilometers yet to travel today".

In the early evening they neared *Mision San Luis Obispo.* It was clearly evident that the Mission buildings were seriously deteriorated. But they were sure that they could find a place in the *pueblo* to rest for the night and likely find food and *vino*, as well as hay for their horses. It had been almost seven years since secularization, that is, the dismissal by the Mexican government of the right of the Franciscan Order to administer the Missions. But even before the 1834 decree, Padre Martinez, realizing that the Mission would soon be ordered closed, discontinued any attempt to maintain the property. Martinez himself, like many of the other *Padres,* had abandoned the Mission and returned to *Mejico.* Thus ended the long existence of one of the earliest Missions, the fifth in the chain, established in 1772 by *Padre-Presidente* Junipero Serra himself.

There remained in the *pueblo* a few of the former Mission craftsmen and their families, as well as a few of the neophytes. All were eking out a living by raising a few cattle that had been taken from the once huge herds. All of the rest of the herd had been sold by the government to important *peninsulars* and a few *creoles,* friends of the new government. At its peak, the *Mision* had almost nine thousand animals consisting of cattle, swine, horses and mules. All were now scattered. And the many hectares of land were also divided amongst the governmental friends. It disheartened Morgan and Juan to see the condition of the once beautiful Mission, and when they learned that the government could not even find a buyer for the buildings, they were even more dismayed. They felt that even a non-religious buyer would at least maintain the property. They knew that with each year of neglect, the Mission would certainly deteriorate beyond repair.

Early the next morning Morgan and Juan set out again. They hoped to reach *Mision San Miguel Arcangel* by early afternoon and possibly *Mision San Antonio de Padua* by nightfall. Although the many Missions had been spaced to be a day's walking journey apart, the distances could now be covered in less than half that time on horseback. Most of the journey was carried out in silence by the two men. Sometimes one would bring to the attention of the other a particularly beautiful view, or an amusing action by some animal, but most of the time each man reminisced as they rode along. Occasionally Morgan would remind Juan of an earlier visit in the area, or he would narrate to Juan how he and *Padre* Payeras had walked this part of the trail many, many years earlier.

And as they traveled they could see the cattle herds that formerly belonged to the Missions but were now owned by the new *hacendado* of the area. Sometimes too, they saw natives that had built themselves tule shelters, in the manner of their forefathers, and were attempting to assimilate a lifestyle that was a mixture of their forefather's culture and that which they had learned at the Mission.

They did pass *Mision San Miguel Arcangel* in the early afternoon. They stopped for their usual midday meal, then rode on to attain their next objective. As evening approached they reached the former *Mision San Antonio de Padua*. At both Missions they found the same conditions as at *San Luis Obispo*, and as *La Purisima* and *Santa Ines*. Each had the same misfortune and neglect once the decree of secularization had been enforced. Each had been abandoned or sold to uncaring speculators and the herds and land divided.

On the third day they passed by *Mision Nuestra Senora de la Soledad*. They did not stop because, as the name implied, it was a lonely place. It had almost always been so. There were a few good years, the years in which the *Padres* were able to tap the Salinas River to irrigate the fields. In those years the Mission flourished. It had many cattle, sheep, swine and horses, as well as excellent crops. And many neophytes also. But the river that nourished the land was also the cause of the Mission's downfall, since it flooded over many times. After each flood the Mission had to rebuild part of its compound. Even before secularization the Mission was beginning to deteriorate because no *Padre* could remain so as to establish continuous direction. Many *Padres* had come and gone, each having a feeling of despair, as none could again make the Mission to prosper. Sensing this attitude of the *Padres* the neophytes too, abandoned the Mission.

Morgan and Juan recalled how when they had passed by many years earlier, the Mission did indeed seem to have attained the expectations of its founder *Padre* Fermin Lasuen. But the fact that Governor Jose Joaquin de Arrillaga had died there in 1814, and that *Padre-Presidente* Vincente Francisco de Sarria had collapsed and died there just a few years earlier, caused the Mission to carry a stigma of evil in the minds of the few remaining neophytes.

The two horsemen continued on, reaching *Mision San Carlos Borromeo de Carmelo* by early evening. Here the miseries of time had not affected the Mission quite so badly. But the neglect of only a few years was nonetheless evident. As they approached they were halted by several *vaqueros*, wanting to know their business there. After explaining that they were only journeying through to reach San Francisco, they were allowed to continue towards the church. But they were strongly advised that all the land around the church was now in private hands, that they must stay within a few feet of the front of the church or be seized as trespassers. They did as they were told. They rode to the church, tied their horses very close by and went inside. Both Morgan and Juan went to the spot of

Padre Serra's entombment, offered a quick prayer for his soul and left the church. They decided that if they spent the night here, one of them would have to be on guard all night to prevent the theft of their horses. They decided to move on. They rode for about one hour further. It was now quite dark, but they found a spot which was a little sheltered by a clump of pine trees. They quickly tied the horse to the tree branches, unsaddled the two that they had been riding, and fell to the ground. After a few minutes of rest they quickly devoured some hardtack and wine, nestled themselves in the pine needles, and quickly fell asleep.

They got an early start the next morning with the hope that by nightfall they would reach *Mision San Jose*, although they instinctively knew that the Mission would not be a suitable place to stay. As they ambled along each man was absorbed in his own thoughts, as on the previous days. Morgan reminisced about his boyhood in Sturbridge, his brother Albert and the rest of his family. He wondered how his brother George's family might now be faring. He thought about how long it had been since the letter from George' widow had arrived. It was many years now. Although he had been learning of events in the United States from travelers, he had no idea of what his own kin were enduring. Then he recalled his father and step-mother. He felt badly that he had not given them a proper farewell when he left home. "But my God!' he thought, 'I was only fifteen. I didn't know any better.'

To break the monotony he called to Juan. "What ya thinking about, Juan?" "Oh, I was just kind of wondering what might have become of my father", was Juan's melancholy reply. "Well I'll be darned",

Morgan replied. "I was just thinking' 'bout my father too." Another long silence ensued. The horses kept loping along. The day dragged on. At noon they took a short stop for lunch and to change horses. They were now getting more anxious to reach San Francisco. If the could reach San Jose by nightfall today, they could arrive in San Francisco during daylight the next day. That would allow them some time to search out Manuel Castellanos.

And so it was that on the fifth day of their travel they did reach the *pueblo* of San Francisco but now it was more like a city. Neither had been there for many years. They were dumbfounded to see how much it had grown, how much more activity was taking place, and how many more people were bustling about. The Mission complex was now completely surrounded by buildings of every sort, from *cantinas* to boarding houses and to outfitters of ranching and farming equipment.

As at all the others, the Mission complex had been sold to be used for various enterprises. But the church itself was in surprisingly good condition. Morgan and Juan went inside but could find no one present, not even a *padre*. They studied the condition of the beautiful adornments, the altar and *rererdo* which did show some neglect, perhaps just dirt accumulation. Of course the golden vessels and candelabra decorations were now gone. The two men looked at each other with sadness in their eyes. They recalled earlier days when the Mission was "home" to several *padres*, many craftsmen and their families and several hundred neophytes. After their customary prayer they left the church. On the street before them, in addition to the many, many pedestrians, they could see many on horseback traveling the street and many wagons being drawn along the street, with both human occupants and commercial goods as their cargo. They even saw tethered oxen and black bears, which they later learned were used by the men for amusement, by letting the animals pull against each other.

Standing for only a few minutes, they decided to travel to a quieter street so that they could decide their next step. Rather than stop to ask every white-skinned stranger of the possible whereabouts of the *padres*, they decided that the natives, who might have been earlier neophytes, might know the answer which they were seeking. Each time that a native came nearby, or as they rode along, they spoke to them in their own tongue. Most did not even answer except for a glare. Morgan and Juan realized that many of these natives did not miss the *padres*. They recalled having heard of the several small revolts that had taken place over the years and the overly firm actions of the soldiers in subduing the natives, killing and wounding several.

Finally they encountered an old native, one with patience in his eyes. He said that he knew many of the *padres*, and he knew that several had returned to *Mejico* by ship after the Mission ranches were sold and the neophytes scattered. In answer to the question by Morgan about a specific padre, one who used to roam the streets of the *pueblo*, the native said that he recalled that *padre*, and that he had been sent to a new Mission further north. The man said that about twenty years earlier a new Mission was opened across the bay that was to house the ill neophytes, those that had contacted the white man's diseases. He said that he also heard that about fifteen years ago another Mission, even further north, was established. He remembered that the street *padre,* they called him Manuel, had left *Mision Doloros,* as it was called by everyone, a few years before the Mission closed.

Morgan and Juan were elated that they seemed to have received reliable information. This fine old native, they believed, would not provide false information. They sought out a livery stable and an inn where they could spend the night. They found one that was more suitable than several others which they had passed, but decided that they would have to share watch duty during the night because they were fearful of horse thieves. It was about nine in the evening. Morgan said that he would take the first five hour stint, until about two in the morning, then Juan would watch until dawn.

Arising as soon as the sun was up, Morgan went to the livery barn where Juan had already saddled two of their horses. Morgan went back inside the inn, purchased some hardtack and rum. Sharing the biscuits with Juan as they mounted, each took a swig of the rum, placed the bottle in a saddlebag, and left for the waterfront. They had learned from the Spanish innkeeper that there was a ferry raft that crossed to *Punta Saucelito* directly north. Had it not been for this. Morgan and Juan would have to ride another six days to get to the same point, all the way back around San Francisco Bay and San Pablo Bay.

They reached the *Saucelito* land point in late morning and began their ride northward immediately. They were hopeful to reach the *hospital asistencia,* named in honor of *San Rafael Arcangel,* before nightfall. When they reached the Mission it had been abandoned like all the others. But they found friendly natives and a few *Mejicanos* nearby who greeted them warmly. They were offered a warm meal and some *vino*, both of which they gladly accepted.

As they sat around a camp fire in the evening the natives and the Mexicans told them the story of the Mission, how it was established as a hospital for the sick natives of *Mision Dolores,* how the diseased natives recuperated well at this higher and sunnier site than San Francisco. They spoke kindly of *Padre* Juan Amoros who came two years after the founding of the hospital. Under his guidance the station had grown and was then accorded the status of a Mission. "*Si, Si,* I am interested in this, but do you know of a *Padre* named Manuel?". Morgan was beginning to get impatient. Was he on the right track or not? Should he go further, or was it a useless venture? "Oh, *si*", one of the natives spoke, as the others nodded agreement, "This *padre* named Manuel, he was here for a while, many years ago. But he was sent to the next Mission, further north, they call it *Mision San Francisco Solano.* At first there was nothing there, but then the *Ruso* soldiers and fisherman came nearby. They built a fort of big logs. They do not want *Mejicanos* or *nativos* to go there. Our soldiers go once or twice, but they come back. They no want to fight *Ruso* soldiers. But General Vallejo, he tell *padres* to make a church there. He say *Ruso* no attack church."

Now Morgan was in a quandary. Should he believe these natives? Why not. How would they know the name Manuel unless he was here. But even if it was Manuel and we go further to this Mission called *Solano*, will Manuel be there? Is he still alive? It'll be another day's ride north. Should we do it or not?. Morgan turned these thoughts in his head several times, even after retiring for the night.

In the morning Morgan said, "Juan, I decided we should go to *Solano.* We've come all this way looking for Manuel. If we're this close we might as well keep going to find out. So far, God has been with us. Let's hope that He will see us through." Juan replied with complete support of Morgan's decision, "*Si, Sharlezz.* It is good that we keep going. If we return home now, not knowing if Manuel is there, we will be angry with ourselves later."

Bidding *adios* to their new found friends and thanking them for their hospitality and information, Morgan and Juan rode off, as the locals called out the usual, *"Vaya con Dios."* Morgan mumbled a low voiced remark to Juan, "I certainly hope so!"

Riding north they encountered individual natives that were busy tending a small flock of sheep or fowl, or tilling the land. To each they asked the same question, "Do you know a *padre* named Manuel?" Most said *"Ninguno senor"*, but as they neared the *Mision San Francisco Solano,* one native farmer said, "Oh, *si senor.* I knew him until a few years ago, but he left the *Mision.*" "To where?" Morgan asked anxiously. "Some said that he went to the east, toward the *Rio Sacramento*", the man said. So onward the two riders continued. This time inland toward the valley of the river.

In the late afternoon they encountered another native tending a few sheep. *"Amigo!* Do you know of a *padre* living anywhere near here?" Morgan called out. The man shrugged, then replied. "There is *uno hombre* living a few kilometers from here. He wears a brown robe with a white rope around him. Some say he is a *padre*, some say he a *diablo*. I don't go near him. He is *loco* I think." As Morgan and Juan urged their horses into a gallop they called back, *"Gratias, senor, mucho gratias!"*

"Do you think it's him, Juan?", Morgan asked. "We'll know soon, *Sharlezz*", was Juan's reply. They galloped on for several kilometers. It was getting darker. Just as they were about to stop for the night they saw a figure in a tattered brown robe near the edge of the woods, not far from the trail. They rode full speed towards the man. The brown-robed man looked frightened. He called out, "Don't hurt me. I have nothing to take. I am a simple hermit. Don't hurt me!" Morgan dismounted quickly. "Manuel! Is that you?" He couldn't tell because the man had a long unkempt beard and hair down to his waist. The man looked stunned. At first he stared at the man approaching him. "Oh, *mia Dios*. It is you *Sharlezz*?" "*Si*, Manuel! It's me, your old friend, Morgan." The two embraced heartily. Juan dismounted and came forward. He too embraced Manuel. "Juan! It is you. My two old friends. Oh, *gratias Dios*. This is a day for which I have prayed."

Morgan was elated. "Well, finally, after all this time, we have found our dear friend Manuel." The three men continued their embraces and their words of disbelief. Finally Manuel said, "Come *Sharlezz*. Come Juan. I will take you to my humble *casa*. I now live as a hermit. No one wants a *padre* anymore." They tethered the horse and walked a few steps into the wooded area. A simple shack made of poles and branches came into view. "This is my home. It has been so for twelve years now." Morgan spoke in reply, "Well, Manuel, we have new plans for your future. And you will soon be working as a *padre* once again!"

CHAPTER EIGHTEEN
Things Are Not Always As They Appear

The three arose at dawn the next morning. Manuel immediately separated himself a little and knelt in prayer for some time. Morgan and Juan also said a much briefer prayer to themselves. When Manuel returned to the others, they all ate some hardtack, drank some wine, and prepared to leave the site. As poor and dilapidated as Manuel's shack was, he seemed sad to leave it. "I came here twelve years ago, after the last Mission at which I was serving closed. Did you know that there was a *Mision* called *San Francisco Solano*? It was named for our Order's founder, St. Francis of Assisi. For a time he lived as a hermit, over six hundred years ago. When the Mission closed and was sold to irreverent strangers, I had no where to go. So I decided to emulate this wonderful man, St. Francis. At first I wandered, but then I found this lovely spot and decided to stay here. Did I tell you that I have been here for about twelve years. I know because I have marked a calendar on a stone in the back of my hut".

"Yes, you told us Manuel.", Morgan replied. He looked at Juan who had the same questioning look on his face. 'Has Manuel gone *loco,* like the old native said.' Manuel saw the look exchanged by the two. He explained, "I have seen few humans in the last twelve years, and I have spoken to almost none of them. I am afraid that my memory may have lapsed some, for lack of use, you understand?" Morgan and Juan nodded that they understood and recognized that what Manuel said would be true. Talking to no one for such a long time would certainly let the brain get lazy.

But now Morgan hoped to excite Manuel by telling him of the new assignment that they had prepared for him. He described Anna Maria's meeting with the Bishop and the Bishop's approval of Manuel's new assignment. He made it sound as if the Bishop himself had selected Manuel, hoping that this would cheer him. "Oh my, *Sharlezz*, I am not sure that I am capable of fulfilling such a responsibility." "Oh sure you are Manuel", Morgan assured him, "you just need a little time to get used to living at a Mission again, like you used to." Manuel looked pensive, "But *Sharlezz*. I was never happy living in the Mission. You know that I always liked working outside, with the people that needed help in their troubled life. And I really came to like my life as a hermit." Morgan wanted to close the subject, "Manuel, in this new assignment you'll be helping many young men in their troubled life." Manuel smiled a little but said nothing.

Morgan spoke again, "Manuel, is there a stream near here? Is there a place where we can clean up a little." He used the word "we", but he really meant "you", for Manuel was indeed as smelly as an animal. "Oh, *si Sharlezz*. Just a few steps down this path will take us to a lovely little stream. It has clear water and many fishes. That is where I obtain much of my food." The three men went down the path. Morgan and Juan began to undress. Manuel looked embarrassed. Morgan said, "Manuel, if you prefer, why don't we move down the stream a little and let you bath here in your usual place." As he said it, Morgan wasn't sure that Manuel had a usual place to bath, or any place for that matter.

He was beginning to wonder if Manuel would still be a capable *padre*, one who could educate young men. Or has his life of solitude affected his once brilliant mind.

After their cleaning chore, the three men mounted the horses. Morgan and Juan agreed to let Manuel have a saddled horse, and they would take turns on the use of a saddled and a non-saddled horse. The fourth horse would be exchanged periodically, to let one horse rest some. As they left the camp-site Manuel looked sad. Morgan wanted to cheer him, but he wasn't sure of what to say. "Manuel, you will be surprised to see my son Carlos. He is a grown man, a real *hombre.*" "Oh yes", Manuel replied, "I had forgotten that you had a son. And *Sharlezz,* how is your wife, ah…" Morgan knew that he had forgotten her name. "Anna Maria is fine", Morgan completed Manuel's thought. "Our son Carlos is married to a lovely woman and we have two wonderful grandchildren." Manuel replied without much enthusiasm, "Oh that is wonderful, *Sharlezz.*" Morgan sensed that Manuel was more saddened about leaving his hermit's life than he and Juan had realized. He looked at Juan, hoping that Juan would add some encouraging words. "When you see *Mision Santa Ines* you will be pleased, Manuel", Juan stated. He said this assuming that Ignacio and Roberto and the others had accomplished at least some of the repairs while Morgan and Juan were away, for it would be almost three weeks by the time they returned to *Rancho del Sol.* Morgan picked up the thought, "Yes, Manuel. The *convento* is being refurbished as the new *colegio.* We are sure that you will like it there."

The three men rode on. They had decided to follow the trail that would take them southeastward, into the Sacramento River Valley. Morgan wanted to see for himself some of those yankee settlers, to find out about their long trek and about where they had originally come from. They traveled two days before encountering their first *Americanos.* As they approached the two men who were tending cattle, the men looked toward them, then towards their muskets that were leaning against a nearby tree. Morgan recognized the men's concern. "Hello there", Morgan shouted ahead. The men looked harder as if to see if they had heard correctly. "Well hello", one replied, "are you Yankees?" Morgan waited until he was closer so the men could see him better. "Yep. I'm a Yankee, originally from Massachusetts." The man who spoke came a few steps closer. "Well I'll be damned. You are a Yankee!"

Morgan dismounted. He introduced his friends to the settlers. The newcomers told Morgan that they were from New York State, Columbia County, south of Albany. Morgan replied. "Yea, I know of that place. I ain't never been there, but I heard about it, before I left home almost forty years ago. "My god!", the other man spoke, "forty years ago? How in the world did you get out here then?" The five sat under the tree to get out of the hot sun. Morgan related his whole history. Then he went on the explain about how he met Juan and how *Padre* Manuel was one of many Catholic priests that had helped, or at least tried to help, the natives. The men said that they had never before seen a Catholic priest. Were they something like their ministers back home? "Kind of", Morgan replied.

The settlers then related to Morgan and the others how they traveled west. It was a perilous journey. A man named Sutter had come out to California earlier and built a saw mill so that there was plenty of lumber to build homes and barns and all. Sutter also sent word back of how fertile the land was, and how spacious. It sounded like heaven to these men and many others from their area. They were joined by another group as they passed though Pennsylvania. As they went westward, more families joined the train from Indiana Territory. These had gone there eight or ten years earlier, but they wanted more land of their own, so they joined the wagon train also. They said that there were forty three wagons in all. A few broke down up in the mountains, but they transferred the families and the goods to other wagons. They said that the trip took almost eight months, through the spring, summer and early fall. They were lucky, they said, that they didn't lose time and have to cross the mountains in the winter. They said that they had been here about a year now and that their families were real happy here.

They told about this feller Sutter building a big fort further north, in case there was any trouble with the "injuns" or maybe the "ruskis". Juan asked if they had any trouble with the natives in the area. The men replied that they all got along fine, so far. Morgan asked Juan, "What tribe are they around here, Juan?" Juan's reply was general. "They are Miwoks. But there are many groups of them, from here to the coast. I am only generally familiar with them. I think I could speak with them. Our Chumash language has some similarities.":

371

After a few more minutes of comparing the earlier lives of the settlers and Morgan, the three Californians moved on. They kept to an old Indian trail that followed the Sacramento river to the south. There were no major settlements along the way, not like the coastal trail with its many Mission stations. Occasionally they did spy a few natives in the field. The exchange of waves between the two groups assured Morgan and the others that these were peaceful natives. The travel was interesting to Morgan and Juan because it was new territory to them. They were seeing the coastal mountain range from the eastern side, not from the west as they had always seen it before. Manuel seemed not to notice any of the scenery. It was evident that he was praying a lot, but without rosary beads. Morgan remembered, as he thought about it, that Manuel never seemed to have the rosary beads at hand as did all the other *padres*.

The next two days went on pretty much the same. New scenery, very few humans, and occasional attempts by Morgan or Juan to make conversation, and to involve Manuel in this conversation. It was difficult to draw Manuel out. Very often Morgan and Juan exchanged questioning looks. Was Manuel ever going to become the vibrant person that he once was? Did the solitary life that he led for twelve years permanently affect his personality?

They had been following the river known as *San Joaquin* but they decided that they had better head westward, to try to find a pass in the mountains that would bring them out onto *El Camino Real*. They did not realize that they had gone as far east as they had. The following day they did see a pass to the west.

They traveled half a day to get to it and another full day before they reached the Salinas river. They camped for the night and in the morning they headed south again. In a few hours they reached *Mision San Miguel*. They were finally on the *El Camino Real*. They would know their way home from here, but there was two days of riding yet to go.

Each day they started out right after sunrise. By mid-day of this twelfth day since they had left, they were approaching *Mision San Luis Obispo*. After taking a break for a little hardtack and water, and while Manuel was occupied saying his mid-day prayers, Morgan pulled Juan aside. Quietly he told him, "Juan, take the saddled horse and leave out ahead of us. Hurry along to home. I want you to get there ahead of us." Juan looked puzzled. "Why? *Sharlezz*." Morgan explained his reason. "Go first to Carlos and tell him we are coming. Tell him that Manuel needs some fixin' up before Anna Maria gets to see him. Go to Rosa Remirez. Have her make a new robe for Manuel. He's about your size. I hope that she still has some material left from when she used to make the *padre's* robes. Then have Carlos meet us late tomorrow afternoon a kilometer or so north of the ranch. Tell him to bring his best razor. We gotta cut Manuel's hair and trim his beard. We gotta make him look like a *padre*, not a *vagabundo*." Juan nodded, "Oh, *si, Sharlezz*. You are right. I'll leave now quietly. You make some excuse to Manuel. *Adios*."

By the time that Manuel had finished his prayers, Juan was out of sight. At first Manuel did not seem to notice, but as they went along the trail a while, he asked Morgan, "What has become of Juan?"

Morgan replied casually, "Oh, he's gone ahead a little to check on a place to camp tonight." Manuel seemed satisfied and did not bring up the matter again.

All that afternoon and all the next day Morgan and Manuel rode along, with the usual rests periods. There were no intruders on the trail and no incidences to concern them. Thus they reached the northern boundary of *Rancho del Sol*. But soon, as they moved along, they heard horses hooves ahead of them. Carlos, Juan and *vaquero* Martinez greeted them. *"Buenos tarde, Padre"* Carlos called. Then he added, *"Bien venido, Padre* Manuel." Manuel looked up but showed no sign of recognition. Morgan shouted, *"Buenos tarde,* Carlos. *"Hola!* Juan. *Hola!* Martinez."

Morgan introduced Manuel to Carlos and the others. Then he explained to him why he must change clothes and trim his hair and beard. "We want you to look like a fine *padre*, like the *padre* that you are!". Manuel seemed to understand. In any event he was cooperative as Carlos shaved him. He then went behind a bush to change into his new robe. When he emerged he was smiling broadly. He seemed now to realize how sinister he must have looked.

When they reached *Rancho del Sol* many from the *pueblo* came to greet them. Shouts of *Bien venido!"* were offered by everyone. Finally, Anna Maria came to greet Manuel. He appeared nervous. "Oh, *Senora Sharlezz*. I am so happy to see you again. It has been many years, has it not?" *"Si, si, Padre* Manuel, many, many years", Anna Maria replied. Then she wanted to immediately clear the matter of the past hostility that she had shown towards Manuel. "When last we met, we had some small differences, did we not? Now we

374

realize that they were insignificant. We must forget them, *si?*" Manuel smiled, and seeming to be much relieved, he offered his approval of her suggestion, "Oh, *si, Senora*. Those were minor differences. They are long forgotten." She continued her explanation, "You see, Manuel, I took a long journey to visit the Bishop, and to obtain approval for this new *colegio*. While traveling I prayed to *Jesuschristo* to give me understanding. He told me that I must forgive, just as He forgives. So I think of all to whom I have been intemperate, and I realize that I am not following the wishes of *Dios todopoderoso*. So I am now of a forgiving heart. I feel much more *feliz*, more happy."

Morgan wanted to disperse the crowd. He said, "Manuel, we should take a few days rest. Then we will visit Santa Ines and soon Santa Barbara." Manual complied, "Oh, *si, Sharlezz*. Whatever you think best." But Anna Maria was more impatient. "Why can we not visit Santa Ines *manana, Sharlezz?* Do you think that you can travel tomorrow Manuel? We can check the progress of the preparations. And *Sharlezz*, why do you wish to visit Santa Barbara?" Morgan replied in a matter of fact tone, "Because, *mi amore*, we need the material and spiritual support of *Padre* Rodriguez." "Alright, *mi amor*," Anna Maria retorted, "we will travel to Santa Barbara in two days. But tomorrow we can visit Santa Ines, is it not so?" Morgan conceded, "*Si*, we can visit Santa Ines *manana*, but we need more time to prepare our trip to Santa Barbara." Everyone looked at him quizzically. "Because", he continued, "we must prepare for the wedding." Now everyone was awaiting an explanation. "Juan, are you prepared to propose to Magdalena? Do you not believe that your courtship has progressed enough that espousal to your lovely *amor* is a now appropriate?" Juan reddened, "*Si, Senor Sharlezz*. It is the honorable thing to do. And I am mucho *en amor!*" Now Magdalena came forward. "Do I not have a choice in this matter?" Everyone laughed, knowing that she would be happy to accept Juan's somewhat forced proposal. All the men cheered and the ladies smiled and laughed.

After the merriment settled and the crowd dispersed, Morgan went to Manuel. "Manuel, I would like to speak to you privately. Will you join me in the shade over there?" He pointed to a bench that Ignatio had made and placed in the shade of a fine old oak tree. When they sat, Morgan glanced all about to be sure that only they would hear the conversation. "*Padre,* I wish to make my confession. Will you hear me?" Castellanos recognized the seriousness of Morgan's voice. "Of course, *Sharlezz*. I do not have a confessional stole, but I'm sure the Lord will grant me this privilege."

Morgan then confessed his affair with Martha. After concluding his sinfulness, he stated, "And Padre, I am guilty of causing Martha to also commit a sin. This is most unforgivable on my part." The *Padre* spoke, "First, *Sharlezz,* In the name of the Lord, I forgive you your sin. The important thing now is that you do not again commit such a trespass. As for both you and Martha, we can hope that the Lord understood your human weakness, and will forgive you both." Morgan appeared relieved, "Thank you Padre, but please do not make Martha feel uncomfortable if she does not make her own confession." Castellanos showed a little indignity, "Of course not, *Sharlezz*. I'm sure when an opportunity arises, Martha will also confess her involvement. It will be of her own will, at the time of the Lord's inspiration."

The next morning a rather large group rode to *Mision* Santa Ines. Morgan and Anna Maria led, followed by Manuel and Juan, as well as Martha and Magdalena, who were curious to see how the *convento* now looked. After viewing the repairs made by Ignatio and others, all were very pleased. "So", Anna Maria spoke, "we are now about to open a seminary for the training of several priests. Now we need only the candidates." At that point, the younger Ignatio and one other of the *vaqueros* who had working on the repairs, came forward. "We would like to present ourselves to *Padre* Castellanos, with the hope that he will allow us to participate as seminarians." Everyone cheered and congratulated the two young men. Ignatio the elder came to his son with tears in his eyes. "My son, why did you not tell me that the Lord had called you to become one of his disciples. Oh, I am very pleased. And your mother will also be happy!"

Two former neophytes that had been helping with the rebuilding then also came forward to declare their intention to become priests. The crowd again cheered loudly. Morgan laughed, "My word, Anna Maria, *Padre* Manuel, it seems that you have much work ahead of you!" As the full entourage rode home there was much joy and laughter among them.

When the group reached *Rancho del Sol*, and as they were dispersing, Morgan noticed Martha speak quietly to Padre Manuel. The Padre nodded agreement. He then looked towards Morgan with a slight smile and imperceptible nod. Morgan knew that Martha had requested an opportunity to confess to Padre Manuel. With this, Morgan was much relieved that now both he and Martha would have a clear conscious in the matter of their mutual wrong-doing.

Several days later, when Morgan and the others reached Mission Santa Barbara, they explained their plan to *Padre* Rodriguez. He was not as enthusiastic about the disclosure as they had expected him to be. "Naturally", he stated, "I cannot offer support of any kind until I receive such instructions from Bishop Moreno. And *padre* Manuel, I do not know you. I do not know your credentials. While I may not doubt them, I nevertheless must receive assurances that you are indeed a *padre* in good standing in the Church." The entire party let out a soft moan. Morgan spoke, "Your position is understandable *Padre*. We will take immediate steps to obtain the necessary ordinances. We will dispatch riders to Los Angeles immediately after the wedding." "Wedding?", *Padre* Rodriguez asked. "Yes, we have two wonderful people who are much in love with each other, and they desire you to marry them." The *Padre* smiled, "Oh, I am happy to do so." Actually, Juan had hoped that *Padre* Manuel would perform the wedding, but he was not willing to wait until Manuel's credentials were clarified. After the wedding, Morgan dispatched the two young Mexican men, those who wished to become priests, to ride to Los Angeles to confer with the Bishop. Morgan thought that it would be wise for the Bishop to meet these two men in person. He thought it best to have the two neophytes confer with the Bishop later. He didn't want it to appear to Bishop Moreno that he was being pressed into a hasty decision.

The two young candidates returned in three days. They had been assured by Bishop Moreno that the seminary would open and that the letter that they were to deliver would authorize *Padre* Remirez to assist the establishment of the seminary in any way that he could. The two young men had mentioned to the Bishop that there were two neophytes also wanting to enter the seminary. The Bishop said that he wished to interview them before agreeing to their admission. Morgan arranged for their immediate departure to Los Angeles.

Morgan himself, taking Manuel along also, delivered the sealed letter to *Padre* Remirez. As Remirez read the letter, Morgan and Manuel were smiling in anticipation of Remirez's involvement. Their smiles changed abruptly when Remirez told of the letter's content. "Good Bishop Moreno advises that he did approve of the establishment of a seminary, temporarily at *Mision Santa Ines,* until the land granted to the Bishop by Governor Micheltorina, will be prepared to become the permanent site of the *colegio.* Further, because he requires some time to obtain the ordination decree from *Espanol* for *Padre* Manuel Castellanos, he has assigned two *padres*, Fra Juan Jimeno and Fra Francisco Sanchez, to inaugurate the studies at the *seminario.* The two young *Mejicano* men are approved for admission, but the Bishop wishes to interview the neophytes, the native young men, before granting his approval for their admission."

Morgan and Manuel were stunned. Manuel looked devastated. Then Morgan spoke, mostly to Manuel, but also to Remirez. "I should have known that this whole matter would require the approval of the Church hierarchy. I'm sorry to have involved you prematurely Manuel. We must all adjust to the new Bishop's control. The Franciscan Order is no longer able to make decisions as it did in the past." Looking very disheartened Manuel spoke, "*Si, Sharlezz*, I too should have known that such credentials are necessary. After all, for twelve years I myself have not been in touch with the *Padre Superior* of my Order. I must now journey to *Ciudad de Mejico* to receive his approval, and a new assignment." Morgan knew by the look on Manuel's face that he wished that he had remained a hermit.

The two retuned to *Rancho del Sol*. After informing Anna Maria of the Bishop's directives, Morgan arranged for his *vaquero* Martinez, to accompany Manuel to Mexico City. It was a sad departure because everyone knew that they would never again see *Padre* Manuel Castellanos.

The College of Our Lady of Sinners, the first seminary in *Alta California*, was thus opened in June, 1844, remaining at *Mision Santa Ines* until 1846, when it was then moved to the new College Rancho nearby.

Matters at *Rancho del Sol* remained static for the next several years, but Anna Maria, who was saddened that she had no more involvement with the seminary, ultimately became ill with attacks of heart pain. In September 1848, Morgan's beloved Anna Maria passed away in her sleep. She was buried in the cemetery at *Mision Santa Barbara*, along side her beloved child, Maria Consuela, and her parents, Juan and Maria Ortega. At the time of the funeral, Morgan commented to his son Carlos, that upon his death he wished to also be buried there. He stated that he had one more matter that he wished Carlos to execute. He wanted to grant acreage to Juan and Magdalena, so that they could have a small home of their own, and enough animals to begin their own rancho. Ignatio and Roberto were assigned to help Juan erect their *casa*.

During the next few months, riders who were traveling from San Francisco or Monterey, and headed to the south, carrying information to Los Angeles and San Diego, would stop at *Rancho del Sol*. The news that they carried, while disturbing to many residents of Mexican and native cultures, was pleasing to Morgan. For these riders told of an American Captain, John Fremont, who led a group of soldiers to Monterey Peninsula, encamping there. He declared that he was there to protect the many American settlers in the area. More and more of these settlers had arrived during the last few years. Mexican General Mariano Vallejo had ordered Fremont to leave, but instead Fremont raised the American flag on a peak about 40 kilometers from Monterey. In May, 1846, Mexico declared war on the United States. In June of that same year many of the American settlers attacked and captured the Mexican Army outpost at Sonoma, raised a home-made flag bearing a likeness of a bear, and declared that California was now a Republic.

Soon, another rider came racing in to tell of the American Army defeating the Mexican and In February, 1848 the Treaty Of Guadalupe Hidalgo was signed. Mexico had officially concedes *Alta California* to the United States. All of this was startling news, for in the course of only a few years, California's Spanish Missions and all of its *pueblos* and culture had come under American jurisdiction. The changes happened so quickly, it seemed, that Morgan wondered if he had dreamed the whole transition.

A month before the rider from the south had arrived telling of the Treaty with Mexico, another rider had arrived from the north. His information was even more startling to Morgan and the others. A man working for the saw-mill owner Sutter, discovered gold. Most of the American settlers who were growing crops and tending their herds quickly began to search for gold on their property. As more was found, word reached other Americans who were on the trails heading west. They too, came hurrying in, to prospect for their fortunes.

Carlos, Juan and many of the *vaqueros* and craftsmen began to wonder if they too, should not join these prospectors. Morgan urged his son to remain on the *rancho*, but declared that any other men that wished to go north, seeking their fortune, were free to do so. Carlos and Juan realized that their good fortunes were associated with *Ranch del Sol*, but a few of the others did travel north. Some returned in a few months, others never. Those returning told of the hundreds and hundreds of Americans, and others, who were pouring into San Francisco and all of the area to the north.

Morgan thought, 'I had wanted California to become part of the United States, but I never expected it to occur in such a disturbing manner.' The next few years were tumultuous, not only for the new settlers and prospectors, but also for the original ranch owners and Californians.

In September 1850, news was received that California had been admitted to the United States, as the 31st State. While Morgan was glad to learn of this, most others, including his son Carlos, were apprehensive about their futures. Morgan tried to assure them that all would be well, that their voices would now be heard, through the election of a Governor and other office holders.

For the next few years tumult was the word describing California's growth. Former *pueblos* became bustling cities. Newly arrived farmers were planting many kinds of crops. Others were raising cattle herds, sheep, hogs and horses. Farming and ranching methods that had been carried on by the *padres* for the previous seven decades were continued and greatly expanded. Unfortunately, most of the Chumash and other natives were not to benefit from this new growth. Most retreated to land that was granted them by the United States government. This land was usually the most unfavorable.

Morgan was now elderly and unable to perform any ranching tasks. He enjoyed sitting on his *portico*, viewing the lovely scenery and observing his son and the other cowboys toiling in the work that they loved. Morgan continued the routine of his daily journal entries. More and more, now, he reviewed the previous pages, reminiscing about the many events and people that had occurred in his life span. He felt sorrow each time that he thought about his beautiful Missions and of their accomplishments, positive accomplishments, he believed.

On October 15, 1859 Morgan was seated on his *portico*. Carlos rode at great speed from the corral. A rider had arrived with news that he knew would make his father very happy. *"Padre!, Padre!"*, he shouted as he dismounted his horse. "I have wonderful news for you! President James Buchanan has restored *Mision* San Gabriel to the Church." Morgan's head was down, journal on his lap, apparently napping as was most customary for him these days. As Carlos hurriedly approached he was still announcing the latest news, "*Padre*, did you hear me? It is believed that Buchanan will restore other Missions to the Church. And it is believed that his elected successor Abraham Lincoln, is also sympathetic to this restoration policy. *Padre,* is that not wonderful news?...*Padre*, did you hear me? Are you awake?" As Carlos reached his father, he placed his hand on Morgan's shoulder. Morgan slumped forward, having died sometime that afternoon, in his favorite spot, his *portico*. He never learned of the restoration of the Missions. Morgan was almost 77 years of age, a very old man for that time.

EPILOGUE

On May 23, 1862, President Abraham Lincoln signed the decree which returned Morgan's beloved *Mision Santa Ines* to the Catholic church. By that time the buildings had badly deteriorated. For the next few years several interested people worked on restoration of the buildings. The Church became a parish church, but never again to be serviced by the Franciscan Order.

In July 1904, Father Alexander Buckler was assigned to the Mission. For the next twenty years, he and his niece Miss Mamie Goulet, worked on the restoration of the buildings, the vestments and art pieces of *Mision Santa Ines*. Today, the Capuchin Franciscan administer *Santa Ines* Parish. Visitors may view this beautiful Mission nearly in the state as Morgan knew it. It will celebrate its bicentennial in 2004.

Old *Mision Santa Ines* (sometimes called Santa Ynez) is located near Solvang, California.

Mision La Purisima Concepcion which stood empty until the 1930's suffered perhaps the greatest deterioration of all the Missions. During the active period of the Civilian Conservation Corp (the CCC) work was begun on the Mission's restoration. During World War II the restoration work was discontinued but in the 1950's the National Park Service assisted the California State Parks Department in continuing the restoration. As far as was possible, all materials, tools and techniques used by the padres and the Native Americans was utilized. This Mission compound is open to the public. It is located near Lompoc, California.

ABOUT THE AUTHOR

Edward G. Schultz was born in Pittsfield, Massachusetts. Following graduation from High School he enlisted in the Army. After discharge he became a self-taught draftsman, then a sales technician and ultimately a sales manager.

In these occupations he was required to do much technical and proposal writing. He enjoyed these activities and found that he could combine this avocation with his love of history. Often having to travel to California for business reasons, he visited and studied the California Missions and their effect on history. He was surprised when one day he discovered the grave of a "Yankee" pioneer among the Spanish inhabitants of Mission Santa Barbara. This and other related historical facts led him to write "Morgan's Mission."